Journey on the Estrada Real:

Encounters in the Mountains of Brazil

Other Books by Glenn Alan Cheney

Law of the Jungle: Environmental Anarchy and
the Tenharim People of Amazonia

Quilombo dos Palmares:
Brazil's Lost Nation of Fugitive Slaves

Ex Cathedra: Stories by Machado de Assis

Thanksgiving:
The Pilgrims' First Year in America

How a Nation Grieves: Press Accounts of the Death of
Lincoln, the Hunt for Booth, and America in Mourning

Journey to Chernobyl:
Encounters in a Radioactive Zone

Promised Land:
A Nun's Struggle against Landlessness, Lawlessness,
Slavery, Poverty, Corruption, and Environmental
Devastation in Amazonia

Love and Death in the Kingdom of Swaziland

Frankenstein on the Cusp of Something

Passion in an Improper Place

Acts of Ineffable Love: Collected Stories

Poems Askance

Neighborhood News

Life in Caves

Journey on the Estrada Real
Encounters in the Mountains of Brazil

Glenn Alan Cheney

New London Librarium
Hanover, Conn.

Journey on the Estrada Real:

Encounters in the Mountains of Brazil — Second Edition

New London Librarium,

Hanover, CT 06350

NLLibrarium.com

Portions of this book have appeared in *Moondance, South
Carolina Review,* and *Bee Culture.*

The First Edition of this book was published by
Academy Chicago Publishers in 2005.

ISBNs

Paperback: 978-0-9905899-3-8

                   0990589935

ePub: 978-0-9798039-7-0

      10 9 8 7 6 5 4 3 2

for Lázaro

Foreword

This book reports on a hike I took along the Estrada Real, from Mariana north to Diamantina. I walked the first half — from Mariana to Itambé do Mato to Dentro — in 2000. I went back to Brazil and finished the journey in 2002.

The first edition of the book was published by Academy Chicago Publishers in 2005. I was less than happy — in tears, actually — with the many editorial changes the editors had made without consulting me. Some of the scenes and incidents that meant the most to me had simply been cut. I was also disappointed with the illegible map they used. So I was delighted when they agreed to return the publication rights to me in 2013. This second edition presents most of the original narrative with some of the editing that Academy Chicago did. There are no good maps focusing the Estrada Real, so I have drawn one.

The second edition is also available as an e-book. That edition has photographs. Photographs are also posted at the New London Librarium website, NLLibrarium. com.

Words in italics — that is, words in Portuguese — are defined in a glossary at the end of the book. The use of the word "*mulato*" is intended to reflect the common Brazilian use of that word, which is merely descriptive and not derogatory.

I returned to the Estrada Real in 2014, retraced much of my route by car. I was sad to learn that most of the older people I had interviewed had passed away. These were the people who remembered Minas Gerais in the early part of the twentieth century, decades before the arrival of electricity, asphalt, telephones, fast food, and television, back when transportation was almost exclusively by horse, mule, or ox cart. Though it was sad to see their body of knowledge disappear, it was gratifying to know that at least a little of their knowledge had been preserved in this book.

Among the deceased was Lázaro Francisco da Silva, who was by no means old. He'd been a friend for many years, as related in the first chapter. He was a historian of everything from local lore to the course of human events. He did what he could to stave off the modernity that has degraded the town of Mariana so much. I dedicate this edition to him.

Glenn Alan Cheney

N

Diamantina
São Gonçalo do Rio das Pedras
Milho Verde
Três Barras
Serro
Itaponhoacanga
Tapera
Córregos
Conceição do Mato Dentro
Morro do Pilar
Itambé do Mato Dentro
Senhora do Carmo
Ipoema
Bom Jesus do Amparo
Cocais
Barão de Cocais
Santa Bárbara
Santa Rita Durão
Bento Rodriguez
Camargos
Mariana
Ouro Preto

Serra do Espinhaço

State of
Minas Gerais

Belo
Horizonte

Congonhas

Tiradentes
São João del Rey

Caminho Velho (Old Road)

Caminho Novo (New Road)

← Estrada Real →

State
of
São Paulo

São Lourenço

Serra da Mantiqueira

State of
Rio de Janeiro

Juiz de Fora

Petrópolis

Paraty

Rio de Janeiro

Portugal →

Atlantic
Ocean

Contents

Introduction

The Royal Road

In 1697 or so, the Crown of Portugal ordered a road built from the port of Praia dos *Mineiros*, where the Rio Inhomirim met the Atlantic, to Diamantina, where creeks were exposing diamonds to daylight. The Estrada Real, the Royal Road, was to surmount the Serra do Mar that stands steep, dark-green, and misty about Guanabara Bay, then probe north into the region known as Minas Gerais — General Mines. The Royal Road was to connect the cities producing gold and diamonds as nowhere else on earth. Tunnels dug into hillsides were turning up just about every type of gem known to man. São João del Rei, Tiradentes, Congonhas and Vila Rica were already thriving cities. Vila Rica was becoming the largest city in the Americas, and its name would some day change from Rich Village to Black Gold – Ouro Preto. Diamantina, in northern Minas, was rising from the muck of a diamond mine in a gully to become a Portuguese outpost worth the wealth it was sending south to Praia dos *Mineiro*s — Beach of Miners – later to be called Rio de Janeiro. From there the wealth of Brazil sailed to Lisbon.

This winding dirt road connected some of the world's most miserable people to some of the world's wealthiest — the slaves in the mines of Minas Gerais to the Portuguese Crown, the ultimate beneficiaries of everything that could be stripped from the land of the ember-colored *brasa* wood — Brazil.

The Estrada Real was to restrict as much as facilitate transportation into the interior. The Crown did not want its colony to develop industrial capacity. It was to continue completely dependent on Portugal for food, metals, tools, nails, ammunition, equipment, and supplies. The Brazilian economy was to be based almost exclusively on the export of gems and gold. The Estrada Real, therefore, was to facilitate the inward delivery of manufactured goods to the interior while speeding the outward flow of mineral riches. The Estrada was also to remain the only route of transportation, making it possible for Portugal to control development and exploitation.

In a certain sense, the history of the Estrada Real

is the history of Latin America. Unlike the settlers who came to North America from industrial nations, the colonizers of Latin America came from feudal lands. They came neither to build nor to stay. In Portuguese, the verb *explorar* means both explore and exploit. The language has no other word for either activity. As if by lingual necessity, the Portuguese did both at the same time, exploring a region so vast that even today it has not yet been fully mapped, exploiting the land and ungodly number of native and imported people. Once the gold and jewels were gone, the people who remained were left with magnificent churches and abandoned mines but no infrastructure for any but an agrarian economy.

That situation hasn't changed much. At the beginning of the twenty-first century, the Estrada Real of the seventeenth century is still there. Most of the road is dirt, dust, or mud, though it becomes cobblestone as it passes through towns and villages. Many of the villages have a toehold on the twentieth century — undependable electricity, a single phone, two television channels, visiting doctors with medical degrees — but the lives of the people there haven't changed much since the seventeenth century. They still cook on open wood stoves, and they travel by horse, mule and foot. They treat their ills with roots and herbs, and they pray for rain. They live in houses built by their grandfathers and sing in churches built by slaves. They still have no infrastructure for any but an agrarian economy.

This is the cradle of Brazilian culture. It all started here, in the mountains of Minas Gerais. As urban Brazil struggles into modern times and the global economy, its slow, quiet past still lives along its first road. How has it survived? How long can it survive? Should it survive? What, if anything, can save it? The search for the answers — a walk down the road — turns up the seeds of an odd revolution. People who have yet to benefit from the global economy are already struggling against it. Some, poor as dirt, ignorant of the world, are satisfied with the happiness they've found in God. Others, more aware, appreciate the wealth of their ancient culture. And some, of course, want to trade their antiquated ways for the commerce and industry that brings the money that buys the stuff that promises to make life better.

This book is about the people, culture and history of the Estrada Real. The people are changing, some by resisting change, some by embracing it. The culture is in the balance. The history is there, as immutable as it is unfinished.

Chapter One

Mariana and Bento Rodrigues

I begin my journey on the Estrada Real in Mariana, Minas Gerais, for two reasons. One is that once upon a time I lived here, trying my hand at banana farming. I never knew that from my front porch I could see the oldest road in the Western Hemisphere rising over a hill to the east and north. The other reason is that there is no map of the entire Estrada Real, no guide book, no signs along the way. There is, however, a rough and often erroneous guide for the road from Mariana to Diamantina, its northernmost point. So, after fifteen years away from the place, I return, look up an old friend, Lázaro Francisco da Silva, tell him my plan, and spend the night at his house.

The plan I arrived with was to buy a no-frills horse and a basic two-wheel cart, called a *charrete*, and simply flog my way toward Diamantina. What a way to travel! Just sit there watching the scenery go slowly by. *Charretes* are fairly common in Brazil, but not, it turns out, in Mariana. We look around all day but find nothing. Lázaro has an alternative idea: a sedan. He happens to have one under construction — not a two-door car but a historically correct replica of a eighteenth century vehicle, a passenger booth on poles. It's the way royalty used to travel on the Estrada Real — carried by slaves, watching the scenery go slowly by. Instead of slaves, Lázaro suggests, we could hire a dozen beautiful women. It would pay off in publicity. Television coverage would be guaranteed. It was a tempting idea, certainly better than looking at the back-end of a horse for a couple of months.

But my budget did not afford the cost of a dozen beautiful pole-bearers, so I decided to just walk. My brother-in-law, a highly domesticated apartment dweller in the state capital, Belo Horizonte, calls my plan a *programa de índio*, an Indian plan, by which I think he means a plan that is not especially well thought out, more an idea than a plan. But what kind of planning can you do when you're going to a place that has no map? I load my knapsack, the same one I used on Boy Scout hikes thirty-five years ago, with toilet paper, a change of clothes, a sleeping bag, an umbrella, a bottle of water, a few other essentials, and a little duct tape just in case of disaster. Lázaro takes me into town to buy a straw hat. The spring sun is hotter than usual, he says, and the rains have yet to arrive.

But they arrive that very night, a ripper of a thunderstorm, an inauspicious introduction to a long hike. I awake when the neighborhood roosters start to crow, which must have been at about three o'clock in the morning. I roll around in bed in unquenchable anxiety, imagining the many ways in which I might be bushwhacked on the Estrada Real. Everyone, without exception, has warned me not to go walking alone in the outback. The crime rate in Belo Horizonte rose ninety-four percent in the past year, and the major daily newspaper, the *Estado de Minas*, always features a story of a purposeless murder. I think they have a special page reserved for reports of homicides and daring robberies. In general, across Brazil, the homicide rate is five times that of the United States. The rural areas are not subject to the same type of urban crime, but the Estrada Real does run through a region still relatively rich in gold. That's exactly why the road's there. The gold is in scant supply these days, but prospecting is still a last resort for men who can't find jobs. They muck around in the streams, panning for infinitesimal specks. Long-term investment in infrastructure is the last thing on their minds. To survive, they need gold, and if they don't find enough — and no one at any time in history has ever found enough — they are perfectly willing to steal gold from anyone else who has been lucky enough to find some. And of course the gold miner's code of ethics is silent on the issue of robbing tourists on a road far from town. Even a grubby, tattered backpack is worth more than the air in their pockets. Or so I have been warned by those who know.

I have a lot of faith in humanity, especially in Brazilian humanity, but I also know that all it takes is one bad apple — and Brazil has no shortage of those — to ruin a trip and leave a gringo dead in a ditch for buzzards to eat. Buzzards hold a strong presence in my pre-dawn fears, and they are also waiting at the place where the dirt road of the Estrada Real meets the paved road that goes out of Mariana toward the Timbopeba and Samarco hematite mines. If I were writing a work of fiction about a trip down this road, I would never dare have the protagonist begin his trip under the gaze of a dozen urubus perched on rocks and fence posts, enjoying the stench of something dead. They look like glum funeral directors who have been interrupted in the middle of a meal. They stare at Lázaro and me as we shake hands and slap each other on the back. He takes my picture, then drives away with a toot and a wave out the window. The urubus watch me as swing my pack to my back and trudge toward points north. I can say with authority that the gaze of a buzzard is palpable on the spine.

It takes me all of ten minutes to forget about being murdered. The tight weight of the pack is as welcome as a fatherly embrace. Birds chatter in the low, dry brush on the hills on both sides of the road. The only other sound is the crunch of my feet on the quartz gravel of the road. The road climbs through a series of switchbacks, then tips through a pass that looks over a wide view to the east. The downhill side of the road is dense with old eucalyptus and, farther down, the general *mata* of natural forest. Way down there, monkeys hoot up a mad orgy of excitement that suddenly quiets down, then rises into a another frenzy.

At the highest point I stop to take a few notes that might improve the SENAC guide book. It's already apparent that its author wasn't a very intelligent person and may well have been inebriated as he described the route. He refers to things that weren't there, such as the Fazenda Gualuxo and the bridge over the Rio Gualuxo do Norte. He is inconsistent in references to such landmarks as entrances to farms, sometimes noting them, sometimes not. He writes little paragraphs such as "Turn left. Go straight. Keep right," without reliable reference as to where these turns might be made. Often "turn right" seems to mean "don't turn left." In most cases, "Stay on the main road for the next ten miles" would suffice, and that's exactly what I do. Still, a little confirmation now and then would be comforting.

I soon give up trying to correct the guide book. I also give up trying to describe the scenery. I can generally describe the road as winding along the side of hills. The view to one side is usually a vista of ten or twenty miles over hills of varying shades of green that gradually blend into hazy purple. The other side of the road is the mountain I am walking around, usually a moderately steep incline with lots of rock, dried grass, low brush. Sometimes, though never for long, second-growth forest crowds in from both sides. By ten o'clock in the morning, cicadas crank up their whine. The road surface varies from red clay to white sand to brown gravel. On this first stretch of road, from Mariana to Camargos, half a dozen cars go by in four or five hours, raising dust in their wake. The passengers seem to be Mariana people on their way to picnics or the little farms, called *sítio* s, that Brazilians often keep just outside of town. I wave at them all, and they all wave back. A couple slow down and offer a ride by holding an up-pointed thumb out the window, but I wave them off with a wag of my forefinger.

Coming into Camargos, some ten or fifteen kilometers from Mariana (the guidebooks says 22, but I'm sure it's wrong) the road forks. I choose the one that doesn't go uphill. Camargos is just a hamlet of a few dozen houses, a town without sound. I soon come to a man who was fooling around with a bucket at a public spigot. A church, large but simple, stands atop a hill on the other side of the road. I ask the man where one could eat a meal in Camargos. He said there is nowhere. We talk a bit. His name is Fernando. He tells me Camargos was the first district of Mariana making it one of the oldest towns in the state. The church, Nossa Senhora da Conceição, is over three hundred years old. It's locked until the priest comes, which won't be that day. Still wary of thieves, I haul my pack up the long, steep stairs to the church, poke around, then come back down and continue on my way. I soon come to Fernando again, now with another man. He expresses his regret that the town has nowhere to eat, but he says he has some coffee, if I want some. Hungry and weak, needing the sugar, I accept and step into his house, which is flush up against the road. It's a simple and immaculate place many decades old. The floors are of a hardwood that no longer exists, at least not in the width of his floorboards. His living room walls have pictures of a saint, a cross, a prayer in a frame. Fernando explains that he gets his lunch from his *companheira*, and therefore he has no cooked food in the house. He pours me a generous dose of hot, sweet, strong coffee from a thermos and insists that I take at least three crackers from a package. We chat a bit about the wealth of the United States. And

11

then off I go.

I soon come to a sign that says "Honey for Sale." Being a beekeeper, I want to go see. Honey for lunch is better than no lunch. I poke around a little lane that winds through the grass along a brook. A dump truck stands at the brook, its motor running, apparently there for the water. I ask a kid if he knows about the honey. He doesn't, but I see another sign that points over a pair of logs that cross the brook. I go across and head toward the only possible place with honey, a kind of shack next to a kind of corral under a kind of roof, a functional, slap-dash kind of place. I clap and call out, but no one appears until a few seconds after I turn around to leave. It's a tall, bearded man, dirty with work in the sun, his arms thick from the kind of work that might well include the cutting of trees, the pounding in of fence posts, lifting of calves.

"Do you have honey for sale?" I ask.

"I have.'

"You're the beekeeper?"

"I am."

"I'm a beekeeper, too."

That gets me a big smile and a strong, gentle handshake of apiary brotherhood. His name is Fernando. He says, "Come on!"

He opens a barbed wire gate, takes me back to his little shack, along the way asking, "You had lunch?"

As a matter of fact, I hadn't. I smell wood smoke.

His shack doesn't quite qualify as a shack. I guess it's more like a hut, just some corrugated asbestos planks over a frame of poles, some plastic and sheet metal and cardboard around the sides. In one corner he has a jury-rigged, waist-high wood stove of sheet metal that once served for something else, a functional mess, a lot of stuff not out of place but hung and stacked wherever it goddam well belongs. His bee hat and veil are on top of a stack of stuff too vague to identify. His pots and pans are upside down on a plank of wood outside, black on the outside, shiny on the inside.

Lunch is a *mexido* of rice, beans, okra and herbs all mixed up in a pot, a delicious expediency typical of Minas Gerais. The first Portuguese *bandeirante* adventurers who came here carried shovels and muskets but no food or plows. They had come for gold. They had no time to plant. They learned about living off the land from the Indians, a people without alimentary taboos. They ate fruits they'd never heard of — *pitanga, araticum, bacupari, jatobá, guava, pequi, cagaita.* They ate fiddlehead ferns, wild squash, bamboo shoots, gooseberry leaves. They ate *tanajura* ants and *bicho-da-taquara* larva. They ate fish wrapped in leaves. They ate their corn raw, ground, boiled, baked, or roasted. They hunted alligator, monkey, quail, rabbit, dove, deer, armadillo, tapir, wild pigs, snakes, lizards. The ate manioc root baked, roasted, boiled, sweetened, ground, souped. From annatto seeds they made medicine, colored foods, decorated their bodies and defended themselves against bug bites. Of all these foods, only the *bicho-da-taquara* larva have fallen from the *mineiro* menu, though it was once a delicacy. They were mashed and boiled, their fat skimmed off for a tasty butter. As they were an ocean away from their women, the men suffered insomnia caused by "excesses of love." To get a good night's sleep, they ate dried larva with the intestines intact but without the head. The meal gave them wonderful dreams of brilliant forests where they ate delicious fruits.

Mineiro food, famous throughout Brazil, was born of hunger, first of the *bandeirante*s, then of the slaves. The slaves ate leftovers, the hooves and ears of the pig, the guts of the cow, the collards that grew in easy abundance, the corn mash that the horses didn't finish, and spices that came from the woods. Hunger necessitated invention, and the African women were culinary geniuses. The best foods on the contemporary Brazilian menu were concocted in miserable kitchens of slave quarters.

Fernando's mexido is manifest proof of the flexibility of *mineiro* food. He assures me that the pot is dirty on the outside but clean on the inside. I can help myself, have all I want. He rinses off a plate at a spigot fed by a tank up on the hill. It's good, hearty stuff, truly delicious. I've never tasted the herb that's in it, and the cook doesn't know what it's called.

Mariana and Bento Rodrigues

Fernando lives in Mariana but comes out here on the weekends. He once wanted to build a house here, but his family doesn't like the place, so he comes here to be alone and is happy here, happy as a pig in mud, a man in his place. He used to work with a company messing in some way with environmental issues, but he lost the job, and now, it being hard to find another job, he spends his time on his little plot of land in Camargos, messing with a few cows, some bee hives, an organic garden. "*Sou homen do mato mesmo,*" he said - a man really of the woods. He loves his grubby little place. I can't say it's dirty though I'm eating thirty feet from a corral with a cow in it. The big box of fine soil beside my foot, I'm told, is full of worms. But worms are not dirty, and I'll take cow-dirt over diesel fumes any day.

Suddenly I remember a beekeeper I used to know, an old guy named Ciro who sold his honey at the Saturday market in Mariana fifteen years ago. Ciro surprised me by speaking English when I complimented him on his honey. He was Brazilian but had worked for GM in Michigan for many years. Then he raised bees in a hamlet an hour outside of a town that was two hours from a state capital that no one outside of Brazil has heard of — Camargos, the place I have just walked through. Now Fernando tells me that Ciro died a few years ago. He praises Ciro very highly as an intelligent man who did things right. With deep nods over his plate of mexido, he emphasized how

15

Ciro was good and smart.

Before he fetches some honey, Fernando rinses off a ladle and brings out a pot of milk still warm from his cows. It's good milk, creamy and earthy and warm. The only honey he has is a plastic container of one kilo, about four times the weight I want to carry. I costs five *reais* — two and a half dollars — which we agree is cheap. Any price for Brazilian honey is cheap because it's made by killer bees. Fernando and I have both had the painful pleasure of raiding their hives and extracting their honey. The price of killer bee honey is always too cheap.

Fernando tells me there's no hotel in the next town, Bento Rodrigues, but there's a little restaurant run by a guy named Juca. Juca is a fine fellow and will see to it that I don't have to sleep in the *mato*.

And off I go. Within a hundred yards I come to the most delightful little cascade, clean water pouring over rocks worn smooth. I change into trunks and wade into the main flow, which bounces horizontally through a sluice in the rock. I let the water pound down on my shoulders, which feels mighty good. Over to the side a lower flow sends a flood of bubbles swirling around under a pummel of water.

Along comes a young man with a very pretty young lady on his back. She strips to a tiny bikini and enjoys the water. He invites me to a place a few yards upstream, where they and some friends are cooking meat and

16

drinking Cuba libres from an aluminum cup. With ice. They insist I sip a little. The coldness of it is very fine. They give me some chunks of chicken shaved from a spit. That is fine, too. The girls slide down a sluice in the rock, slowly, giggling, ignoring all orders and advice from the guys who are attending to the meat and the rum.

Then I take what I later find out was the long road to the village of Bento Rodriquez, a hot and winding road that curls high around a sierra. It's too high for tall trees, which means nice views but no shade. Much of the road surface is fine, white sand, which reflects the early afternoon sun up into my rapidly toasting face. What a glorious feeling it is to come around a bend and see Bento Rodrigues at the far end of a deep valley, still far away but within sight. With the Igreja São Bento at the center of town and fields all around, it's just as cute as can be, a place for Hobbits or fairy tale people. My feet hurt as I plod into town. At this late moment it occurs to me that I haven't walked this far in one day since adolescence some thirty-five years ago. Teetering with exhaustion and thirst, I pull up to the first bar and order a bottle of Skol beer. Then I sit down and drink it. It is cold and wet and good. I watch as rowdy a group plays pool at a little billiards table.

I inquire about Juca and am directed up the street to a bar that is just a small room that is filled to capacity by about ten guys playing a boisterous game of cards.

17

At the crucial moments of laying cards on the table or transferring funds or resolving a dispute they're loud to the point of hurting my ears. They rather effectively pretend not to notice that a stranger has just walked in. At the little counter in back I introduce myself to Juca, make the connection with Fernando and in that instant obviously gain Juca's favor. When I ask him if he has beer, he gives me an answer that I've often heard and always thought would be a good line in a commercial for Antarctica beer: "We only have Brahma."

Brahma's the exact same thing as Antarctica, Skol, Kaiser, Bohemia and every Bud, Busch and Miller made in the U.S.A. — a light, hop-free, rice-based beer that is very, very good if too cold to taste on a day too hot to tolerate. Beer's a rich man's drink in the interior of Brazil. The guys playing cards are drinking *cachaça*, a drink so cheap that it rhymes with *de graça*, which means "free." It also with *desgraça* — misfortune with implications of disgrace. Rich guy that I am, and hot and thirsty, I opt for the Brahma and take a seat on a bench just outside the front door. I am sitting there, writing notes and resting my poor feet and wondering how to go about asking where a person can sleep around there, when along came an old, skinny black man with eyes that obviously can't see much and a knot of mutilated teeth at the front of his black and ragged gums. He asks if I am a "gringo" and offers his hand, which wavers about eight inches off course. He is not only half blind but three-quarters drunk. I shake it. In his garbled, gummy peon lingo, he asks if I'd buy him a *cachaça*. I cannot say no to a man who looks so poor and miserable. He should be entitled to every drop of *cachaça* he can hold. I tell him to tell Juca I'll pay for a dose. He goes in and tells Juca. Juca comes out to confirm. He has a game leg that isn't good for much except as a prop to keep him from falling over. To walk he has to swing it around with one hand. I tell him I'll pay for the drink if he wants to sell it to the guy; it's up to him. So he goes and gets a half a glass of it — a good four or five ounces - but he holds the glass out into the street so the guy has to physically leave if he wants to drink it. The guy downs it in one gulp, thanks me and, to my relief, leaves.

I then use Fernando's reference to ask Juca where a person can sleep in Bento Rodriguez, strongly implying that Fernando has passed this responsibility on to him. He indicates a Manoel Muniz, who lives down a grassy lane that runs beside the church. My weak and shaky legs stagger me on over there, arriving just as Manoel is coming through his gate with four plastic milk pails. A certain semi-mute I had seen in the first bar, who talks by huffing and squeaking and waving his arms around, is there with Manoel, apparently advising him of my imminent arrival. Manoel eyes me up and down as I explain myself and my mission and give Juca as my reference, strongly implying that I am here at Juca's request and recommendation. I recognize Manoel as a good man, the type with Christian love in his eyes, an older guy who still gets to do things with milk pails.

Manoel is a little concerned that he'll have to feed me. I say I'll eat at Juca's. He asks if I'm alone. Yes, I am. He asks how long I want to stay. I say I'd be out of there by dawn. I tell him I only need a little space on the floor. I just don't want to have to sleep in the *mato*. And in case he can't tell, I also need a shower, though I can certainly wait until he gets back from his milk business.

Well, he reckons he can put me up, so he takes me through the gate and around to the back of his house to where his wife is pushing coagulated milk into round cheese molds with her fingers, making the famous *queijo mineiro* - cheese Minas-style, a soft, salty cheese that can be anywhere from dripping wet to grainy dry. She is old and heavy and coughing and waving flies off her cheese. She shows no reaction to my presence. Manoel takes me to a bedroom, then leads me to the bathroom, a convoluted trail through the living room, kitchen and dining room. He shows me where all the light switches are, in case I have to get up at night. He explains that the hot water comes from a *serpentina*, a pipe that runs through the grill of the *fogão a lenha* wood stove, then up to a tank over the ceiling. The boiling water circulates itself up to the tank while drawing water down from the same tank. He doesn't need to explain that the supply of hot water, therefore, was limited but would be plenty hot. He also didn't need to tell me that the toilet might need an extra flush or two to really do its job. I can tell by looking at it.

It's a nice, clean, *casa mineira* with tile roof and blue trim around the doors and windows. The windows have no glass, just heavy shutters to swing shut at night. In this house, they swing into the room to open. In some houses, they swing out. The living room furniture is cheap and simple, just a leatherette couch, a chair, and a coffee table with a big Bible on it. The walls sport pictures of Nossa Senhora da Conceição and Santo Gabriel, a battery-operated clock in antique style, five starfish, a heavy-duty, oversized, only-for-show rosary, a picture of Jesus with arms held out to a nice lake, and the inevitable old photos of a husband and wife. I think just about every house in the interior of Minas Gerais has one of these pairs of photos in an oval frame. They are strange photos from deep in the past, often with formal clothes painted below the photo of the face. Someone told me that the photos are blown-up prints made from tiny contact prints. The rosiness in the cheeks is water color. Manoel tells me the photos are of him and his wife, taken fifty years ago, just after they were married. By the looks of the wife, she's been in a bad mood since day one.

Not just a bad mood, it turns out. Manoel tells me she's got mental problems.

It turns out I'm not the first foreigner to stay in this house. A guy from Germany, a backpacker who looked a little like me, was here not long ago, and a couple from Europe somewhere, and a whole busload of people from São Paulo who called beforehand and arranged to rent his whole house and *quintal*, where they slept and camped. They were friendly, peaceful people, members of a church. They had their pictures taken beside him beside his flowers, his chickens, his house and the little cow barn.

Manoel has a great *quintal*, a word for which there is no translation besides, inadequately, backyard. The *quintal* of a rural house in Minas Gerais is a lush area planted with food and flowers. In Manoel's case, it includes not only bananas, *jabuticaba*, lemons, limes, oranges, pitanga berries, mulberries, tangerines, and a lot of flowers but five dairy cows, three pigs, and twenty-one piglets that have been timed to reach table-size by Christmas. The *jabuticabas* are ripe, an event that takes place twice a year for about two weeks. These odd, black-purple berries grow right from the trunks of the many-stemmed tree, and a given tree produces far more than a family can consume. They can't be frozen or stored, though they can be made into a liqueur or jam. You have to eat them when they're ripe. They're a good fruit for eating outdoors because they involve a lot of spitting. You take each berry, which is a little larger than a marble, bite it hard enough to break the skin, then suck out the insides. You squeeze it to get the pit and pulp out, suck the pulp off the pit, then spit the pit out. There's probably a delicate way to do this, and I suppose it could be done indoors with a bowl on a table, but it's far more efficient and satisfying to project the pit into the great outdoors. As if the taste were not enough, the guilt of having a tree full of *jabuticaba* drives everyone to eat as many as possible. As with potato chips, it's hard to eat just one, or even just a pound, though as you binge toward a kilo, a certain limit is reached, usually all of a sudden. After two weeks of this, everyone's glad the season is over.

Manoel is seventy-six years old. He has a head of hair thick and black. One lens of his black-frame glasses is dirty and spotted with what seems to be white paint. He lives in a house with a roof that's a hundred years old, the house where his father was born. He's a fine fellow who loves his wife, his fruit trees, the chickens and ducks that peck around his sandaled feet in the *quintal* as he flicks corn scooped up in a blue plastic hard hat. He loves the piglets he will sell come Christmas. He loves Fernando of Camargos; he loved Ciro, the smart beekeeper who died, as I now learn, of a heart attack at the gate of his farm as he was about to leave for Mariana. Manoel loves his twenty-one grandchildren and the great-grandson who just turned one, at which point he had his little existence confirmed and glorified in a laminated card the size of a post card with the young lad bright-eyed and optimistic, looking for all the world like someone destined to become the mayor of a place with pavement.

We sit at Manoel's big dining room table, eating crackers and his wife's *requeijão*, a *queijo mineiro* that comes out soft and almost spreadable because at some point in its making it has been boiled. We also eat creamy *doce de leite* caramel that originated in his own cows. He gives me some manioc soup that had been warmed all day on his wood stove. We drink coffee which I believe he thinned down with water so there's be enough for both of us. His wife, suffering from a fever, keeps to her bedroom.

Ever-so-sore from my long hike, I sleep in exquisite soreness, window wide open, barely aware of the chilly fog that wafts in. It takes four hours of cock-a-doodle-doo, starting long before dawn, to get me up. For breakfast, Manoel makes me strong coffee — much stronger than that of the night before — with cheese and requeijão and store-bought cookies. It's good. He also boils me two eggs, serving them in a state barely beyond raw, which is the way I like them. One of the eggs had a greenish shell, the other a splotchy tan, both typical of the *ovos caipiras*, the eggs of truly free-range chickens who live off not chicken feed but whatever they can scratch up in the *quintal*. I contribute some of Fernando's honey, but it turns out Manoel has honey from a grandson who messes with bees. He has a vial of store-bought propolis, too, for medicinal purposes.

Before I leave, I ask if I can fill my two-liter plastic guaraná bottle. (Guaraná is a popular soft drink made either from the mildly stimulating seeds of that plant or from an artificial version of it. It's the only drink in Brazil that outsells Coca-Cola, though the Coca-Cola company has now come out with a guaraná drink of its own.) Of course Manoel is glad to provide me with water. In fact, he chills it for me by bringing from his freezer a block of ice in a war-torn aluminum pot. He draws water from his clay *filtro* tank and lets it cool over the ice before he pours it into my bottle. We fill the bottle in two batches, but that isn't enough. He uses a hammer and a lot of thumping to get the block of ice out of the pot. Then he cracks it into slivers that he slips into the mouth of the bottle. Presto! Cold water for my journey.

Then I ask him what I owed. Well, really, he says, nothing. If I write a book and bring more tourists to Bento Rodriguez, maybe some great-grandchild of his might someday open a little hotel in his house. It would be a great thing if that happened.

But I insist, and he finally says that any little thing would be fine. I slap him around the shoulders and tell him what other foreigners — the German, the Europeans, the church people in the bus — have told him: He knows how to work but he doesn't know how to charge. I give him ten *reais* — about five dollars — and he says it's too much and won't take it so I press it to the granite of his kitchen counter and tell him that's how much he gets.

And off I went with five pounds of cold water and the comfort of knowing I have to walk only nine kilometers to Santa Rita Durão. It's mostly uphill, however, and before I am a tenth of the way, I stop, dump my pack to the ground and drink as much of the extra weight as I can. A man comes up the road from behind me, a scythe and ax over his shoulder. I offer him water. He says he's hard put to swallow water. Just can't do it. I joke that *cachaça* is better, but he tells me he used to drink too much of it. A little dose (three or four ounces) in a glass wasn't enough. He needed a full glass, to the top. But then he decided to become a man again. He said that if you drink too much, you trade your friends for *cachaça*. So he stopped, and now he's going up the road to cut some firewood.

Chapter Two

Santa Rita Durão

The walk becomes agonizingly long. I'm still tired and sore from the day before. Most of the trip is uphill, curving around a mountain, and then the extended decline is just as painful. I'm still tired and sore from the day before. Much of the road is through a forest of eucalyptus that has been planted for use as charcoal. The road of wide, smooth dirt passes no houses. Every half hour or so a truck stacked with logs goes by. I'm walking toward the imposing range of the Serra do Caraça, a massif of semi-naked rock stretched into a series of vegetated peaks. Near a mine of the Vale do Rio Doce company I pick up dusty asphalt that goes into Santa Rita Durão. I pass the Igreja do Rosário, the church built for slaves in the eighteenth century, then the Igreja da Nossa Senhora Nazaré, where the white people worshiped. Not far beyond is a little restaurant, the Restbalanche Restaurant, so named because, the owner, Sr. Edval, tells me, it used to be a *restaurante*, bar and *lanchonete*. But the bar part was creating too much trouble, and the luncheonette wasn't worth the effort of offering snacks all day, so the place now just serves one meal to anyone who walks in.

The meal this day meal includes a formidable amount of food served on individual stainless steel platters: rice, beans, beef, spaghetti, collards, stir-fried cabbage, a fried banana, a few leaves of wet lettuce with two slices of a tomato that seems to have led a long, sad life in a town whose last name is the superlative of "tough." That, with a dose of *cachaça* and a beer, costs me $2.15. I chat up the waitress, a solid woman blessed with a moderate portion of African genes, wide hips, love in her eyes, and a warm smile unimpeded by a need of dental work. She, it turns out, is the wife of Sr. Evaldo himself. I ask her where in town a person can sleep. She says there really isn't anywhere, though just up the street a certain Dona Cota used to take in boarders, though the place is of dubious living condition. Worst case, she says, if necessary, I can sleep on the floor of the restaurant after they close.

Hoping to decline that offer, I leave my pack in the restaurant and go look for Dona Cota. Her house, a humble two-story building on the Nossa Senhora Nazaré, is run down to the point of seeming uninhabited. Steps in front lead up to the second floor, but the doors and windows look like they haven't been opened in years. I poke around the side and find the ratty remains of a door so full of holes that I can see it leads to a dim place in serious degradation, a place a lot like an old basement. I bang on the door — carefully — and soon a shy but smiling little girl creaks it open. She's wearing a school uniform that's the same deep blue as the trim on most of the houses in town. She says her mother's working, won't be back 'til around five o'clock. I ask if her father's home, and the answer is as I expected. She has no father.

So I wait around all day for Dona Cota to come home from work. Back at the Restbalanche, a nice guy named Inhô, offers to take me up to the Igreja do Rosário to see if it's open. The carved altars there, he says, are the most beautiful in all of Brazil. We go, but the church is closed. Deathly sore, I need to lie down, so I go around to the back of the church to lie in the shade of the eave of the roof. I try to make my muscles sleep. Meanwhile, people are arriving and climbing over the wall behind the church to pick *jabuticaba* berries from several tall trees in somebody's yard. They climb back over with a lot of chatter to the effect of hold this/let go/ now the other leg/ leave me alone, I can do it. I ask a lady for some *jabuticaba*, and before I can stop her, she just about fills my straw hat. She doesn't want money — after all, she's basically stolen them. But her labor was worth something, and getting her stout body over the wall had surely cost her something, so I press a couple of coins into her hand. She says God will pay me.

I eat too many of the addictive little fruits, then I teeter my aching bones back to Cota's. She's still not home, so I retire to a shady patch of grass beside a trickling fountain in front of the church, which is surrounded by barbed wire and with a sign that says "Entry Prohibited." A mangy horse and some mangy dogs keep me company. The horse looks pretty bored, but the dogs are engaged in complex and mysterious canine politics. There I lie in stuporous anguish for as long as I can stand the tickle of ants that apparently were waiting for somebody to come along and lie down on the ground. I reflect on the apparent fact that in Santa Rita Durão there is not one book, magazine or newspaper for sale anywhere. Not one piece of writing is for sale. No one in this town reads.

The town also has only one brand of cigarette, Broadway, which I've never seen anywhere else. And it has just one beer (Skol), just one place to eat, and one place to sleep, maybe. There's one bar with one pool table, and another bar that has nothing but a concrete counter to lean against as you down a *cachaça*, of which there are several kinds, none with labels. One is flavored with health-inducing herbs, twelve cents for all you can take in one gulp.

All afternoon I keep checking back for Dona Cota. I really need to take a bath and lie down on something soft. Each time, the little girl tells me not yet. I ask where Dona Cota works. The little girl tells me, "*lá no mato*," out there in the woods. As the day wears on, I feel sorrier and sorrier for the poor woman. I wonder what she does out in the woods.

I drag on over to the bar with a pool table to get a cold Skol to help me feel sorry for poor Cota. I notice how everyone here needs to chatter all the time, like the flocks of parrots that swoop around town to raid *jabuticaba* trees. Such simple lives they have, yet they have so much to tell each other! From the bar I watch six or eight people chattering as they pack themselves into a VW bus, on their way to a four-o'clock-to-midnight shift at one of the mines. No doubt they do this same thing every day, yet it takes an unbelievable amount of talking and shouting, passing bags in and out, people trading places, deciding to go or not to go, dashing across the plaza to resolve an issue with someone peripherally involved in the trip. Then they finally drive off, their huffy VW engine whistling into the distance, their tires raising more dust than you'd expect to come off asphalt.

Darkness seeps into Santa Rita Durão. I go back to

the Restbalanche to maintain my relationship there, the one which might win me a spot on the floor if things don't pan out with Dona Cota. I have dinner, another overkill of six or seven dishes, twice what I need. The evening *novela* — a soap opera that lasts for months — comes on the TV. It seems to be counterposing life in the jungle with life in the urban upper-middle class. The scenes alternate. Now it's people arguing in a house with a swimming pool. Now it's a couple of hunky guys in loin cloths chasing a buxom woman in a wet t-shirt through Amazonia, with an occasional comic intervention by a fat Indian chief and a pair of Indian maidens in grass skirts and no shirts, their modesty preserved only by their long hair. The *novela* is called *Uga-Uga*.

Just up the street, the minuscule one-room Igreja do Evangelho Quadrangular, has cranked up a mid-week celebration of its personal version of God. The door's wide open. Inside, a dozen people clap a regular beat and sing the glories of Jesus and the certainty of peace hereafter. The preacher, short, black, clean-cut, in a tie, leads from up front. Three little girls in dresses help him. As I pass, I smell soap. The Church of the Quadrangular Evangelism is the sweetest smelling place in town.

Cota arrives while I'm sitting on the doorstep of the Restbalanche. I'm sure it's her. She carries a stack of long logs on her head, balanced with one hand as she moves forward at a slow, onerous plod. She's barely five feet tall, stocky in the way of peasant women. I watch her to see if she goes into her house. She doesn't seem to, but when I show up a while later, the logs are leaning beside her door.

She doesn't seem too pleased at the possibility of a guest. The place is dirty and disarranged, she says. She really isn't in the business anymore. People kept staying there, then leaving without paying. They stole the blankets and mattresses. I'm not one to insist, but I plead my case with a certain desperation. Its hard to hold her attention because she's trying to hold a five-year-old still enough to dump some medicine down his throat. He whines and runs away. She chases him and drags him back. She finally asks how long I'd be staying, warning me again that the place hasn't been cleaned. Giving up on the sick kid, she takes up a thermos and shakes it. It's empty. "Sure would be nice if I came home and had some coffee waiting for me," she says. "Everything's on my shoulders, the firewood, the rice, the sugar, it's all on me." She slams the thermos down. I offer to get her a coffee from the bar across the street, but she won't hear of it. She and two kids take me outside and up the stairs to the second floor to the former dormitory. It is indeed grubby. It was grubby long before it got to the state of needing cleaning. The wooden floor is thickly littered with dead bugs and flecks of paint from the woven *taquara* bamboo ceiling, which is frayed with age, stained with roof water, and sagging with the weight of antiquity or dead rats. The two beds in the biggest room look like cadavers. One has a foam mattress in the late stages of disintegration. It makes the other one look good. Cota and the kids take the clean mattress downstairs to beat the dust out of it.

Cota has pretty much given up on trying to run a *dormitório*. The last time she had people here, two men, they ran up a big bill, then left without paying. Whenever she made a little money, she always had to spend it on something of more pressing importance than the business. Now the place is run down just about as far as a place can run. The roof leaks. The big concrete sink in the back is all globbed up with some kind of compound. The brass faucet is stuck into a PVC pipe and secured there only by a string that's about to rot through. A section of garden hose leads from the faucet to the faucet of the twin basin, where a complex arrangement of rags and plastic and an old stainless steel tea tray minimize drips and feed what escapes into the other basin, no doubt because the plumbing below also leaks. The feeder hose comes in through a window from a PVC pipe that wends its way down to a lean-to kitchen on the back of the building, where the pipe trickles constantly, filling a big, old five-liter cooking oil can on a counter next to the wood-burning cook-stove.

The electrical system is just as precarious, with wire of extension cord quality strung expediently from point to point by the shortest route possible, even if only neck high across the center of a room. Its insulation is cracked and graced with dusty cobweb, and the wire itself is just twisted around connection points without benefit of insulation, joining a light bulb socket to a wall switch and then up a wall to snake through the ceiling over to the next room.

The electric shower head is part of this jury rig and itself has been stripped to a minimum, the housing over the electrical part having no doubt been stolen by the same guys who took the blankets and mattresses. The wires connected to the heating element are exposed, and the little brass knob that turns the water on and off is layered with a thick wad of electrical tape, probably because the shower is grounded to the plumbing. Which means that if I get a little too exuberant in the washing of an armpit, I could electrocute myself and die in the slime of guys who swipe blankets and don't pay their bills.

I feel so sorry for Cota. She works harder than anyone I know, gets ripped off by her few customers, and has three young kids, one with a wicked cough. When I tell her she should fix the place up, she says her husband always said, "You need to have money to make money."

Cota and a couple of kids sit on the bed with the rotten mattress while she tells me these problems. I egg her on, hoping to find out what had happened to her husband, though in all likelihood he just ran off and probably hadn't even been the kind of husband who is actually married. Before I get to ask, the lights go out. The whole town goes dark. Cota says it's strange because there are no thunderstorms around. She fetches a candle from downstairs, though by the time she returns, I've got my own lit and melted into place on the windowsill. In a globe of yellow light, at a pace slow enough not to blow out a candle, she shows me around the *dormitório*. There really isn't much to show — some empty rooms, the odd deployment of light switches, the grimy bathroom. With a yank of the string, she flushes the toilet, though it really doesn't need it. It's just a gesture, all she can do on such short notice.

As soon as she's gone, I light a mosquito coil and collapse on the bed. All night long I keep rolling over, groaning as I adjust my bones. The smoke of the mosquito coil, undoubtedly carcinogenic, makes the inside of my lungs itch. Morning takes a long time to come.

Next day, I meet Inhô at the little restaurant. I'm not sure how to spell his name, but neither is he, and besides, his real name is Raimundo. The poor guy has very bad teeth. The few that remain, protruding from isolated places in his gums, are tilted and black. He offers to take me up the mountain that stands above the east side of town. There's a tunnel up there, he says, dug by slaves in the search for gold. He can take me to see it. Despite my sore muscles, I agree to go. We walk out of town and uphill for as far as I care to go, following a path of packed graphite bordered by hardscrabble grass and weeds. Inhô points out a gulch two or three hundred meters long slashed straight up a cliff of rock. The bottom of it ends at a swampy stream. The tunnel, he says, cuts diagonally up to the top of the gash like this — he holds his arm at a forty-five degree angle. The slaves dug out the tunnel and dumped the rock down the gulch into the stream. There the rock was crushed, washed and separated from the gold.

Just above the swamp, we probe into a dense little jungle of trees, vines, spider webs and brush. After a few false forays, we find it, a rather perfectly carved door-shaped opening in the rock, an oval as tall as a slumping slave and wide enough for two of them to pass each other. It's too dark inside to go more than a few meters, the floor strewn with fallen rubble. Inhô tells me it's blocked. Disappointed, I figure that's the end of it, but Inhô leads me up a narrow path across the side of the cliff. It rises at the same angle as the tunnel inside. My legs are wobbly, so I cling cautiously to every tuft of grass and knob of rock I can reach. Soon we come to a gash in the rock that reaches into the tunnel. The opening is fifty feet wide, six feet high or so, its ceiling supported by quartzite pillars that the slaves chiseled around. The tunnel passes at the bottom of the gash, too far in to see. Inhô heaves a rock into the gash. We listen as it tumbles into the darkness. Inhô marks the thumps with his hand while his eyes tell me to listen. Each thump seems to be the last, but then there's another...and another...and ...another. It's a deep gash, but Inhô's been down there. Vale do Rio Doce, which owns several mines in the region, hired him to accompany some geologists into the mountain. They were assaying the site for gold. Their painted marks on the walls and pillars still remain. Inhô rappelled into the mountain with the geologists. They poked into every nook and crack, mapped the whole thing. He knows the mountain inside out. He shows me three types of rock that make up the mountain: very hard quartzite, something soft and red, and sandstone. The gold is in the quartzite.

The mountain holds a lot more gold, Inhô is sure. The Portuguese dug one tunnel and cut out a few slices that lead into it. But it's a big mountain. They got only a little of it.

CVRD did not treat Inhô well. Once he cracked open a piece of quartzite and showed a certain golden chunk to the geologists. They said it wasn't gold, but they put the rock into their pouch, and that was the last he saw of it. When he asked a geologist about it, the geologist said that he shouldn't ask questions like that. If he'd asked anyone else, the geologist said, he'd have been fired on the spot. Asking questions hinted that the peon might be interested in doing a little mining himself. Inhô didn't like that attitude. He figured the geologists should have taught him geology so he could help more.

One time he found a big, wine-red rock. The geologists said it was nothing, but they put it in their pouch. He was sure if they'd cracked it open, they'd find a topaz inside, worth a lot of money. He's sure the geologists sold it.

As soon as the geologists were done with their survey Inhô got laid off. He thought that was pretty rotten. He'd worked well, taken risks, and offered expertise that few others had.

He takes me farther up the cliff. My legs get wobblier as we go. A slip to my right would send me tumbling a hundred feet almost straight down, at best slowing myself by grabbing grass or digging my fingernails into rock. We stop at more gashes. At some points we can see the tunnel below. We toss in more rocks, hear them tumble down, down, down.

I say, "Imagine how many slaves died in there."

A lot, Inhô says, his face crushed with seriousness. "*Muitos.*"

We squat on the path, look out and down across the unending green waves of hills of the state of Minas Gerais. Smoke rises from a broad area three or four hills away — a charcoal operation turning eucalyptus trees into fuel for steel mills.

Inhô tells me that his great-grandfather, who might

39

have been alive not long after slavery was outlawed in 1888, told him how the Portuguese disposed of slaves who didn't work well. Down in the tunnel they unchained them and brought them up to where we are now squatting. There, as Inhô demonstrates, they put a foot on the slave's back and pushed him over the cliff. Down below, other slaves received their dead and buried him somewhere out in the *mato*. Inhô sweeps his hand over a vast area to show me where thousands of unmarked graves lie. It's the slow, broad gesture of a priest blessing a congregation.

Farther up the path, we come under a rock from which hangs a strange, white substance the size and shape of a large pillow. Quartz? No, Inhô whispers — bees. The white stuff is honeycomb, and the dark stuff killer bees. He cautions me to walk and speak softly.

"*Muito africanizados*," he says. "*E bravos.*" Very Africanized, and mean.

All wild bees in Brazil are, to come extent, Africanized. NonAfricanized bees would be the relatively docile Italian bees that are raised, and wild, in North America. But in 1957, twenty-six African queen bees and their entourages escaped captivity in the state of São Paulo, where they were being studied for their unique characteristics. Among those characteristics are stamina, aggressiveness, and a tendency to attack en masse. The African bees are stronger, so when an Italian queen is in heat, it is inevitably an African that catches her in her mating flight. He's sorry, of course, because it is his genitalia that get ripped out once he's filled her spermatheca, but his offspring are half African, and theirs will inevitably be three-quarters African, and as the generations purify toward the African, they get just as mean as can be. I once raised these bees in Brazil, and I know how they can be quite docile one day, but another day, maybe due to internal politics we can never know, they don't want you anywhere near their hive. Every once in a while somebody gets killed, often not by the stings but by their desperate attempt to flee. In this particular case, on the side of this particular cliff, the escape route is either over the cliff and down to the swamp, or into the gash in the mountain to hide in the darkness, where bees will not go. Or one can whisper and walk softly. Thanks to the sweat and blood of a thousand slaves, we are able to get around the hive by going through a hole that has been carved through an outcrop.

During this hike up the mountain and back down, Inhô keeps stopping to talk. He tells me things several times, and he acts a lot of it out as if in charade. This is good because he's hard to understand. In quick, *Mineiro* peasant dialect, he rattles his words fast, smearing the vowels and using peasant slang that I often don't understand. He talks a lot about the rotten deal he and everyone else got from working with the CVRD mining company. They really worked hard. They went down into these gashes, hauled up bags of sample rock on their backs, slipped along the path when it was raining, got paid little and only for temporary, contracted work, without benefits, and had his undoubtedly valuable rocks stolen by the geologists. He suspects he got fired for inquiring about his topaz. He recently became entitled to retirement payments form the government, but he's been waiting for his check for five months. He leads me into the same conclusion I'd thought of earlier, one which I didn't think he'd figure out: that slavery has not ended. Maybe they don't push you off a cliff when they're done with you, but destitution is basically the same thing.

He also talks a lot about his desperate financial situation. He has five kids, all of them sick with a flu of the chest, no doubt the same one I've been feeling for the past three days. Sometimes he doesn't have food for them. Crying, they ask for food, but he has to explain that he doesn't have any, not 'til his retirement check comes in.

But he won't steal! Não senhor! he wags his leathery finger at me and raises his chin with pride. His father on his death bed told him not to steal, that something stolen never leads to anything good.

Inhô is priming me, of course, for a generous payment for his services, and of course I'm glad to make my contribution. Halfway down the mountain, he points across Santa Rita Durão, over to the section on the other side of the river, where the little houses are hard to see under the trees. A van from CEMIG, the electric company, is parked next to a utility pole, and there's a guy in a yellow hardhat up there doing something.

"They're here to shut off my lights," Inhô says. "I got my last warning yesterday."

Inhô and I have lunch at the Restbalanche, and then I go looking for some nice sponges. I need them to pad the shoulder straps of my pack. The straps appear to have had padding back when I was a boy scout, but the last thirty-five years have turned it to something with the consistency of mushy sand. The years haven't been much kinder to my shoulders, and the twenty-mile hike into Santa Rita has rubbed them raw. They feel bruised. So my plan is to tape some sponges to the straps. But just try to find a decent sponge in a town like this! There's just one store, and its sponges are only a quarter-inch thick. The store has a few fruits and vegetables, however, so I inquire about limes. I want to make a *caipirinha* with the little Coke bottle of *cachaça* somebody gave me at the Restbalanche, the product of his father, made from a recipe that goes back at least three generations. It is indeed very good, with a secret ingredient. The conversation associated with the transfer of this fine stuff circled in on the likelihood of that ingredient being *jabuticaba*. There are no limes in evidence, however, so

I ask. Limes, it seems, have just gone out of season, but the store owner thinks he may have one or two on his tree at home. He dispatches a small boy to lead me there, just up the street and around the corner. An older boy at the house leads me into the *quintal*, where we shake a tree for the last of its limes, just three or four that have blackened on the outside but not rotted on the inside. They are an orange kind with a flavor that is good but have the flavor of neither a lime nor a lemon nor an orange. The store owner refuses to accept payment for them.

Back at Cota's I borrow a glass. She takes a long time to find one that is worthy of her guest. Before I go up to bed, I ask her how much I owe. I plan to leave for Catas Altas as early as possible the next morning so I can arrive there before the heat of noon. Dona Cota has no idea how much to charge. She really doesn't want anything. I get her to tell me how much people used to pay, or would have paid if they hadn't skipped out. She tells me it varied, depending on whether it was CVRD or the individual guest that was paying. She vaguely remembered something around the equivalent of four or five dollars a day, depending. So I pay her twice that, figuring her kid's got a cough and that it sure won't break me. I wish someone would give me the job of walking down the Estrada Real and handing out spare change to people who need it, except of course that's everybody, and if I ever finished that project, there'd always be

Bombay and Ouagadougou needing it just as much.

In my room, I set up shop at a little table that's about a meter square. I squeeze the lime into the glass, add a couple ounces of *cachaça* and a big spoon of Fernando's honey and mix it up. It's warm and littered with little seeds but tastes and feels very good. I like it because the *cachaça* has a secret ingredient and no brand name, the lime did not come from a store, the honey came from a guy who gave me lunch, and I'm drinking this fine stuff from a jelly jar.

I like my little office-of-the-day, too, my little table and the section of log on which I sit, and the single unfrosted light bulb that hangs by a wire from the ceiling. The table has a history of labor spread across it — a field of old white paint with some areas of light green and some intriguing blotches of red that isn't paint. It has been scratched with knifework and general use. It's a bit sticky where I sliced my lime. The top is of two wide boards, one of which has split. The nails are old and rusty. Maybe it's the *cachaça*, but I think that if you hung this tabletop in a nice museum, people would have a hard time telling it from art. And if we can assume for the moment that it is indeed art, placed here in Dona Cota's Museum of the Unstolen, we would nod slowly and call it beautiful.

Chapter Three

Catas Altas And Santa Bárbara

Before dawn I'm out the door. I grab a café com leite at the Restbalanche and cadge a liter of cold water. The road out of town is dry dirt of hematite and clay. Buses, cars and trucks serving the local CVRD mine raise waves of red dust that coats me like a disease. This would have been a good section to cover in a bus except that I'd miss the spectacular view of the Serra do Caraça. I walk below a sheer cliff that must be a kilometer straight up. It's a good range to pass slowly. Its rock face is sharp in the clear morning light, and its peaks condense the air into plumes of thin, horizontal cloud. It's massive yet isolated and small enough that one can get the sensation of walking past a whole mountain range. It started distinctly at Santa Rita Durão, and Catas Altas, ten miles ahead, is about halfway along its length. Somewhere up there is the monastery known as Caraça, where monks still live, supporting themselves with a rustic resort and a variety of fruit preserves. Those who have been there recommend it. I haven't been there, but I recommend it anyway.

And if I had taken a bus, I wouldn't have stopped at Morro da Aqua Quente — Hot Water Hill — a village that looks like it might have a food supply. Somebody tells me there's a little restaurant just a hundred meters up a certain street, but it turns out to be at least a kilometer, all of it uphill, a long way to go to get ripped off for two pieces of bread and some coffee. The kid who brought it to me charged at least twice the reasonable price, keeping half of it for himself, I'm sure. But I really got my money's worth out of the bathroom, which featured a toilet seat, soap, and even a little mirror over the sink. I left a lot of red dust there.

And if I hadn't walked up that hill to that restaurant, I wouldn't have strolled into the Capela do Nosso Senhor do Bonfim. I almost passed the place, which didn't look like much, but then decided I really ought to at least have a look. Turns out it's under restoration. A crew of seven is working on or near scaffolding up behind the altar. Our Lord of the Good End, life-sized, agonized, is nailed to a cross laid over the tops of several pews. A shroud protects Him from the dust of restoration. A tenor sings something beautiful from a boom box. It's the only music I've heard in several days and the first time I have heard classical music in Brazil anywhere outside of a concert hall or someone's home. It's a nice place to sit a while and an interesting place to take a photo at a slow shutter speed, the camera supported on the back of a pew as I try to hold my breath and make my heart not beat for about three seconds.

I'm about to leave when the head of the crew comes back to ask if I'd like to know anything about the project. His name is Maurício Lins. He has an interior decorating business in Salvador, Bahia, but he has a degree in the restoration of antiquities from the Universidade Federal de Ouro Preto. Whenever he can, he takes an assignment restoring an old church. Little by little the government and a few private-sector companies are trying to save the hundreds of rural churches that are fading and falling apart. In some cases, beautiful paintings on altars and walls have been covered with plaster. Beams are rotting. Roofs are leaking and falling in. Icons, carvings and fixtures are being stolen. At the moment, Maurício is repainting the altar, carefully cleaning the paint that remains and adding paint to fill in spaces where the original paint has flaked off. He is not, he points out, covering original paint with new paint.

Maurício suggests I walk to Catas Altas via the train

track, which is just above town, just below the Serra da Caraça. It's a better walk, he says: no hills, lots of shade, nice views. Along the way to the tracks, I can stop at a water tank and take a bath. so that's exactly what I do. It's a nice bath, but by the time I get to the tracks, it's noon and very hot. I lie down under a high bridge to rest. Two big diesel trains full of iron ore rumble by. I throw a rock at an ore car just to see what a rock bouncing off a train looks and sounds like. The route ends up having no shade whatsoever. A shy, skinny horse follows me, staying about fifty meters behind, stopping when I stop. It wanders off by the time I get to Catas Altas. The tracks pass above the town. This, I decide, is the best way to arrive at a place, from an elevation that lets me see the shape of the town as it lies across its hills. I can see its steeples, *praça*s and woodsmoke. I can hear its barks and cock-a-doodle-doos and feel the humanity of the place.

I come into town hot, tired, sore and dusty. I awaken a dog who's sleeping in the middle of the street, a classic dog of the interior, lying on his side across the cobblestones, legs out, not worried about cars. He barks at me, and then all his friends come to bark at me. They follow me through town, everybody barking, gathering more barkers as we go. It's quite an escort, very cool, a full-blown barkarama.

Taking Maurício's advice, I seek out the *Pousada* Municipal, a small inn operated by the town government.

It's a good choice, right on the plaza of the Igreja Matriz de Nossa Senhora da Conceição, right over a little post office and an office that serves the town legislators. (*Igreja* means church; the *matriz* is a town's main church.) The building is at least two centuries old, with tall windows closed by heavy shutters, tall doors of wide boards, wide floor boards, high ceilings, a long dining room table that must weigh a ton, everything waxed and clean. A room without a bathroom, but breakfast included, runs about five dollars. I suppose I could afford the extra two and a half dollars for my own private bathroom, but there are no other guests in the place, so why waste the money? The proprietor, a classically interior Brazilian in black pants, white shirt, dark necktie, trim mustache and neat, moist hair, leads me to a corner room that overlooks the *praça* on one side, the Serra do Caraça on the other. The view of the mountain to the west promises a constant evolution of visual entertainment. The *praça*, however, threatens to ruin the ambience with constant noise.

I'm wrong about the *praça*. It's a quiet *praça*, sloping westward from the church, with only one or two vehicles in it at any given moment. The stores around the edge are sleepy, small, and, inside, dark. The church is majestic up against the eastern sky. The *praça* itself is a serious deployment of chunks of dark gray granite laid out by slaves sometime in the century before last or the one before that. Though all the stones are the same color, their rectangular shapes are set in patterns that radiate from the church.

The *praça* is clean, too. The whole town is clean. Coming into town, I did not see a speck of litter anywhere, did not catch a whiff of burning trash. I've never seen such a thing in Brazil. On the way into town, I noticed yellow trash barrels — sawed off oil drums — every twenty or thirty meters, each stenciled with the initials of the municipal government of Catas Altas. In this town, there is no excuse for dropping a piece of trash in the streets.

But somebody did. I didn't see it happen, but somehow, perhaps by accident or emergency, a plastic soda bottle came to rest in the street beside the church. More surprising than that anomaly was the teenager who came along and took two steps out of his way and leaned all the way down to street level to pick up the bottle and carry it with him to the nearest yellow barrel.

The mayor of this town is serious, I can tell. His town is clean and his people are inspired to keep it that way. His municipal inn is beautiful. The town just feels like a nice place to live. It may be a bit short on amenities, such as restaurants, but it's big on peace and quiet. My guidebook lists two restaurants, one of which, according to the nice lady at the post office, either never opened or isn't open anymore or if open is certainly not worth eating at. She's a pretty, vivacious and sociable post office lady who obviously would never lie about a restaurant.

The open eatery is indeed a nice place. Most of the tables are outdoors, under a tile roof, and on this particular evening I'm the only diner there. The waitress seems shy and excited to be serving someone with a foreign accent. I request a local *cachaça* and some *caldo de feijão* bean soup. I like to mix two or three spoonfuls of hot soup into the *cachaça* and drink it in two gulps. Nobody else in the world drinks *cachaça* this way, but they should. Then I have some fried manioc and a bottle of beer while I write a letter that gushes with the good feelings I have about this town. I can hear three sounds: the delicate song of a bird in a cage next door, an argument among geese in the yard across the street, and, in the kitchen, the hot dialogues of the *Uga-Uga novela*. I note the nice lady from the post office coming home to her house on the other side of the little *pracinha* in front of the restaurant.

Then I go back to my *pousada* and sleep well. I sleep with the windows and shutters wide open. The *praça* — the whole town — is so quiet I can't resist getting up in the middle of the night to look out the window. The town is still there, the *praça* dream-like under the limited illumination of street lamps. The whole town is asleep, every person, dog, and rooster. It is perfectly silent. It's almost too good to sleep through.

I want to meet the mayor of this place. Something tells me he isn't in the business of ripping off public funds.

Actually, it was Mauricio, the church-restorer, who told me that. So I find town hall — it's diagonally across the *praça* from the *pousada* — but the *prefeito*, Juca Hosken, is out until next week. The best his secretary can offer me is some printed matter about the town, including the October 2000 issue of Catas Altas Informa, a four-page bulletin with news about the town. The October issue has the election news. Here I learn that Catas Altas is a new town. Until 1995 it was part of Santa Barbara, the next town up the Estrada Real. Hosken was its first elected *prefeito*, and in the elections of October 1, he was reelected with 1,477 votes, 56.94% of the total, 360 ahead of the runner up. So he's in until 2004, and he promises more of the good works he has started. It was the first election by electronic polling, putting Catas Altas two generations ahead of Florida, which, a week after I arrived in Catas Altas, would impose its corrupt and erroneous election results on the rest of the United States.

The newsletter reports the latest census data. Catas Altas now has 4,160 residents, a ten percent increase in four years. In September, a *Casa* do Professor was inaugurated as a meeting and research place for teachers. One school in town now has sufficient water thanks to a new well; no longer will a certain farmer have to contribute water to the school. And speaking of water, right outside my *pousada*, in the middle of the *praça* in front of the church, there's a lone pillar, about seven feet tall with a brass faucet. Water trickles from it into a stone basin. According to the newsletter, this *chafariz* is part of the town's cultural wealth. It dates back to the town's founding in the early eighteenth century, when the fountain was the town's central water supply. Documents indicate that slaves were tied to the fountain and punished.

Also happening in Catas Altas today is the repaving of streets, not with asphalt but with stone bricks typical of the town. And the area's vintners are getting organized, as are the town's potters and those who offer services relating to crafts and tourism.

This is a rebirth for a town which 301 years ago got off to a questionable start as a gold-mining town when Domingos Borges first raised the Portuguese flag at the site in 1702. The first baptism came ten years later, and in that year construction was begun on the Igreja Matriz de Nossa Senhora da Conceição. It wasn't finished until 1780, about the time the gold mine petered out and most inhabitants went elsewhere. The remainder lived by subsistence farming and small-scale gold prospecting. It's rather amazing to think that a few hundred people were using a church that rivals many in Rome.

The town was largely ignored by the government of Santa Barbara, so when Hosken became *prefeito*, he had plenty to do. He immediately set out to restore the town's many historic buildings and its three historic churches.

According to the booklet, there is not one child between the ages of seven and fourteen who is not in school. The town has eight schools, six of them in rural areas. There are 265 students in the rural schools and 500 in town. Two hundred students use school buses. By law, the town must spend 25 percent of its budget on education, but Catas Altas spends 30.95%.

The booklet gives the Igreja Matriz just two short paragraphs, neither of them attempting to describe the indescribable interior. Words fail me, too. I simply cannot believe that human beings carved something of such beauty and intricacy. The overall effect is dizzying. The effect may be all the more true of the Igreja Matriz because each of the lateral altars was financed by a different family, so each has its own style, adding to the sense of swirl and turbulence. Neither the mind nor the eye, let alone the camera, can take it all in and knit it together. While each detail is infinitesimally precise, every aspect of the overall design seems aimed at confusing the eye. The pillars of the altars, and even the supports of banisters, seem twisted into thick spirals. The cherubs look off balance. The gold leafing dazzles the eye. The ceiling tricks the eye into seeing the depths of Heaven and history. There are no straight lines anywhere to give the eye a sense of horizon.

And if one could believe, for the sake of argument, that human beings actually created this place, one would have to ask why it could be done in the eighteenth century but not in the twenty-first. Faith, I suppose, has something to do with it, as does a change in public finance policy. I suppose the international space station could be said to be, in its own way, as intricate and complex as a Baroque church; it's simply in adoration of a different god.

Groping from the church into the hard light of day, I cross the *praça* to the post office to see the nice lady and get directions to the "*sítio do japonês*," the little farm of the Japanese guy, which I've heard about from several people along the Estrada. His place is just twenty minutes away by foot, she says, so off I go, down some streets and onto the paved highway that goes on to Santa Barbara and back toward Belo Horizonte. I can see the *sítio* well before I get to it, an impressive plantation on the side of a hill above the highway, a neat arrangement of fruit and coffee trees, garden greens and outbuildings. As I come up a long driveway, dogs come to warn me off, but I call their bluff and press on. I ask an elderly Japanese woman where I can find "*o famoso japonês*," and she asks me whether I want the older or younger one. She indicates the younger, over yonder in a tall, open garage/workshop. He's busy roasting coffee in a crusty old gas-heated drier that growls as it rotates and exhales blue clouds of acrid smoke. He seems relieved to see that he can hand me off to his father, and he hustles off to fetch him.

The elder Japanese, Nitaro Mori, a solid-looking

man in his late sixties or early seventies arrives from his garden. I explain that I'm researching the Estrada Real and that he is apparently one of the monuments along the route. At that, he just starts talking but in a direction I hadn't expected. I'd expected his philosophy of planting. Everyone has told me that his farm products are unexcelled, that he gets his fruit to grow out of season, that he shames the rest of Brazil by showing everyone what can be done with land if one applies a little intelligence to it.

He does indeed have a very nice little farm, but it isn't the Eden I'd heard about, and planting is not what he chooses to talk about. Nitaro Mori's schtick is shiatsu massage and herbal remedies made of, especially, comfrey and aloe. He has a little flier, a photocopy on half a sheet of paper, that lists what he can cure. Depression heads the list, followed by two biggies: cancer and AIDS, then bronchitis, nervous disorders, emphysema, thrombosis, inflammation of the digestive tracks, rheumatism, colic of the kidneys, menstrual colic, hypertension, diabetes, pains and inflammations in general, sciatica, bursitis, tennis elbow, colitis, gastritis, gastric and duodenal ulcers, lung infections, asthma, wounds that will not heal, angina, hormonal dysfunctions, chronic cystitis, prostate problems, hemorrhoids, sinusitis, slow mental or physical development, learning difficulties, bed-wetting, all emotional and mental problems, grip, obesity and, last but by no means least, hepatitis, not to mention half a dozen ailments I cannot translate.

A lot of these cures, he says, are only promised in books he's read. He hasn't had enough patients to test all the indications. Depression heads the list because that's the latest thing he's cured, but cancer and AIDS are right up there for the same reason. Yes, he has cured AIDS, but no, he doesn't know why the patient never came back with others. Obesity he is about to move up to the head of the line, that having been another recent cure. He's going to add headaches, too, because while I'm sitting there, someone calls up to say that her migraines have disappeared.

Nitaro has bags of herbal mixtures for tea, bottles of aloe-comfrey snake oil, jars of garlic in vinegar. He lets me drink a little cup of something just so I could see how terrible it tastes. It has two herbs, horsetail and broomweed, in it. It does taste like something that surely must be healthful. He shows me how to massage my wife's foot to help her relax, how to knead her calves to relieve her depression, how to unknot her spine with my thumbs. If I want to bring my relatives in for treatment, he'll charge me nothing if he doesn't cure them on the spot. He'll even take a shot at my sister-in-law's schizophrenia, though he's never tried that before. He doesn't offer a guarantee on that one.

I'm not sure how much of this to believe. For some

odd and stupid reason, his being a very nice man and a little on the old side and Japanese — or really, the son of a Japanese couple who came to Brazil before World War II — lends a lot of credence to his claims. The Japanese are renowned in Brazil for being able to do things right, especially in agriculture. Brazilians use Japanese-Brazilians as an example with which they can flog themselves for their own inadequacy. One thing's for sure: As soon as I get home, I'm going to plant a lot of comfrey.

Nitori discovered the miraculous powers of aloe and comfrey quite by accident. He mixed them with *cachaça* — his son has a small distillery — and used them to successfully cure his own dandruff. He tilts his pate to me, points to a place that has little hair. There is no sign of flaking.

* * *

The next morning I head for Santa Bárbara. My guidebook promised a "parkway" between Catas Altas and Santa Barbara. the only thing park-like about this asphalt highway are the occasional virgin trash cans with the name of a mining company stenciled on the side. Apparently there's a plan to build a bicycle path along the road, but unless it's a hundred yards away, it won't be a path anyone would want to use. Trucks and buses barrel past me, missing me by only three or four feet. It's truly terrifying. For all my fears of bandits, snakes, and exposure to the elements, this stretch of paved road is by far the most dangerous part of the Estrada Real. At one point, I see a car passing another car as it comes around a curve while from the opposite direction a bus comes tilting around another curve. With uncharacteristic quickness of thought, I dash into the deep grass beside the road, getting as far away as I can before the collision. With a lot of vicious honking, however, they three vehicles manage to get by each other.

I'd be glad to have skipped this stretch of the Estrada, but if I'd taken a bus, I would have missed the singing street cleaner of Santa Barbara, a slender and very black woman with a battle-weary wheelbarrow, a broom, and a scoop with a long handle. She sings beautifully as she flicks bits of litter into her scoop. When she sees me coming along with my pack, her pretty faced lights up with real happiness. She pauses her song long enough to say *"Bom dia!"* like she really means it. And indeed my day is made good, the tense headache of my hike assuaged.

Except for the singing street cleaner, Santa Bárbara isn't a very pretty city. It's grown a bit beyond my preference. It's pretty and peaceful right in the center of town, between the Igreja Matriz de Santo Antônio do Ribeirão de Santa Bárbara and the town hall just across the street, but within a few blocks the town turns commercial. The town is big enough to have a few banks, shops for just about everything I could want to buy - just a pad of paper is all, really, but if I wanted new shoes or a radio or a bicycle or a plastic doll whose eyes close when you lay her down, I could get them here. The products are of the low, tacky quality that finds its way into the interior of Brazil. You don't see these products in the big cities. The products come in plastic bags foggy with age and small-town dust.

It's a loud town. I don't know why, but the sounds all seem magnified. Televisions seem louder. People talk louder. Music from unseen sources is not only loud but bad, imitations of Euro-American pop rock junk. It seems that an unusually large portion of the cars are Volkswagen bugs with thin mufflers that take unusually long to sputter out of earshot. It must be something about the stone streets or concrete buildings that makes the noise echo and intensify. Maybe it's the contrast with the very quiet Catas Altas. I don't know. The city is simply a din.

I book into a small *pousada* just off the main street. The city noise penetrates my little room. The TV in the other room booms and barks and rattles with commercial urgency. I write a little. I take a book on Tarot from the room with the TV and look for wisdom in it. I go out and walk round, but it really isn't an interesting town. At night, a lousy rock band cranks up on the sidewalk just up the street, and some goon spends the night making ugly noises into a microphone, complaining, I'm sure, about how awful life is.

There's one person I want to meet in this town: the owner of the Mackllani apiary. I've been seeing his honey products everywhere, from Belo to Santa Barbara. In fact, he's got a big billboard just outside of town, announcing that Santa Barbara is honey country. The owner of the *pousada* takes me to his back porch and points out the Mackllani building, just half a kilometer away. He even lets me use the phone to call and make an appointment with Renato, the owner. And the next morning, I go to see him.

Renato Fonseca Oliveira was studying accounting at a university in Belo Horizonte when he discovered bees. At the time, he was also trying to run a flower shop. It was a lot of head-work, studying numbers and running a one-man business, but some people are like that, and Renato was certainly one of them.

This was back in 1982, when the beekeeping industry in Brazil was just beginning to develop. A state industry association, APIMG, offered a demonstration course for beginning beekeepers. As if he didn't have a enough to do, Renato took the course. That was the end of his career in accounting.

Despite the vociferous remonstrations of his mother,

who'd been looking forward to having a son with a nice job, Renato dropped out of school, returned to his native town of Santa Bárbara, bought three hives and declared himself in the bee business.

He learned the details. He processed his honey in his mother's kitchen. He worked without help. To sell his honey, he filled empty liquor bottles. He put the bottles in a bag and hitchhiked twenty-five miles down a dirt road and another fifty miles down asphalt to Belo Horizonte, where honey fetched a fair price — if the honey of killer bees can possibly be said to have a fair price.

Having sold his production, he "capitalized his revenues," an accounting term meaning "bought more hives." Two years later, having expanded his business and left his mother's kitchen spotless, he earned a government award for Excellence in Rural Productivity. He sold his flower shop and bought a VW bus. And more hives. Over the next few years, he won more prizes, including a magnificent trophy named Rosângela Maria Gonçalves, whom he married. He started packing his honey in plastic containers. He printed up labels that said, "Mel Santa Bárbara." (*Mel* is honey.) He won a trip to a conference in Switzerland. Three times he won an award for Excellence in Commerce and Industry.

Don't underestimate the labor involved. By necessity, all beekeepers in Brazil work with Africanized bees, some more African than others. They're the only ones that can resist diseases, which in Brazil include the varroa mites and foulbrood bacteria that have made wild honeybees almost extinct in North America. Mackllani uses no medications to protect its bees.

Except for ants and a rather scarce cousin of the skunk, wild pests don't mess with African bees. The African bees work harder than the wimpy Italians that populate North America. The Africans go to work earlier in the morning, work harder all day, and work later into the evening. Italians queens are available in Brazil, and they can be installed in a hive of African worker bees. Within a few weeks, all the bees in that hive will be nice, gentle Italians. But when a new queen comes to power, she will mate with the first drone that can catch her, inevitably an African. The next generation in that hive will be *mestiços*, and each subsequent generation will be increasingly African. For this reason, attempts to supplant Brazil's killer bees with gentler strains have failed.

Just as Brazilian bees work harder, so do Brazilian beekeepers. Their suits are heavy canvas that zip up tight and reach down over heavy rubber boots. Renato works in the hills of Minas Gerais, but still, it's Brazil, and the sun is hot. And the bees are aggressive. A few always manage to wiggle into the suit. Once they're in, there's nothing the beekeeper can do but wait for the sting.

Renato's company, Apiários Mackllani Ltda., has

grown consistently from day one. Even today it expands by an awesome 80 percent per year. Today it's the largest supplier of bee-related products in Minas Gerais and one of the top five in Brazil.

Much of Renato's success is in the variety of his products, which may well exceed that of any similar company in North America. He offers over 90 different products, and his strategy is to offer something new every month. He sells honey, pollen, propolis, royal jelly, honey with royal jelly, honey with propolis, honey with propolis and eucalyptus, honey with propolis and extracts of any of a dozen herbs and spices that include ginger, mint, garlic, watercress, salvia, pomegranate, strawberry, lime, and Brazilian plants you've never heard of. He sells soaps, shampoos, cosmetics, salves, pomades, candles, perfumes, liqueurs and candies. He sells honey sticks and little packets that hold a tablespoon of honey mixed with the aforementioned extracts. He sells long chains of these packets. He sells medicinal sprays. He sells trinkets and statues and paperweights that glorify the bee. His factory and shop are the fanciest things in Santa Bárbara. Tourists in buses come to see where their honey comes from.

His sales reps roam over much of Brazil. They offer a nice, big wooden stand that holds all the Mackllani products. The retail price of straight honey is about two dollars a pound. Of course he has a website: www.

melsantabarbara.com.br.

Renato affirms that killer bees don't go flying around looking for something to kill. Sometimes they set up shop on a cliff or under the eaves of a church and hang there for a few months, gathering nectar 'til they've filled the available space, at which point, OK, maybe, sometimes, yes, they might get a little irritated with the noise of a festival or a church service and decide to chase off the faithful, but the faithful understand that God works in mysterious ways, and bees are one of them.

These really aren't bees for the backyard, Renato says. You keep them out in the woods. You can get near them, but not real near. When one of his workers, a metallurgist manqué named Regismarlon, takes me to one of several bee yards, he speaks in a hushed and respectful voice. We approach with caution, ready to run. We get a warning shot. One hits me behind the knee. It hurts. We get into the truck. We leave.

It isn't every day somebody gets killed by these bees. It's a rare event. Renato can remember only a couple of recent cases. In one, someone captured a swarm and was taking it home in a small hive when for some reason he left it on the side of the road. He told a local farmer not to mess with it. Along came a highway worker on a tractor, mowing grass. When he hit the hive, the bees exploded. The farmer told the worker to run. He did — faster than the farmer, may he rest in peace.

In another case, somebody had a hive in their backyard. For some reason, the bees turned mean one day. They attacked the owner. He ran, tripped, hit his head on a rock and died. Technically, and mercifully, he died of a concussion, not stings, though if the concussion hadn't killed him, the stings would have.

That's about it for bee emergencies around Santa Bárbara. Besides that, the 150 beekeepers who supply Mackllani with honey have had no serious problems. Regismarlon says he rarely gets stung in the field, probably because he wears a no-nonsense suit.

Raising bees in Brazil isn't much different from the way it's done in North America. The hives sit on steel monopod stands that have a basin of motor oil around the leg to keep the ants out. A plank of asbestos — a common roofing material — keeps the sun and rain off the hive. Though Brazil has no winter to speak of, the bees are inactive from October to January, spring in Brazil, when rain and lack of blossoms keep the bees home. It's good to feed them then and to leave them stocks of honey to see them through temperatures that can plummet into the fifties. Mackllani's hives have odd feeders that hang down from the front door, plus a standard entrance feeder that's inserted in the side of the hive.

Africanized bees tend to swarm more often than Italians. That's both good and bad. It means you can easily lose a swarm, but you can just as easily capture one by poking a hole in a box and leaving it in the woods. A little wax inside helps. So does lemon grass. The best box is the special cardboard express mail box provided by the Brazilian post office. It's cheap and it's coated with something that makes it waterproof.

Mackllani operates about a thousand hives, and beekeepers throughout the region sell their honey to the company. Three people do the uncapping, by hand, with forks. They have a single 32-frame extractor. The rest of the process is efficient, automated, and clean. A decrystalizer heats the honey, sends it by pipe to a pasteurizer which sends it in a continuous flow to tanks that hold pure honey, honey with propolis or honey with pollen. From there the blends go on to be mixed with the various flavors.

Mackllani distributes the products to seven states in Brazil, and retailers in other states order products by mail. In many areas, it's the only bee products available. Some of the competition produces more honey, but none offers such variety.

Mackllani is adding value to its products by promoting the concept of Santa Bárbara as the land of good honey — a convenient coincidence to Minas Gerais being Brazil's main dairy state, making this the land of milk and honey.

Journey on the Estrada Real

Chapter Four

Cocais

It's a moist walk from Santa Bárbara to Barão dos Cocais – Saint Barbara to Baron of Coconut Groves. The rainy season has arrived suddenly and thoroughly, so I am suddenly thoroughly wet. But I do believe I'd rather walk in rain, holding my little blue-green, busted-rib umbrella, than suffer the heat of an unbroken sun. But I'm mighty chilled and wet as I slog into Barão dos Cocais, a relatively large town of 25,000. I walk through town for half-an-hour before I come to the main *praça*. A kind-eyed lady in a pharmacy tells me where it is and explains how I have to go next door and call over a gate and ask to talk with Senhora So-and-so about a room.

Senhora So-and-so, or her son, actually, takes me up to a very simple room with a simple bed and a window looking into a simple air shaft. The bed sheets are clean and tightly tucked. The floor is well waxed, and the towel on the bed is fanned artfully, perhaps to distract the eyes from its threadbare condition. The bathroom, just across the hall, is clean, too, though the toilet lacks a seat. Senhora So-and-so's son collects my five *reais* (two and a half dollars) in advance. No breakfast included in this deal, and if I should leave early the next morning while his gate is still locked, I should just lob the key in.

Barão dos Cocais is probably an ugly, industrial town in the best of times. Under a cold rain, it's perfectly miserable. I rest in my cell, but after a while I have to get out. I have no long pants or anything dry, so I tread around town cold and wet, which isn't so bad as long as I keep moving. The centerpiece of the local economy is a loud and smoky steel mill with a billboard out front proclaiming the company's love of the environment. Walking past the wall that surrounds it, I can see and hear the white-hot crackle of something being done with melted steel. Viscous yellow-gray smoke hemorrhages from a low, fat smokestack and blends into the low-lying clouds. The place hums with industrial power, and sometimes something weighing a few hundred tons clanks against something hard.

But that's not the worst noise in town. That record

is held by an ice cream shop on the plaza in front of my *pousada*. A single, large speaker stands on the sidewalk, blasting out the worst of Brazilian rock, horrid stuff imitating American punk. In a little *barzinho* next door to the *pousada* a man expresses his irritation with the noise. Everybody in town hates it, he says. The music is not only loud but terrible, some kind of ersatz punk made worse by a cheap, low-fi speaker. And there's nobody in the ice cream shop. It's just a take out place where you pick up a cone and go somewhere else to eat it. I ask him why nobody does anything about the noise. He says nothing can be done.

Next morning, more rain. Not long after dawn I have some bread and butter and café com leite at a little bar, then head in the obvious direction of Cocais, which is to say toward the end of town I didn't come in on. But it's not the right direction. In the not too distant past – just a few weeks ago, really – I would have gotten extremely upset, depressed even, at walking in the wrong direction through the rain for a mile or so, delaying my journey and wasting my energy, but on this particular day, despite the ten-mile hike ahead of me, I just turn around and head the right way. No problem. I'm glad it's raining and glad I'm going somewhere with a pack on my back.

I have to tromp through town for a couple of miles, gradually rising toward a forested ridge. The next several miles are cobblestone through a eucalyptus forest planted to provide charcoal for the steel mill. The drizzle stops and starts, making it difficult at any given moment to say which is happening. There's not quite enough room for both me and my pack under my little folding umbrella. I let the rain drip off the front for a while, then off the back, getting myself and my pack equally soaked. The road climbs steeply for miles. I have to lean into it to keep my pack from tipping me over backward. The extra work keeps me from freezing in the mist and fog, which gets chilly at the top of the ridge, where the wind blows clouds against me.

It's a very peaceful walk, however. The forest is perfectly quiet, with hardly a tweet of bird to break the hiss of rain. I pass no houses, fields or pastures until I come over the ridge and out of the eucalyptus. From there the road, just mud, descends. I'm startled to hear a sound behind me, a man on a bicycle who must have just pedaled up out of Barão de Cocais. He had a little basket on the back of his one-speed bike and a corn husk black-tobacco cigarette in his mouth. We exchanged quick pleasantries, or at least I assume he spoke pleasantries. I couldn't really understand the quack and huff of his peasant dialect.

No more monoculture of eucalyptus. This side of the mountain is humanized, with a little farm every mile or so. The first is the Sítio Laranjal, a pretty little place of coffee, cattle, various fruits and a simple house tucked under mango trees, and hidden behind an upthrust veil of banana leaves. It looks like a nice place to beg a drink of water — for the conversation as much as the drink. I whistle and call from the gate but get no response, probably because of a radio that's playing loudly. I walk on down toward the house until three half-deaf, cross-bred, ill-kempt dogs suddenly take notice and come charging out like wolves with turf issues to resolve. I show them the palms of my hands and talk sweetly to them, agreeing with everything they say but not panicking. Before too long a short, solid woman in a raggedy sweater and black rubber boots comes out and yells at them. She's friendlier than her dogs, I can tell. She has the teeth and smile of a simple woman who knows how to live and tend to life. She yells at her dogs sweetly, and they obey. I'm sure she has cows somewhere and a personal relationship with each of them, as she does with her chickens and garden plants and God. She asks me if I'd prefer my drink of water cold.

She brings me a big aluminum cup of cold well water. I drink it slowly as we talk. She doesn't own this house, it turns out. She's the caretaker. The owner lives in Belo Horizonte. She's been here for twelve years. I compliment her on her productivity and the organization of the place, and she gives me a big, shy smile.

A couple of hours later I come to a relatively new house made of unpainted cinder blocks in the low, wide proportions of a shoe box. The roof is of corrugated asbestos, not the algae-tinged clay tiles of older houses. A bike leans against the front of the house. It's the same bike that passed me up on the mountain, and the same man comes out to see what his dogs are barking at. He invites me in for coffee.

Inside, the house is one large room that looks inhabited by someone who doesn't really live there. The floor is concrete. The furniture consists to two beds — he has a roommate, he tells me — a chair, a little gas stove with rusty burners, and a sink. He uses his fingers and a trickle of water to sterilize a glass, then pours me sweet, thin, blessedly hot coffee from a thermos. He gives me some little bananas for my journey. As we part, we wish each other the assistance of God.

The village of Barra Feliz sits about halfway between Barão dos Cocais and Cocais. It apparently earns its miserable little keep by sustaining a smoky mill of some sort. The town sits in a crotch of muddy hills with the factory up on the side of one, looking grumpy and foul, like an old mother-in-law with bowel problems. Barra Feliz looks like a nice place to shake the rain off my umbrella and take a quick hit of coffee. I pull into the first *barzinho* I come to, but the guy says he has no coffee. I consider a dose of *cachaça* just because it's raining and my shorts are wet and it's that kind of town, but I can't bring myself to do it quite so early. I tromp along, soon to enter a tolling of church bells. It's Sunday and the mass is about to begin, so I slink though the door, lean my pack against a wall and take an unobtrusive seat in the back pew.

I don't know why, but I like to hear peasants sing hymns. Maybe it's their voices, which blend in a high pitch to sound like children. Maybe it's because I know they're desperate, singing to their only hope, loving the one thing that they can have without buying it. The congregation has a gentle little band, a soft drum, a tender tambourine, swishing maracas.

The people of Barra Feliz are rich in voice, but their glory is cleaved by the booming, nasally drone of a priest with a microphone connected to two huge speakers, megawatts of overkill in a church so small that even the flimsiest of voices could be heard front pew to back. His booming voice crushes everyone else's. If there's any holiness in this church, he is pounding it like a tough steak.

This church is relatively new, probably built in the past fifty years. Unlike the churches of centuries past, it is simple and efficient. Which is to say it lacks artistry and any sign of effort, which I suppose translates into lack of financial application. The crucifix is a two-dimensional cut-out of either plastic or laminated cardboard. The art on the walls is not the work of devout families who have dedicated generations of effort to the cause. Rather, artwork dedicated to the Lord consists of eight-by-ten pictures in plastic-gilt frames, representations of the stations of the cross. They look pathetically small on the vast, tall walls. If the forebears of this place, those who built the magnificent churches in larger towns, saw this, they would have to suspect the influence of the devil. Which, of course, is what I suspect — something devilish, anyway. The economic power of the region is surely at least what it used to be, but it is not dedicated to the church. It is dedicated to sewers, running water, gasoline, satellite dishes, medicine — stuff good and bad, useful and useless, vain, necessary, ephemeral, with little or nothing of aesthetic or spiritual appeal.

In other words, they don't make churches like they used to, and that's good and bad. Either way, the priest's microphone is an ugliness in a place that is, however stripped and simple, beautiful because it is full of people and they are singing.

* * *

Good-bye Barra Feliz. I walk for a few miles more. I can see Cocais for over an hour as I descend slowly the last few miles past pastures and rock outcrops. Its nice to descend into the sounds of settlement, the chopping of wood, a bark, a shout, a cluck-cluck here, a moo-mOo there, a toll of church bells, somebody hammering something.

But the sounds of Cocais cower under the thunderous chunk, growl and crunch of a gravel mine on the other side of the valley, slightly above the town. This mechanical beast pounds at the town all the time. It's horrendous.

I feel like I'm coming into town through the back door. I come to a church from the rear of it, and from there can see the rear of another church. Not knowing which way to go, and not wanting to walk all the way down into town only to learn that the only *pousada* is up from whence I just descended, I sit on a bench in front of the Igreja da Santana, which is very old and in desperate need of maintenance. In several places its thick plaster has broken away, exposing the simple humus of its adobe brick. The dark mold on its walls and twin bell towers give it the mask of an old man who's been left outdoors too long.

Sitting there for twenty minutes or so, I gradually realize how little movement there is in Cocais. There are plenty of houses in the neighborhood around the plaza in front of this rather large church, but it's twenty minutes before someone comes along, a little girl who has no idea where there might be a *pousada*. Since she's obviously headed toward a nearby house, I ask whether her mother's home, and then follow her to her gate. Her mother directs me to the Pousada das Cores – The Inn of Colors — just up the street.

The Inn of Colors, a new, ell-constructed establishment, aims to become a regular resort. It has two dozen rooms in a long, two-story building. Each has a door in one of five or six bright colors, and each is named appropriately. I am assigned the Canary Room, the one with a bright yellow door. It's small but well furnished, with a towel on the bed fanned to the shape of a broad palm leaf. Beside it lies a little bar of soap like you'd find in an American motel. The clean, tiled bathroom features a toilet seat, the first I've seen since Mariana. But such luxuries don't come cheap. This is by far the most expensive place I've stayed at – US $17.50, but that vast sum includes not only the soap and the toilet seat but three meals.

They turn out to be gourmet meals served out on a patio on a table of fifteen-foot planks of thick wood supported by the legs of old sewing machines. Lunch takes over half an hour to prepare, but then it just won't quit. I'm the only guest in the place, and the lady who cooks is pathologically shy, perhaps in some way mentally limited. She wears a baseball cap over her frizzy hair. She goes to tremendous effort to prepare roast beef with onion glop, a *farofa* of manioc flour stir-fried in butter with egg, raisins, carrot, bacon and whatnot, okra, rice, brown beans, French fries, and a salad. Dessert is candied figs, *doce de leite* caramel, and *mineiro* cheese. A can of Skol costs a dollar extra.

Cocais

Over the course of the next few hours, Cocais impresses me as a place where people really seem to be a little soft in the head. I don't mean that as an insult or complaint. It's just that everybody I talk with — the caretaker at the *pousada*, the cook, the lady at the post office, someone I asked for directions, the lady with the key to the Santana church — they are all hard to penetrate with the simplest of questions. At first I thought they might be deaf or that my Portuguese had deteriorated in the mountain cold. As soon as I determined that they weren't deaf, it seemed they were speaking or understanding a different language, and then it seemed they had merely heard a question I hadn't asked. Luiz, a boy of about eleven or twelve, the son of the cook, has a speech problem, a hesitant stutter, though as soon as he gets the words out of his mouth, he seems plenty sharp. He understands my questions and gives me good answers. His first question for me is whether I'm a writer, which strikes me as pretty astute. (On my way into town, an old guy herding a cow up the road detected an accent in my speech, a pinkness to my face, a reddishness in my gray hair, and asked me if I was Chinese.)

I want to know more about Cocais, so I ask around to learn who might know something about the town. The consensus is that Ivone is that person. She works at the post office during most of the day, though not at the moment I'm there to mail a letter. At other times, she's

81

the town clerk. She lives in a tall, somber, ponderous house that has been a central town building since well before George Washington was born.

As soon as I see her behind the very old counter of her clerk's office, I know I've found a person of brains. She has a short and stylish haircut and eyes alive with intelligence and consciousness. She talks with me from behind a wooden counter upon which exchanges of slaves have been recorded. Behind the counter is an old table with an old manual typewriter on it. Neither her office nor her home, upstairs, has a phone.

As soon as I express my interest in the history of the town, she launches right into it. Cocais was founded in the 1600s by three brothers who were deported from Portugal for political activity. They settled in a place that was impressive as a forest of coconut palms - cocais. Unlike most Portuguese, they started farming rather than looking for gold. One of their nephews, who would go on to become the Baron of Cocais, entered into a joint venture with some Englishmen who wanted to mine gold. Most or all of the gold ended up in London, where it remains until today despite some attempts to have it returned. During a war between São Paulo and Minas Gerais, in 1842, he fought valiantly along with the famous Duque de Caxias. He lost, but, being a friend of Don Pedro II, he was given the title of Barão and made governor of Minas Gerais.

Against her will and better judgment, Ivone ran

for *vereador* , a legislative position in the municipal government. She doesn't consider herself the type to enter politics. She doesn't like the disloyalty of politics, she doesn't lie, and she doesn't want to go after the money needed to get elected. But she agreed to be one of sixty people put up for nomination. When it boiled down to five, she was one of them. She didn't campaign. She lost and she's glad.

Ivone kind of confirms my unspoken observation that people around here might not be real bright, or, as she puts it, they are people who need to be "*conscientizados*," that is, made conscious of a situation, made aware. The *não-conscientizado*s don't know for whom to vote or why. They have no concept of improving the town, no idea that it could be done or that it should be done. They just expect someone to come in to town and do it.

The biggest employer in village of Cocais is the municipal government of Barão de Cocais. The mine that digs up the raw material of gravel and cement employs another twenty. There are about ten commercial establishments in town — a minuscule general store, a store for farm materials, a bakery, a few little bars, and the *pousada*. To earn money, people have to go elsewhere.

Ivone takes from her desk two old books. Their leather covers are turning to dust, but their pages are in amazingly good condition. Perfect frilly script fills their pages. One calls itself a book of sales and purchases.

Its earliest date is in 1834. One paragraph relates the liberation of a slave woman, "more or less sixty" years old, who was to be given freedom for having served her masters — a man and his sister — so well. The woman was to be liberated as soon as the man died.

Ivone invites me to come back after dinner, which I gladly do. When I arrive, she is rather spruced up and a little anxious. She introduces me to her husband, Raimundo, a jovial, portly fellow with a grizzled mustache. They talk about how hard it is to get the local people to raise their standards, to not depend on the government or the church for handouts.

For five years Ivone headed a church group that helps the poor, checks up on children, gets food where it's needed, gets a door or window fixed for someone who can't afford it. Recently she quit the group, not wanting people to think she was latching on to the position.

She's seen the town's two churches get ripped off plenty — not the poor box but the furniture, fixtures, saints, icons, carvings, the silver chandeliers. The culprits include a few priests — not priests from Cocais but from outside who come to say mass. They help themselves to sacred stuff and sell it in the city. One priest, over in Bom Jesus do Amparo, didn't even bother to show up to steal stuff. He just sent a truck, told the men to pick up a silver lamp, a magnificent table, a diamond brooch that some rich lady had draped over a statue of the Blessed

Virgin Mary. But for once, miraculously, the people actually rose up and did something. They stopped the truck, demanded the return of the loot. When the truck got away from them, they called the police, and the police got some of the stuff back.

What's most amazing about this incident isn't that priests were stealing and selling sacred objects from the church. It's that the people got up and did something about it. That was probably the last time, but theoretically, Ivone says, it could happen again.

Ivone and Raimundo live in what may be the oldest house in town. Raimundo, recently retired and good with his hands — he was a machinist, and his hobby is making miniature tools — is trying to fix the place up with what little money they have. The house is sparsely furnished with furniture of the lowest quality, but these people are not in any way "poor." Ivone says that municipalities are given money for fixing up the "patrimony," but none of it comes their way. Their house is called a *sobrado* because it has two floors, both of them with ceilings at least fifteen feet high. Some of the *taquara* ceilings are painted and are now flaking. There's no replacing them because no one around there weaves *taquara* anymore. Raimundo plans to put in wooden slat ceilings. The house has twenty rooms. It would make a fine *pousada*, but Ivone and Raimundo really aren't interested in having guests.

Now that she's off the church committee, Ivone

is considering an offer made by Everton, the owner of the Pousada das Cores. He'd like her to head up a Friends of Cocais association that would organize cultural events. One cultural event, created by Everton himself, is the marriage of the *lobisomen* wolfman and the *mula sem cabeça*, the headless mule. Both are old mythological figures from the region. Another town had started a festival of the *lobisomen*, so Everton decided to adopt the *mula-sem-cabeça* as the town mascot. The first celebratory event was the marriage of the two, right there in Cocais, with the climactic event taking place at Everton's *pousada*. It turned out to be pretty big, with people coming from afar to witness or participate in the pageantry. Even the *Fantástico* TV show, ever on the lookout for non-news, showed up.

Everton, a free-lance journalist by profession, is a dedicated Cocais-booster, and I suspect his heavy investment in a medium-high-class *pousada* isn't the only reason he's trying to get the town to save itself. He also just plain likes it here. He wants the place to be quaint, cute and quiet. Quaint and cute it already is. The streets are just little lanes with grass among the cobblestones. Pink bougainvillea spill up from yards like cumulonimbi at sunset. The two churches are as old as God. It's quiet except for the damned gravel mill. Some of the houses are a little rundown, and if the people aren't careful, they will keep running down. The town is poised at a turning point. It can let itself deteriorate, or it can recognize what it has, and hang on to it. With a little raising of awareness of what they are and what they have, the people of little towns and villages like this can see that their simple beauty and tranquility, their traditions and culture, are things that have value. Their poverty is worth money.

This poverty, of course, isn't the misery of urban poverty. It isn't hunger and tuberculosis. It's the poverty of a family that makes only a few hundred dollars a year but eats a six-dish lunch cooked over a wood fire, where the kids grow up and live within a hundred yards of their parents, where people in bars may well break out in song. It's the kind of poverty that gives a town only two TV channels, both fuzzy, which leaves people with little to do but go outside and talk with their friends over at the gazebo or down by the old *chafariz* where the horses of their ancestors used to drink.

Years ago, Ivone tells me, there were twelve pianos in town. Classy people came here for the quiet. The French composer Fernand Jouteux wrote the opera *Os Sertões* here. Then he went to Belo Horizonte and never came back.

Milton Nascimento, one of Brazil's most popular and respected musicians, visited Cocais, too, and by his specific request he ate lunch in Ivone's house.

I went to see Augusto Bento de Nascimento (no relation to Milton), an old guy who might be considered the town historian. He himself is pretty historical. He used to work with the *tropas* , the mule trains that once transported goods up from the coast and firewood down from the hills. The *tropas* were still active in the decade when men first walked on the moon. Augusto remembers when the first electricity came to town. It was generated at the cascade below the *pedra pintada* rock paintings. The power supply was barely enough to light a light bulb in each house. His father was born in the house where Augusto lives today. His grandfather owned Ivone's house, and had a commercial business there. He couldn't read or write but had developed his own written language of circles and boxes and slashes to keep track of who owed him what. Augusto's father's father's father was the son of a slave and an Indian.

Augusto keeps a little museum of colonial artifacts, most of them of crude cast iron made from local hematite mined by slaves and melted with charcoal made from local trees cut by slaves and hauled around in baskets on the backs of donkeys and mules. He has huge keys that weigh a few pounds, pots, a thing for bleeding a mule to check for illness. In that process, they'd jab a vein, pour the blood into a large leaf where they rolled the blood around to see how it looked. He has a broken sword, spurs, hinges, drill bits and an ingenious drill contraption. He has a stone that was chained to a slave to keep him or her from running away. It still has the chain embedded in it.

The Pedra Pintada — Painted Rock - is one of the archaeological wonders of the western hemisphere. The real wonder is how Brazil can keep it such a secret. Thanks to the vagueness of my guidebook, I walked right past the entrance to the place on my way in from Barão de Cocais. I saw the sign indicating the turn-off, a little metal thing that said "Pedra Pintada" and another sign that said "*Cachoeira*," which means waterfall or cascade. According to the guide, Pedra Pintada was several miles up that other road, farther than I was willing to walk, but Ivone tells me it's only a hundred yards or so off the road. So I hoof three or four kilometers back up to the turn off, taking with me a camera and an umbrella.

The actual entrance is just a farm gate above a little peasant house. A sign says that it will cost two *reais* for the guide to take you to the site. I enter with all due barkarama. The little house has J-E-S-U-S welded across the front door. An old woman with a floppy goiter on her neck invites me in. (Everton, owner of the *pousada*, later tells me that long ago, goiters were considered sexy in women, but this particular one has no such effect on me.) Her voice is loud, gravelly and as pointed as a chisel. Among her first questions is whether I believe in God. I know the correct answer to that one. Then she brings out her guest book. I sign it. She tells me all about her life until her husband, José, arrives. He's a thin, old man with very black skin but the tight facial features of a European. His eyes and mouth are boyish and round. His short gray whiskers are silvery against his dark skin. He's 84 but looks 25 years younger. He's the one who will take me to the painted stone. As we walk through his lush *quintal*, he tells me that he's always busy. There's always something to do up here on his little farm on the *serra*, but he always takes the time to take people to the painted rock. He's pitching to get the two *reais* that was demanded at the entrance, maybe a little extra.

He does have a fine *quintal*, the product of a lot of work indeed. He's got trees of every tropical fruit. A lot of fruit lies rotting on the ground. This couple can't eat a hundredth of the food they produce. Their children and grandchildren and other relatives show up on weekends and take a lot of it. One nephew maintains a few beehives there.

It's a short walk to the rock, and there it is, up on a cliff, under a bit of an overhang, just above reach, twenty feet of drawings not unlike those of Altamira and Lascaux, drawings that might be within my own artistic capability, including a lot of dots that might have been someone's attempt to count days or the dead or the phases of the moon. I guess we'll never know the true message. There are simple drawings of animals, too. As José explains it — and he, a man who cannot read, is the only local source of information — tells me the figures are 8,000 years old. (Other sources say 4,000 and 6,000 years, but all sources admit that no one really knows.) Neither he nor anyone else knows how the images were stained into the rock.

He has this job by default. The police came one day, he says, and told him not to let anyone mess with the paintings. They didn't pay him anything for this service or give him any other instructions or any power to prevent people from messing with the paintings. So an illiterate 84-year-old man, armed with nothing but good intentions and a sense of responsibility, is in charge of Brazil's oldest record of human activity.

Back at the house, he and his wife give me coffee and a puffy, salty pastry that *mineiros* make on their wood stoves. They make an obvious effort to impress me with their poverty, godliness, and sobriety, their hard life on the side of a mountain. Snakes slither into their house. Scorpions tiptoe in. José has been stung by scorpions several times. The couple's only medicine is *cachaça*, and *cachaça*'s only purpose, as far as they're concerned, is medicinal, though it may also have properties of magic. *Mineiro* myth has it that if you get stung by a scorpion, you should catch the bug, insert it into an empty bottle, drip *cachaça* on it until it dies, then have the patient drink it. I can't imagine the difficulty of getting a live scorpion into a bottle, but I suppose the effort will take a lot of attention away from the pain. If that doesn't work, they try herbs. If that doesn't work, they use their nephew's cell phone and try to persuade someone from town to come pick them up.

Chapter Five

Bom Jesus do Ampáro

North of Cocais, bound for Bom Jesus do Amparo, I get really lost for the first time. Good and lost — in the woods, no less. Five kilometers into the trip, the guidebook says (translated), "Beginning of reforestation. Keep left. Repouso do Guerreiro Farm. Turn right. Turn left." Unfortunately, the farm precedes the forest, and over the next mile, there's nowhere to keep left. The turns I see simply don't feel right, but it's an easy walk down a level dirt road through a pleasant-smelling forest of eucalyptus. Suspecting I'm off track and getting nowhere, I flag down the first vehicle to come along, a dump truck carrying nothing. It stops, and the driver explains that I should have turned down a little road about a mile back, just before the Repouso do Guerreiro. I start walking back. Before I get there, the dump truck comes back (still carrying nothing) and the driver tells me I can take a shortcut through the woods, down a trail till I come to some water, at which point I should turn right.

He seems a trustworthy truck driver, so I take the trail. I'm soon stepping over branches and hacking my way through spider webs as the trail closes in. It's a perfect place to get bitten by a snake and die. No one would know for a long, long time. But there are no snakes, and I soon come to a little swamp, where I turn right on a trail that widens into a road. Soon I come to an intersection with another dirt road where I can turn left or right, and of course nothing indicates which way will lead me toward Bom Jesus do Amparo.

Someone once told me that no matter where you are, if you sit there long enough, someone will come along. But for twen ty minutes tyhat doesn't come true, so I turn to the left, and sure enough I come to a little bridge and some of the other vague landmarks that the guide refers to – the rubble of an old mill, the remains of an old bridge, power lines, a road to the right. I'm still on course. A VW bug whistles by, pulling a little trailer with milk cans on it.

Sore of foot, shoulder and stomach, I am more than

relieved to arrive at a paved highway. To my delight, less than a hundred meters away is a big gas station with a *churrascaria* attached - a barbecue restaurant with a *rodízio* deal - all the meat you can eat, served at the table off spits hot from the fire. A patio overlooking a filling station doesn't offer the best of dining ambience, but it's mighty nice to get my feet off the ground and up onto the chair at the other side of my table. I order the *rodízio*, a local *cachaça* and a beer. I eat and eat and eat. I toss bits of meat to a big, skinny dog who's working the gas station. But he pays too much attention to me. The waiters catch on and stop coming around with meat, which is probably for the good since I still have to walk several miles into Bom Jesus.

The *cachaça* buzz burns off after the first mile, by which time the sun is out and blazing hard. Twice I walk up wrong roads and then back. Half a mile off course seems so little in a car, but on foot, it's truly depressing to have to turn around and cover the same wrong ground again. After a sore and sweaty afternoon, I come to a paved road that isn't supposed to be there, just a couple of miles north of where I had lunch. Somewhere along the last stretch of road I missed a turn-off onto a trail. But here I am, not far from where I want to be and not far from where I was a few hours ago. There's a covered bus stop and a sign that points toward Bom Jesus. I decide to wait for a bus and ride the rest of the way into town. When a truck comes along, I stick out my thumb. To my surprise and joy, it stops. Two friendly guys take me all the way into town and indicate the location of one *pousada*, at a truck stop, and the name of another, somewhere up near the center of town.

The place near the center of town isn't a *pousada* so much as a *dormitório* — a crash pad of narrow rooms with little beds and no other furniture. I have to talk my way in. Dona Maria, a sweet elderly lady, says at first there are no rooms, but then she starts asking where I'm from and my purpose in town, how long I'll stay and whether I'm alone. I answer correctly, and it turns out she does have a room, six *reais* (three dollars) for the night, payable in advance, no breakfast, and no toilet seat in the bathroom just a few doors down from my room, a location which can be convenient or disturbing, depending on the bathroom. In this case, it's a convenience.

I take a shower and go out for a walk around town. The population of Bom Jesus is only two thousand in town, another three thousand in the surrounding area. It's just big enough to have a little commerce. The center is pretty with a *praça* of trees and walkways and well preserved old houses and shops. The Church of Bom Jesus do Amparo stands on the corner, looking good on the outside but rather stripped and simple on the inside. The only thing of interest I see in there is a saint I've never heard of — not that I know much about any of them. His name is Santo Expedito, saint of urgent cases, a holy cop, a heavenly paramedic, God's 9-1-1. By the picture on the oration card I find below an altar to Maria of the Rosário, Expedito appears to be a reluctantly eager young man in Roman military garb decorated with cross and palm leaf. He looks a little sad, maybe a little sleepy from being called in the middle of the night, but he is always ready to come to the rescue of those in need.

Beware, however, whosoever may call upon him! Santo Expedito comes with strings attached. It is expected, the card explains, that you will show your thanks by printing and distributing a thousand Santo Expedito oration cards, which can be ordered by sending thirty-eight *reais* to a place which you must call first. The cards will be expedited by overnight mail.

I have just one contact in this town, the woman more or less married to the owner of the *pousada* in Santa Barbara, a woman divorced from a cab driver here in Bom Jesus. Her name is Teresinha. She's a grandmother and a teacher. She had arisen early on the day I left the *pousada* in Santa Bárbara so she could make me some coffee and serve me some bread and cheese for breakfast. She sat and talked and talked and talked. She told me how evil governments are, how unconscionably greedy politicians are, how all the young people in Bom Jesus are smoking marijuana, how much her school needed an encyclopedia, how much she loved an indefinable god while having little regard for religion, how satisfied she was to live in a simple house in a little town. I genuinely agreed with her on every little thing she talked about, every little value and principle and belief. I liked her very much and was sorry to have to leave town shortly after meeting her.

So I try to find her in Bom Jesus, where she spends most weekdays, teaching her elementary class. I walk around to one school, where they tell me she works in the other one. I go there, but they tell me she's already left for the day. Since the next day is the Day of the Dead, there will be no school, a long weekend, so they think she might already be on the bus back to Santa Bárbara. They won't tell me where exactly she lives, but a secretary lets it leak that she lives over on the uphill side of the *praça*. I walk up the only road on that side of the *praça*, asking several people whether they know where she lives. I figure out which is her house. She isn't home, of course, so I write a little note and flip it through her gate far enough to get it under the roof of her carport.

At least twice a day the Igreja Bom Jesus do Amparo plays sappy tunes from loudspeakers on its single bell tower. It's a chorus of women singing about love and Jesus. Judging by the scratchy sound, it's coming off an LP that sounds like it might have been found alongside the Dead Sea scrolls. I suppose it must soothe the populace. It sure soothes me. I can't imagine getting into a fight or pulling off a drug deal while optimistic little marches are underway, though it would make a disturbingly ironic background music for such activities.

Town Hall and the post office are closed for the next three days because of the Day of the Dead. I want to talk with someone about the town, its history and current situation, but it looks like that isn't going to happen. The next morning I rise early and take my pack to the *praça*, where I hope to get a quick café com leite and some bread before I leave on the nine mile hike to Ipoema.

But it's the Day of the Dead, and in all due celebration, the town itself seems pretty dead. Nobody's awake yet. The town's two taxi drivers, one of them the ex- of Teresinha, don't look like they're going anywhere soon. Even the local flies are groggy. It's 8:20 before the steel overhead door on one *barzinho* rattles up and another twenty minutes before they've made coffee. By the time I hit the road, the sun is up, the air already hot.

Chapter Six

Ipoema

It's a pleasant if somewhat hot walk to Ipoema, nine miles of pretty hills with lush pastures decorated with some of the healthiest-looking cows I've seen in Brazil, Herefords and Guernsey's, I believe, real fatsos each and every one. A few of the farms have coffee planted - the first I've seen on this trip — but they are mere patches compared with the huge farms in the southern and western regions of the state. The air smells of grass and flowers. The bougainvillea at several farm gates are shades of purple and pink I've never seen before, some as big as trees, their blossoms great gushes of volcanic colors. Every half hour or so, a vehicle passes. A dump truck, two cars, and a motorcycle stop, unbidden, to offer me a ride. The woman in one car says she knows I don't want a ride, but she felt she should at least offer. The last car is driven by a young man with a big, toothy smile who introduces himself as part of Rádio Alternativa, of Itabira, where he's an announcer. His name is João do Carmo, but everyone knows him as Tangará. He shuts off the engine so we can talk properly. I appreciate that gesture just as I appreciate a place where a person can stop a car in the middle of road for a good conversation with a stranger.

Tangará gives me a brochure that reveals that he also does promotional events, such as rodeos, dirt bike races, concerts and so on. The folder features several pictures of himself in fancy red-white-and-blue cowboy shirt with fringes, and a big white cowboy hat of the sort rarely seen outside of very old westerns. Just about every picture in the brochure includes Tangará up on a stage with a microphone in his hand, or standing with some people who must be equally famous in this part of Minas Gerais.

Tangará recommends I contact a Dona Eleni in Ipoema. She owns a *pousada* and knows a lot about the town and its history. I jot down the name on his brochure.

As I drag my weary dogs into Ipoema, I settle onto a bench in front of the main church. In every town, a bench in the *praça* is a good place to sit for a while. They are usually comfortable, for concrete, having a supportive curve to the back and a slight tilt to the seat that tends to encourage continued sitting. It's also a good place to wait for someone to come along and ask who I am and what I'm doing there. Those won't be anyone's first questions. In fact, passers-by won't do much but nod and say, "*Bom dia,*" unless I ask them a question. They'll then feel me out for my source and objectives. Here in Ipoema, no one comes along, but a couple of men are talking in the shade of a tree in the little plaza, so I go ask them where I can find Dona Eleni. One of the men, it so happens, is her brother, Inácio, and he tells me Eleni is right across the street, at the house of her two aunts.

So we go on over there. She's delighted to hear that I've come looking for her and that I'm researching the Estrada Real. Delight, I can tell, is the default expression on Eleni's face. She and Inácio take me up the street to the *pousada* she owns with another brother, one who, for reasons described as "complicated," does not get along with Inácio. The *pousada* is a new house built in the style of old houses. It has two clean, well-appointed bathrooms, four bedrooms and a light, airy, modern kitchen with a dining area. My SENAC guide refers to another *pousada* in town. Eleni knows of it and would be glad to take me there, it doesn't really matter to her, but she doesn't recommend it. Her place is a little pricey for me at twenty *reais* (about ten dollars), with breakfast, but obviously it's the place where I must stay. I don't know why ten bucks should strike me as expensive for the daily rent of an entire house. I guess I just get used to prices being cheaper than that. Twenty *reais* is fine. Here I stay.

Eleni leaves to attend to business elsewhere. I wash my clothes in a sink behind the house, rig up a clothes line, then eat at a nearby by-the-kilo buffet. Eleni soon shows up to take me to her brother's other *pousada*, outside of town. We go there by car with two other women. All three of these women go to exercise classes to lose weight, and they like to take long walks. The *pousada*, an old farmhouse being refurbished, happens to be a long walk from a restaurant that Eleni's brother is building up on the mountain. Another mile and a half (each way) is about the last thing I want to put on my aching feet, but I'm always glad to go somewhere, even if it's uphill all the way.

It turns out to be more than just a restaurant. They have formed a lake by damming a stream that comes from higher up the mountain. The water comes over the dam into a concrete pool. It's a great place to soak the dust out of my pores, but I can't stay in the early afternoon sun for long or I will burn. I'm already red in the face and arms, and the absolute last thing I need is burnt shoulders. If I can't carry a pack, I'm stuck where I am for at least a week, and though I like it just fine where I am, a week is too long to be anywhere but home in Hanover, Connecticut, USA.

On the walk back down the hill, Eleni tells me how she and her brothers are very active in trying to preserve the nature and history of Ipoema. They are big advocates of the Estrada Real project. (In fact, I believe they are the first people on this trip who have actually heard of the Estrada Real.) She writes, publishes and distributes a newspaper, *Jornal do Rural*, which tries to glorify the rural life, the local culture, the small-town politics, the importance of nature as a valuable resource. This publication was supported by the government of Itabira, but with the recent municipal election, a less enlightened government came into power, and their support is less likely. She needs new sponsors or the publication will die.

So Eleni is a person I can really get to like. We see eye-to-eye on everything, from politics to environment to economics to an appreciation of the simple, rural life. It turns out we're both active in our local Green Party. We are both among those whom she calls the *conscientizados*—those who have been made aware.

She already knows about the little struggles among the Federation of Industries of Minas Gerais, which is promoting tourism as an industry; the Instituto Estrada Real, which is trying to promote the concept of the Estrada in tourists and local people; Raphael Olivé, who is writing and publishing some well-researched guides to the Estrada Real, and is apparently trying to keep the whole concept under his own wing, and the Secretária de Turismo, which, being a state agency, isn't doing much at all. She wishes they'd all just work together. What needs to be done most, she says, is to "conscienticize the people" and train them in the standards of tourism. For the most part, she says, the workers in this trade have never set a table, might not know how to deal with an indoor toilet, have no standards of sanitation. The whole interior of Minas (i.e. the area outside the capital) needs a general raising of awareness and professionalism. And that is going to be a huge and lengthy challenge.

And it could all start, as far as Eleni is concerned, with the concrete benches in the *praça* in front of the Igreja da Nossa Senhora da Conceição. For some reason, people like to sit on the back of the bench and put their feet on the seat. Consequently, all the seats are dirty.

And if anyone in town had any sense they'd notice that the supermarket on one side of the plaza leaves its trash on the back steps where dogs get into it, leaving behind an unsanitary situation that smells bad No one but Eleni seems to realize that the back steps of a supermarket don't have to look and smell like a garbage dump. Eleni is in the process of complaining about it, but Ipoema doesn't really have a government. It's part of Itabira, a town with bigger fish to fry than dog mess in a no-account village far from sight. What the town needs, she says, is a woman in charge, someone who can recognize filth and the need to keep it contained or at bay. The whole country, she says, needs women in authority.

Eleni was a prime mover behind the hiring of an actual garbage collector for the town, a guy with a cart with pneumatic tires and leaf springs that is pulled by an actual mule. The government never thought of such a service. Eleni had to think of it and then make it happen.

Ipoema, she tells me, is a town of *tropeiros*, the people and donkeys who used to haul goods up from the coast and gold down to the coast. The town's economy was based on receiving, feeding, and dispatching donkeys and mules. Eleni would like to make Ipoema a center for the study and appreciation of the *tropeiro* way of life. She and others have a lot of stuff that they'd like to put in a museum.

I suggest to her that slavery would be an interesting theme, too, for a museum or tourist attraction. All along the Estrada I've seen or been told of signs of slaves. The churches and older farm houses were built by slaves. Any church called Rosário was built for slaves, and just about every church has a statue or icon of Nossa Senhora Aparecida who is black. Here and there one can find *galeria*s dug into mountains by slaves. No doubt the decayed bones of slaves lie here and there just a few inches under the ground. Town clerks have written records of transactions of slaves. In Diamantina, the northernmost city on the Estrada, the lifelong affair between the owner of a diamond mine and the daughter of a slave woman and her master is one of the most fascinating romances in Brazilian history. Diamantina also has the Caminho dos Escravos, the trail of slaves. Every person with dark skin is a descendant of a slave. Here and there someone can show you shackles embedded in the foundation of a house. I wonder if a single marked grave of a slave exists anywhere.

Eleni's face blossoms with the suggestion. She knows of all sorts of local reference to slavery, not the least of which was the fact that as a child she'd been cared for by a nursemaid who had been a slave. The farm of the father of the woman who takes care of the *pousada* has stone steps that were carried in by slaves. Someone in town has instruments of torture that were used on slaves. The town clerk Ipoema has a record of a slave boy who was given freedom by his white father as soon as the boy earned enough money to buy himself. Somewhere outside of town there's a hole full of water that's so deep that the bottom has never been found. Once a slave, terribly depressed over something, fell in. A burro fell in, too. Neither was every found.

Eleni likes the idea of a project that features the signs of slaves. No one has done it before. No one really wants to talk about slavery. It's a nasty skeleton in the closet of history — a closet not entirely shut. As everyone knows, she tells me, we still have de facto slavery.

Eleni calls the town clerk, has him open up his little office. Just as in Cocais, the office is minimal, with a manual typewriter, no phone, some old leather-bound books riddled with holes chewed by insects. It also has a rickety office copier. The clerk shows me the page that gave the boy the right to buy his freedom from his father. We make a copy and I shoot some photos of the book.

Just up the street, Eleni and I meet a *benzedeira*, a faith healer who cures people by blessing them. She's as black as can be, old, toothless, diminutive. She wears brass earrings and speaks in a clipped dialect I can't understand despite her grandiose body movements with which she demonstrates how she takes the sickness out of people, even out of a cow that had been bitten by a snake. She keeps gesturing to the sky and telling us how she gets what she needs from "*lá em cima*" - up there. She has never charged for her services. She gets her payment from up there. She cures people of things that doctors can't identify. She makes the hospital unnecessary. About the only thing she doesn't do is births. She says there are doctors for that. She gestures toward the clinic on the *praça*. She got her ability from her mother, and she hopes to pass it on to her granddaughter.

Later, in the car, I admit to Eleni my inability to understand peasants. She says I really should record their voices. Their dialect will be extinct before much longer.

A recording of these voices, of course, doesn't preserve this vast aspect of Brazil, this huge body of people who are not participating in much of the economy beyond their towns, who are barely under the influence of television or anything but their own blessed ignorance. A tape recording would preserve the species no more than stuffing a mastodon. But this doesn't mean it shouldn't be done. The bigger question is how the real and living culture of the rural peasants can be preserved. Their culture — arguably even their special wisdom – is grounded in illiteracy and ignorance of the rest of the world. Are those good things to preserve?

*   *   *

One of the main attractions in Ipoema is *Cachoeira* Alta - High Waterfall. And high it is, a straight, narrow plunge of 318 feet into a pool fifty feet deep. It's awe-inspiring eve now, at the end of an extended dry season. In December and January, I'm told, it's even more powerful as a tremendous amount of water gushes through an notch at the top of the cliff. Eleni's friend Rogério and his very sweet fiancée, a geologist, take us out there. Rogério's father owns the farm where the waterfall is. It's a beautiful farm that has been essentially self-sustaining for well over 150 years. The clay tile roof is 143 years old. On the front porch stands a bench made from hardwood planks at least fifteen feet long. It was made by slaves 200 years ago, on a different farm. The axle of an old waterwheel lies in front of the house. Slaves probably made it, too.

It's a great farm, rich in the aromas of manure and wood smoke. The timbers of the door frames and window shutters are inches thick. The doors are a good twelve feet tall. The kitchen has a long *fogão a lenha*, and outside the kitchen door, under a roofed area, they have a clay brick dome oven where they make bread and biscuits. The lovely grandma-type dona da *casa* has a few servants to help her keep house and process crops into food. On walls and above doorways hang photographs over a hundred years old. Some of the faces have a suit and tie or nice dress painted below the subject's neck.

This is actually the second house on this farm. The first was torn down to make this new one. The old one used to stand over the road that used to go from Ipoema to somewhere which no longer exists. The stumps of two old stone pillars still mark the place where the old house stood. The road is gone too, but Rogério's father points where it wound over hills into the distance.

Rogério's mother brings us *biscoito de polvilho*, an airy, crunchy bread of a fine manioc flour cooked in a ring about four inches in diameter. It's just out of the clay oven, warm and smoky, not sticking to the teeth as it will a few hours from now. There's nothing cooking in the oven now, but it's still hot. They've stacked the next load

111

of firewood inside to dry.

Today the farm has a steel waterwheel with a diameter of a good ten or twelve feet, fed by the water that fell from the *cachoeira*. Before reaching this waterwheel, which is used to press sugar cane for *cachaça*, it passes through a horizontal waterwheel. The water hits flat spokes that are angled to make the wheel spin to turn a round stone that grinds corn.

This is the waterwheel that presses juice from cane that's used to make *cachaça*.

When the cane's ripe, Rogério's father makes 250 liters of *cachaça* a day, storing it in a large wooden boxes that lock shut with padlocks. He pours me a dose from a spigot. It's very good — smooth and light. Rogério tells me they leave it in the wood boxes for six months. Eleni agrees that after that, it takes on too much taste of wood. *Cachaça*s aged in oak for years, we all agree, are not as smooth as what we just slid down our throats.

Eleni's brother, Zé Inácio, comes to the *pousada* to tell me about the glories of greater Ipoema. Above *Cachoeira* Alta, he says, there's another waterfall, and above that there's another, and above that there's a pool, from which water flows over both sides of a divide. One side flows to the *Cachoeira* Alta, through the two waterwheels and thence down to the Rio Poço Alegre, which leads into the Rio Tanque, which flows to the Rio Santo Antonio, which flows into the Rio Doce, which goes through the State of Espírito Santo and into the Atlantic.

From the other side of that pool on the mountain, the water makes its way to the Rio das Velhas, which flows through Belo Horizonte before joining Brazil's second longest river, the São Francisco, which flows northeast across Minas Gerais and on up to the bulge of Brazil that leans out toward Africa, emptying into the Atlantic between the states of Sergipe and Alagoas.

When Zé Inácio tried to explain that to some muckety-mucks from the state tourism department, they wouldn't listen. They didn't see the importance of it. They also overestimated the importance, locally, of Carlos Drummond, a poet and writer of international fame.

"Carlos Drummond this, Carlos Drummond that!" Zé Inácio, says, looking up at the ceiling, his arms rising in cynical worship.

But Carlos Drummond, born in Itabira, left town and never came back, barely even looked back, according to people around here. Carlos Drummond, they say, shouldn't be the raison d'être of the Estrada Real in this region. The real story is the *tropeiros*.

Ipoema was the intersection of *tropeirismo*. From Caeté, Santa Barbara, Diamantina, Nova Minas, Itabira, the mule trains all passed through Ipoema. They brought gold and diamonds from the north. They brought English porcelain, Portuguese port, food from the coast. Santa Bárbara was the commercial center, but all roads led through Ipoema. They used to pass the *Cachoeira* Alta, coming down the road that isn't there, walking under the farmhouse that isn't there, no doubt spent many a night, watered their mules, and sat on the bench that's still there.

Zé Inácio knows what will happen if people don't become conscious of the treasure they have in this town — this fascinating history, the magnificent waterfalls, the traditional architecture. The outsiders will come in, buy up all the beautiful old farms, buy the culture. The locals will be forced into *favela*s. If they don't value what they have, they will lose it.

The Estrada Real, it seems, is paved with politics. Eleni explains it to me. I can't keep track of all the people and organizations and agencies and other interests, but she says that most people are promoting the concept in their own self-interest. They try to keep their name and personal cause in as much light as possible, but this only hinders the project and hurts themselves. Their little conferences and panel discussions have been rather meaningless because the wrong people end up in charge, up at the head table. They don't have plans; they have interests.

I need to think about this. After Eleni leaves, I cut up a big lime, put it in a glass, sprinkle sugar on it, mash it up with the handle-end of a knife, pour off the sweet juice, mix it with some *cachaça*, stir in some honey for purposes of good health, and sit back to figure out what somebody ought to do with the Estrada Real. For one thing, they should put up signs, thousands of them, just little arrows, perhaps stylized in some cute, faux-antique way, if necessary bearing the name of a sponsor. An effective guidebook would sure make things easier. A map would be a big help. They need to designate local historians, and those historians have to be continually educated. They must be given information for their own use and the use of tourists.

Tourists need *roteiros*, routes — either local or general – that include local farms, meals, *alambiques* (*cachaça* stills), historical buildings, waterfalls, and other natural phenomena. Towns need funding for museums and a program to collect artifacts and information.

A great business for someone to get into: tours by buggy or horse cart, with trips off the road, meals in farm houses, lectures by local historians and experts, and academic credits for completion of the program.

They need to coordinate festivals so they are either related to each other or scheduled so something somewhere along the road is always happening. Festivals for *cachaça*s, *batida*s, harvests, foods, crafts, battles of bands, religious revivals, short courses in history, crafts, herbs, nature, geology, cooking, slaughter. They could use the universities to teach local docents.

Computer-access centers in each town, for tourists

to maintain contact with the world, and for locals to share information and access a central website with information on preservation and environmental programs, events, history, tourist accommodations, and so on.

With that latter thought, a crushing depression sets in. Do I really want to see my beautiful Estrada Real gripped in the tentacles of the Internet? Can we not leave it the way it is, isolated and firmly founded in the independence that comes with ignorance of the rest of the world? Or is ignorance a form of slavery? Or is the Internet slavery? Or is no job, no teeth and no hope a slavery of despair? I am not sure. I just don't know. I cannot figure it out. I can't even begin to grapple with the depths of it. (My bachelor's degree in philosophy provides little insight. The more I apply my mind to something, the more complicated it gets. That's about all I've ever figured out.) Would the Pedra Pintada and its simple caretaker, José, be any better off if linked to the World Wide Web? Will Google come up with an emergency cure for a scorpion sting that works any better than *cachaça* and prayer? Will Dona Cota be better off if people can use email to make a reservation for her jury-rigged non-inn? Will a data bank hush the gravel mine at Cocais?

Or will the knowledge that comes with the Internet prevent the paving of the Estrada and make people aware that their simplicity is their gold, that their lack of store-bought stuff is actually worth something? But what happens if we persuade them of that? Then what will they need money for? What will they need the Estrada Real for?

I won't trust anyone who claims to have an answer to these questions. The real questions are too deep and complex to even ask. But to me, it's a big decision, a moral juncture. The Estrada Real isn't a road. It's a fork in a road. Which way to do we go?

I don't know which is the right way to go, but to just sit here and wait for something to come along and make the decision is no more moral than making a best-guess choice. I have to go with my instincts, and my instincts lead me around to the conclusion that any idiot would have reached without a degree in philosophy: knowledge is better than ignorance. If we let ignorance lead the way, the Estrada Real will go downhill. Its people will abandon their dull towns and move to the city, where they will dream about how good it was back home. The *pau-a-pique* houses will be knocked down and replaced by cinder block. Pavement will only increase traffic. Golden arches will welcome the tourist with hygienic nutrition, and all the *cachaça* will be properly labeled.

So yes, the obvious (and to me, tentative) conclusion: Give them the Internet and see if they can put knowledge to good use.

*　　*　　*

Eleni takes me to another farm, one that has prehistoric paintings on a rock. It's owned by a guy named Bemvindo. We have to stop half a mile before the farm because the mud is too deep. The farm is over two centuries old, with an old waterwheel that no longer works. The wide stone steps to the front porch were carried in by slaves, though no one knows where the stone came from. A big extended family lives there, caring for a good number of cows in a corral just outside the kitchen window.

Eleni, half a dozen people from the farm, and I hike up a steep trail, hop over a brook, wind through brush and vines, and pass a little cave of overhanging boulders until we come to a massive granite outcrop with two simple drawings on it. They seem in the same style as the ones at Pedra Pintada. They're oblong and striped, about the size of bed pillows. They look to me like giant, abstract cockroaches. Hanging on the same boulder is a wad of killer bees the size of a horse head, and as soon as I get my camera adjusted, they send a few interceptors out to ward us off. I take a couple of stings while I snap quick shots of the painting. Then we take the hint and hustle back into the bushes. I'm the last one, which means I'm the one closest to the bees, the one who's absorbing the warning shots. When we jam up at a thicket of vines, I forge my own trail around them, smacking my neck, face and arms as I go.

Eleni has one more thing to show me before I leave Ipoema: the inside of the Igreja Nossa Senhora da Conceição. She finagles the key from someone and lets me in. The interior is just as ugly as can be, with big loudspeakers and rows of big fans mounted on the walls and aimed at the faithful in the pews. On the ceiling over the chancel is a celestial scene of Nossa Senhora da Conceição among the angels. It's a very poorly painted scene, probably the work of somebody's sister-in-law or old school chum, and it doesn't help that it's upside down to the people in the pews. Only a priest at the altar could see it right, and he'd have had to look straight up.

"*Incrível, não é?*" Eleni says with an upward, backward wave of her hand. "*Simplesmente incrível.*"

Chapter Seven

Senhora do Carmo

Come time to leave Ipoema, the rainy season has fully arrived. I decide to take a bus the ten miles to Senhora do Carmo. It's a sloppy, muddy trip, and the bus has to slam through deep puddles to keep going. I'm glad I'm not standing on the side of the road with my pack when it goes by. It's a municipal bus, not really meant for long hauls down muddy mountain roads. The driver keeps the engine at high revs but maintains conversation with the conductor, who stands beside him, slouched against the howling engine compartment. They talk to passengers, too, telling them about another bus that was stuck in the mud for three days. When a bus gets stuck on this road, somebody has to walk to a farm that has a tractor or some oxen. Unless the bus has chosen a convenient ditch to get stuck in, a farm with a tractor is probably several miles away.

But we arrive in Senhora do Carmo without problem, and the bus stops at the central *praça*, which sits at an incline below the church. It's a vaguely triangular little *praça*, no wider than fifty feet, perhaps seventy-five feet long, with half a dozen benches under a few trees. On the *praça* are a minuscule Banco Itau, a luncheonette in a little trailer, a *barzinho* called Centric's Bar (the apostrophe being an exotic import that serves no function in Portuguese), a telephone office with barely enough room for the operator and the caller, and the Pousada Neves — the Inn of Snows. The snows are quite liquid on this day, so I'm glad it's a short walk from the bus to the inn, a big old townhouse inhabited mostly by the family that owns it. The house is ancient but they have installed cheap new steel windows, ruining the beauty of the place. They've replaced the curved clay roof tiles with flat "French" tiles, distinguishing it from most of the rest of town.

Just up the street is the town's only eatery, a place of long tables and benches and a choice of chicken or beef with your meal. The ceiling is of *taquara* bamboo. Above it, the roof has a leak that drips exactly where I sit to eat.

I report the fact to the lady in charge, Efigênia. I also compliment her on how finely shredded her collards are. She tells me the compliments should go to her husband, and she invites me to the kitchen to deliver them. I do so, and we get a good laugh when I tell him I shred the collards in my house, too.

Efigênia, it turns out, is the mother of Fábio, a *conscientizado* whom Eleni recommended I look up. Fábio has been consorting with the conscienticized of Ipoema and Bom Jesus do Amparo. He sits down with me while I eat the lunch his mother has made.

Fábio works for the municipal government in Itabira as an agronomy technician. He and a few others in town want to see things valued around Carmo. He wants to see its *alambiques* improve the quality of their *cachaça* by, for example, not storing it in plastic barrels that once held olives. Tourists might appreciate a *cachaça* that looks good in a bottle with a fancy label. This town of under 2,000 people has at least twenty-five *alambiques* distilling uncounted hundreds of thousands of liters of *cachaça*. They sell it all. The average price is under half a dollar per liter, and the average quality is far better than any *cachaça* available in North America or Europe and better than most store-bought brands elsewhere in Brazil. The trouble is, you have to drive several hours down a dirt road to get to it.

Shortly after noon, the loudspeaker in one bell tower of the church plays Brazil's national anthem, which as far as I know is called simply *Hino Nacional.* (My guidebook does not mention a church in this village, but it does itemize seven banks, all of which are apparently invisible but are surely within shouting distance of the town's only phone. I presume the banks are in Itabira. Senhora do Carmo hasn't got enough money to fill a decent-sized piggy bank.) The *Hino Nacional* always sounds to me like music more appropriate for a circus act of overweight Gypsy women in glittery pantyhose doing magic tricks on the backs of elephants and kangaroos, perfectly appropriate for a nation more interested in *cachaça* than war. Then the church plays the *Hino Estadual,* and then the *Hino Municipal,* then some huffy military music. As Fábio explains it, this music is the idea of the local pharmacist, who once taught physical education for the upper grades of the school. But that wasn't the worst of his ideas. He was in cahoots with the brother of a bishop who somehow subdivided the land that's up behind the church. The same bishop may have been responsible for the sale of the town saint, Senhora do Carmo herself, a large wooden carving donated by one of the original settlers. Indeed that donation led to the changing of the name of the town from Onça (in English, Jaguar) to its present name. Everything else in the church, including beautiful chalices, has also disappeared. The stuff in there now looks pretty chintzy to me, hardly expressing the love and faith that went into the original equipment.

Fábio takes me to see an old guy whose latest gig in life is making *rapadura* — molasses sugar, which was once the main source of sweetness in rural areas. The man's name is Gilberto, but everyone calls him Nenêgo. He's 89 years old. He's been a *tropeiro* and a hunter. He started working when he was ten, taking care of other people's cows. By his late teens he was the boss of his own *tropas* , the mule trains that used to haul everything everywhere. As the boss, he was the only guy who got to ride on a mule, leaving the others to walk. He took his mules from Santa Bárbara up to Santa Lucia, Itabira, Itambé do Mato Dentro, twenty mules at a time with two helpers and a cook, lugging *cachaça*, food, and supplies up into the hills. He carried a gun, but thieves were not a problem then. "They did not exist," he says.

The mention of thieves shunts the conversation to recent reports of bandits assaulting tourist buses on the border of Minas Gerais and Goiás. In such a place, they would certainly be Brazilian tourists, though even that sounds strange to me. I wonder if there's a difference between a tourist bus and a regular bus and whether bandits are attacking regular buses.

Nenêgo was a *tropeiro* in the 1930s, but in the 1940s he became a hunter, hunting the pig-like peccary and the capybara, a rodent that can grow to four feet in length.

For a while, the capybara just about disappeared, but when it became illegal to hunt them, they came back strong. They have a lot of offspring. Nenêgo killed one that had seven fetuses. He knows of another that had ten. Today, the capybara get into gardens, even devastate whole fields of sugar cane. They can be raised for meat. With a mischievous glint to his eye, Nenêgo notes that no one could tell whether the meat of a capybara came from one raised on a farm or shot in the *mato*.

Today Nenêgo's got a pretty impressive *rapadura* operation. He brings in the cane on a ponderous wooden oxcart that must weigh over a thousand pounds. At the moment, it's dismantled so he can fix it. It's hard to get parts, he says, because the good trees are extinct. The axle he's making is not of the ideal wood. The wooden wheels, about four feet in diameter and three inches thick, have rusty steel bands around the rim. I ask him how old the cart is. He says he bought it seventy years ago, then adds that he bought it used. He thinks the wheels are probably 150 years old.

His *rapadura* operation is under a wide, four-sided tile roof. The cane feeds into a press driven by oxen that walk in a circle, pushing a wooden bar that turns a wooden shaft that turns the steel gears that turn the rollers that press the cane. You need one smart ox or two dumb ones to make the whole thing work. The *garapa* flows down a wooden spout, through a sieve and into a clay pipe that leads to a copper vat that sits over a fire. The vat is a good five feet wide. The fire boils the *garapa* until it becomes molasses and then *rapadura*. He sells a little of it around town, but most of it is for personal consumption.

Four people live in his house now, or maybe five, depending on how you count them. But at any given moment, twice that many are present. While I'm there, at least fifteen people pass through the little living room, arriving and leaving without celebration.

Nenêgo and his wife produce just about everything they need to live. Salt is about all they buy. They grow and husk their own rice, grow, husk, and roast their own coffee. They make their own sugar and raise all the beans they need. A herd of at least twenty cattle, including a lot of calves, lives literally within spitting distance of their living room couch. If flies were worth money, Nenêgo would be wealthy. Even if money weren't worth money, he'd still be rich. He's got all his bases covered. He either has or can make everything he needs and wants.

Nenêgo's a bit deaf, and his wife uses a cane, but their minds are still working well. When they talk about the old days, their voices peter out and their eyes shift into a focus on memories beyond their words or my imagination. We can never know, nor could they ever tell us, what it was like to take a mule train up and down trails through the mountains of Minas Gerais in the 1930s.

One of Fabio's dreams — and that's what he calls

them — is to buy one of the oldest buildings in town, a grist mill, and make it into a museum. The mill was operating until a few years ago, when it had its electricity cut.

Small world here. Fabio's wife, it turns out, is the granddaughter of Bemvindo, the guy with the farm that has the boulder with the prehistoric drawings on it and who, I now really realize, is the brother of the guy with the farm at *Cachoeira* Alta.

On the way back to the *pousada*, Fábio and I meet an old guy named Luiz at the *praça*. Luiz has a serious *alambique*. He is probably the only guy in town who registers his *cachaça* and gives it a name and a label. He tells me he ages it in oak barrels once used to import whiskey. I say something to the effect of "Wow," so he opens the door of his pick-up truck and takes out a plastic bottle that's about the shape and size of a hand grenade. The liquid inside is quite yellow, a sign of a long time spent in oak. He twists off the plastic cap, lets me sniff. It is the most aged-smelling *cachaça* I've ever smelled. He fills the little plastic cap and has me taste it. It's fine, full of oak flavor. "It's a whiskey" I tell him. "Better than whiskey," he tells me, and he relates the story of an American with whom he exchanged a bottle of his *cachaça* for a bottle of bourbon. The American later wrote back to apologize because the bourbon wasn't nearly as good.

Sunday night, while I'm writing in the half-open kitchen area of the *pousada*, drinking coffee from a thermos, and writing at a little table, a high-school girl who works there, and a younger girl who has the face of a woman in her thirties, and a lad of about seventeen settle onto a couch to talk with me. They present the usual and useless questions about prices and wages in the United States. The boy really wants to go there in a couple of years. He's studying English at a school called Wizard, which he thought meant lightning.

It's dull talk, but finally the boy and younger girl leave. The other girl, apparently the daughter of the owner, lets on that her father is a big drinker. He had a stroke a couple of weeks ago, went to the hospital in Belo Horizonte, spent three days on a bed in the hall, waiting for a room. He recovered the use of his arm but still has trouble talking and walking. The doctor said that if he puts another drop of *cachaça* in his mouth or smokes another cigarette, it will be the end of him. But the first day he got home, he "went into the street" looking for *cachaça*. The girl went around telling people not to give him any or sell him any, but he found it, as he always does. She said that sometimes he socks her mother. Sometimes they get him some *cachaça* so he doesn't go out into the street in the rain looking for it.

The next morning, Luiz is supposed to pick me up at seven o'clock to show me his *alambique*, but as of nine o'clock he hasn't arrived. This tends to happen on rainy days like this one. Nobody's going anywhere. Across the *praça*, people hang out under eaves, waiting for a bus that never arrives.

So I give up on Luiz and walk up the street to one of the bigger houses in town, one with French roof tiles. Though the roof of this house is new, the guy living in it is not. He's 74. His name is Ildeu de Oliveira. He, like Nenêgo, was a *tropeiro*. He'd take trains of 200 mules down to São Paulo, even all the way to Foz d'Iguaçu, the vast and massive waterfall on the border of Paraguay, Brazil and Argentina. He went with guys from town and his brother-in-law, all of them riding mules. It was all *mato* between towns back then, just trails through the forest. They carried guns in case of animals. There were no thieves, he says. "They did not exist." He'd sell his mules in the south, then ride home with all his *reis* in a leather bag. No one ever robbed him.

Ildeu finished school after two years of study, then went to work. He was eight at the time. He hoed fields for a hundred *reis* per day. By the age of ten, he was buying and selling cattle. By eleven, he was a *tropeiro* working with his older brother.

He was a *tropeiro* during World War II, when there was no fuel for vehicles. Mules were in great demand. Everything in Brazil moved by mule.

He also drove cattle to Uberlândia, some 250 miles

to the west. He drove *gado magro* (thin cattle) several hundred kilometers west to Uberlândia to grow fatter, and he'd drive calves up to Nossa Senhora do Carmo to grow older.

His grandfather, Joaquim Antônio de Oliveira, owned the Fazenda da Cobras — Farm of Snakes — and owned slaves. It was a big farm. He was a good man who made his money with *cachaça* and never denied anyone anything they needed.

Ildeu never worked with Nenêgo, who wasn't really a traveling *tropeiro*. The only traveling *tropeiro* around today is Joãozito. They remember a lot of things. The world was different then. There was no fuel and everything moved by mule — the good old days.

Now Ildeu has a prostate problem. He had an operation, but he wears a colostomy bag. It's on his mind all the time, that and the way the world used to be.

Luiz shows up at the front porch. It turns out he's Ildeu's nephew. His full name is Luiz de Oliveira, but everyone calls him Titi. He has big dreams for the tourist industry. He has the basic set-up for his own little business: his mother's old farmhouse, which has spring water right behind it and a *quintal* of fruits. Across the street he has a roofed corral, a pasture, and most important of all, a respectable *alambique*.

Luiz Titi makes good *cachaça*, the best around, he says, and I believe it. It's very good, smooth. His aged stuff is excellent, beyond comparison. This year's vintage, just a few months in barrels of *ipé amarelo*, is already very good. At home, he keeps it in little oak barrels. Even this new stuff is very good, the best *cachaça branca* I've tasted in recent memory.

He thinks he's got a good place for tourists, and I agree. He could receive travelers on horses, take care of the animals, sell some *cachaça* and other stuff. He could take them to the local *cachoeira*s. All he needs is — he rubs the pad of his thumb with his forefinger — money.

His wife, who is somehow related to Nenêgo, teaches at the school, where, it so happens, I have to go to meet Ana Maria Gonçalves, the director and a local historian. So, after a nice lunch at Luiz's house, it's off to school we go.

Ana, it turns out, is expecting me. Eleni has advised her of my arrival. Ana is among the conscienticized, and she is attempting to conscienticize her students. She realizes that it is all but impossible to conscienticize the whole town at once. She is therefore educating the children, and she seems to be doing it well. She has not only given them the good message but organized activities that reinforce the lessons. They practice what she preaches. They celebrate the things that are important to their town. They recognize and celebrate the banana leaf, a shovel, some dirt, a dead snake. They plant trees to replace the *mato* that their parents and grandparents and other forebears cut down in their own self-defense until they had no more wood for ox carts or capybara for the hunt. The teachers fight the shame associated with the *fogão a lenha* wood stove, the *forno de barro* mud oven, and the work in the field.

What an impossible challenge here! They are going to have to adopt the computer and the TV and the telephone. Can they preserve the only beautiful things they have — the slow food, the hard-earned crop, the love of a little rain, the traditional dances, the values and music that have not been corrupted by Hollywood and Motown? The cities of Brazil have been lost. Can the *campo* be saved?

Chapter Eight

Itambé do Mato Dentro

The hike from Senhora do Carmo to Itambé do Mato Dentro is the best and wettest of the trip so far, a quiet road of red-tan mud and a constant mist that often thickens to a drizzle. The hills along the road are steep, their grass trimmed to stubble by cows. The tops of the hills are up in the clouds. No doubt there are cows up there. All the greenery is freshened with rain. Everyone I meet agrees that this rain, light and constant, is perfect — a little late, but arriving at the same rate that the earth can soak it up. It's just perfect.

The vehicles on the road are few. A little pick-up

goes by, then returns with several steel cans full of milk. A spiffy new car goes by with a man driving most expertly through the mud, his pretty-faced passenger looking surprised when she sees me. An old motorcycle goes by with a box of empty two-liter soda bottles in a box on the back, then returns with the bottles full of milk from cows that live in the clouds.

The farms are beautiful, old houses adjacent to muddy cow corrals, lots of palm trees gray in the mist, one especially beautiful place with a driveway lined with towering bamboo that lean in to form a tall, green tunnel. A man walking by in a yellow slicker with his *capa preta* (black cape) shepherd mix tarries to praise the rain and ask my destination. He seems to be the sort of peasant who can't read and might mistake me for a Chinese. To my surprise, he informs me that I am on the Estrada Real, that the old empire has passed here, that it must be preserved, that tourists are going to come. I hadn't asked him about any of this. I can't tell whether he wants to see these farms turned into *pousada*s or whether he hopes that won't happen. The beautiful old farm at hand, with the bamboo over the driveway, was his father's, his family's. He lives just up the road.

Another vehicle goes by, a yellow VW bug purring through the mud in second gear, pulling a little trailer that holds half a dozen milk cans. And that's it for traffic on this day.

My favorite place along this section of road is at perhaps the highest point, the terrain dominated by exposed boulders and rock outcrops. The left side of the road rises steeply into the clouds. The right side descends gently into fog. At this highest point, on the right side, someone's got a little cow operation centered around a cave under exposed bedrock. His fence is a crude stacking of rails. I stop here to look down on it for a while. I peel an orange, leaving the white inner skin intact so I can squeeze it and suck the juice out. Then I fill it with *cachaça*, light a cigarette, and slowly suck out the *cachaça*. It's too early for *cachaça*, around ten or eleven in the morning, but I feel entitled because it's cold and windy and my clothes are almost damp enough to drip.

I descend into Itambé at around lunchtime. It's the first town I've ever seen with a river of steep rapids rushing right under the main street. The water looks surprisingly clean. It isn't a quaint town, but it is quiet and clean and smells pleasantly of dung. Great geysers of pink and purple bougainvillea hint at a people with a sense of beauty. I stop to listen to a little bird which I believe to be a *sabiá*. It seems to tell a little story in a tweety-gurgly sentence about ten seconds long. The town looks a little mopey in the November drizzle, but I'll bet it's beautiful in the sun. People don't seem unhappy with rain, but they move sluggishly under the burden of umbrellas. They're going to be wet for the next two or three months.

I'm plenty wet as I slog into the Pousada Hotel-Bar-Rest, the only place to sleep in town. It's owned by the recently re-elected mayor, Geraldo Mercês. Although rather new, it lacks toilet seats. I book into a room without a bathroom, but the common bathroom has a toilet that doesn't flush right and the shower is cold and asthmatic. I decide to go deluxe and take a room with a bathroom, which costs all of $10.50 a night. Still no toilet seat.

I hand all my clothes, all of them wet, to the cook of the place. Her sister does laundry. All I have left to wear is swimming trunks and a damp, sweaty t-shirt. I urge her to bring the clothes back soon, but she says that depends on the weather. Maybe the day after tomorrow I'll be able to wear something that doesn't stink.

The hotel restaurant serves lunch on a patio under a roof on the second floor above the street. A young girl who looks to be about fifteen years old asks if she can ask me some questions. She wants to know where I'm from, what I'm doing, and how I like the town. She wants to know because she's in town to conscienticize the people about how to use their town as a tourist attraction, and how to keep tourists happy. Her name is Daniela. Bright-eyed and confident, twenty-three years old, she's fascinated to hear that I'm in tune with the Estrada Real program. She invites me to her class that night. I don't know the word for toilet seat and am too shy to take a guess, but it's something she should teach. Lesson one: Install toilet seats. Lesson two: If somebody steals the toilet seat, hunt him down and kill him. If he has already pawned the toilet seat, spring for a new one.

In my wet shorts and wet t-shirt, I go to her class over at the elementary school. It's quite boisterous and chaotic, as Brazilian classes, from kindergarten to college, tend to be. Lecturing over several other conversations, Daniela turns angry every once in a while, threatens not to give anyone their certificates after the course. The consequent silence, however, lasts only a few minutes. I can't entirely blame the students, who range in age from high school to middle age. Daniela is talking too abstractly about the importance of the environment, but these fidgety students need specific, palpable information on what they are supposed to do. They need lists of what the tourists want. They need to understand the financial ramifications of a toilet seat. They need specific suggestions for businesses they can open with little or no investment. She doesn't give them a hint as to how they, the people, can affect government policy. But her ideas are beautiful and true. I like Daniela. I wish I could get up there and show her how to do it. The chaos becomes absolute when she announces a break for snacks. Shivering in my damp clothes, I bail out, go back to my room, snuggle under my covers and sleep well.

*　　*　　*

Celeste works for the Igreja Nossa Senhora da Oliveira. She's about thirty-eight years old, unmarried, living just outside town with her father. I saw her at Daniela's course. She sat up front in a chair for kindergartners, her knees higher than her hips. She didn't say anything, and even if she had, she wouldn't have been heard in the din of unruly students. This morning she speaks in a weak, thin squeak, her eyes milky blue, her lower lip moist and pink. Though taking Daniela's course, she's not so sure that tourism is a good idea. It will bring "movement" and noise. It will ruin the calm of the town. It might bring money, but it's not worth it. As it brings in a lot of people from out of town, no one will know who is good people, who bad.

Nossa Senhora da Oliveira has two small problems. One is that lightning struck the church. The lightning rod had already burned out from a previous hit, so the heavenly juice found its way to the patron saint, Nossa Senhora da Conceição, who stands high — too high — above the altar. The jolt sent a crack down her left side. She's not about to split in two, but the congregation certainly has something to think about. I wonder if there's been any discussion of a miracle.

The other problem is the bells. The church has

two, both in the left tower. (The other tower has two megaphones.) They are very old bells, survivors of extensive refurbishment that stripped the church of most of its ancient beauty. The overall look of the church is of concrete efficiency. The problem with the bells is that to ring them, you have to go up in the tower and stand right up beside them and pull the rope. No one has figured out a way to ring them from down below. Of course it's impossible to stick your fingers in your ears as you do this. Celeste says she's quite deaf when she comes down from the tower. Sometimes it takes a lot of ringing to get the job done, first the big bell, then a lot of tolls on the smaller one, a bonging followed by a lot of banging. The ring patterns are different according to the event, be it funeral, festival, or other announcement. She doesn't like using the bells for messages. The slow rings are too sad.

Celeste got this job after Dona Caetana retired. Dona Caetana, 84, is hard of hearing, deeply wrinkled. She lives right up the street from the church. She hasn't got much to say. She watches church service on TV, the volume up loud. Her husband used to do farm work, but they always lived there in town. She worked for the church for fifty years, at both the Oliveira and a smaller one, the Rosário. She has four children on earth, she tells me, and four in the sky. The ones on earth live here in Itambé do Mato Dentro, except for one who has gone to Itabira. São Francisco de Assis stands on a shelf in a corner of

Caetana's living room, his needlepoint oration above him in a large frame. To the left of that is her diploma, certifying that she finished the fourth grade in 1931.

*   *   *

The *Cachoeira da Vitória* is about three kilometers outside of town, an easy walk up a dirt road, then five hundred meters down a path. The waterfall is beautiful, falling seventy meters in a narrow plume, dissipating into feathers as it descends. When the water arrives at the rocks below, it is barely more than a heavy mist that lands with a pulsating swish. A breeze originates there, swooshing out, carrying cool mist across the pool and down the hill. I take a sip of water by doing a push-up down to the rock basin the water slides over. It's a good place to sit and think about water and to kiss it from rock.

On my way back, hungry for lunch, I find that I can run downhill without my back hurting, the first time I've been able to run in over a year. It's a fine, fine feeling, with my legs feeling tough and strong, my left thigh pleasantly sore from a strained muscle.

Almost into town, I meet Daniela and her local chum Adauto in his little pick-up truck. They're on their way to Cabeça do Boi. Daniela invites me to come along. I ride in back. A light rain falls. It feels good. The scenery is beautiful — increasingly rugged mountains and dense *mato*. Cabeça de Boi turns out to be a little village surrounded by steep, high *serras*, one of them a high cliff that disappears into the clouds. The village is small and isolated, a few dozen low houses huddled on a hill. I wouldn't be surprised to see gnomes in the grassy streets. We go into a *barzinho* for fried green banana chips, coin-sized slices of unripe banana. Outside, the rain comes down hard, making a lot of noise on the roof. We drink three beers and smoke *fumo de rolo* wrapped in corn husk. It's still raining when we leave, so I get to squeeze into the little Fiat cab with sweet little Daniela warm and soft against my left flank, where she can get the full impact of my rancid clothes. We stop at the *Cachoeira Lúcio*. The lower fall is an impressive two-tier tumble of clear water thundering into a pool with a little beach, a lush *mato* closing out the sky. Higher up, the water drops farther into a deeper pool. That pool, too, used to be completely closed in by tall trees, but the electric company cleared a lot of them away for some high tension wires that pass overhead. Above the pool there's a big cave under an overhang. We collect the litter we find there and take it back to Itambé.

Later I stopped by Adauto's little store to buy some honey and some industrial, probably carcinogenic, punk that keeps mosquitoes away. I have to buy a whole kilo of honey. It's good honey, produced by a local guy named Marconi, but even the smallest jar is far more than I want to carry. A tenth of a kilo would be plenty.

Adauto invites me upstairs for coffee. There we meet his father. The *cafezinho* builds into cheese, cookies, crackers, fruit, and juice as Adauto's mother hovers around, thinking of more things she can offer the guest. With a mouth of crackers and cheese, crumbs on his lips, Adauto's father explains to me why George W. Bush is no good. I'm amazed at how closely he reflects my own thoughts. He says that Bush wants to dominate the world with his army and his industry, that wealthy people are ruining the world by trying to own far more than they need, that everyone is entitled to enough food to eat, the basics, and nothing else is necessary or even advisable. Excess and greed cause pollution and wars. Because of television everything has changed. It is ruining the community and its youth. How can you keep kids moral when they see immoral things on TV? They no longer have respect. Parents can't control them. It's the end of the world, no?

I sympathize completely, but no, I don't think it's the end of the world. The world is always ending, I tell him. It's always in a bad position, but somehow it always survives. But yes, much is being lost, and yes, in my opinion, television is the great culprit.

Honey and punk in hand, I head for the post office, where the postmistress spends twenty minutes flipping through huge books and fat files to figure out how much postage to put on an envelope to the United States. She says she did it once before but has forgotten how. She finds the probable answer but then has to dig up an improbable combination of stamps that nearly covers the front of the envelope and which, on second thought, is the wrong combination, so we have to peel them off and do it all again.

Then it's off to lunch. A woman named ZeZé has been much recommended.

ZeZé is the best cook in town. She used to live in the center of São Paulo, where she worked at a *pensão*. She wanted to learn to cook. The cook there said no, ZeZé was much too obsessed with detail for a kitchen that served three thousand lunches per day. But ZeZé wanted to cook, and eventually she got a job at PetroBras, the national oil company, and took courses in cooking and soon was serving thousands of meals per day, and with considerable attention to detail. It still wasn't what she wanted. She moved to Itabira and opened a bar there with her husband, Valdir. It still wasn't what she wanted, and soon she moved to Itambé, a far cry from São Paulo, but it's what she wanted.

Along came Semana Santa - Easter Week. Perfectly typical of this confused and short-sighted country, the whole town closed down from Maundy Thursday until the Monday after Easter, one of three weekends during the year when everybody in town has an opportunity to make a little extra money. Tourists show up to stay for that whole week. A couple dozen stay at the Hotel Estrella. A couple dozen more rent houses. Several score camp in the area, near the waterfalls. The Hotel Estrella is about the only place in town that serves food, but not on the holy weekend. So the owner of the hotel went to ZeZé and suggested that she prepare to serve food for three days. She kind of wanted to but had no money, and all she had to serve food on was three dishes. She happened to know someone who wanted to get rid of some restaurant equipment, including a freezer. He just wanted it moved out of his place. He said she could pay for it when she had the money. So all of a sudden she got a truck and picked up the equipment and went to Itabira and bought sixty kilos of fish and thirty kilos of shrimp and got ready for the weekend.

And she sold all the food. She worked day and night not just on the holy weekend but the whole week before because the guests at the hotel didn't like the disorganization of the place. She made about US\$ 4,000 — a huge amount. And next year, come Carnaval, she drew an even bigger crowd. She had a reputation as a good cook with a lot of food. She bought a hundred cases of beer, fifty cases of soda, and a lot of food. She sold it all and made the equivalent of eight thousand dollars.

She was renting a bar at the time for two minimum salaries (i.e. twice the amount a worker would earn in a month at minimum salary). That was too much, however, so she opened a restaurant in the lower half of her house and outside it, too. Valdir tends to the vegetables in her organic garden. Her specialties are typical *mineiro* dishes, such as *feijão tropeiro*, *abobrinha*, *tutu* and such imported dishes as lasagna and stroganoff. She wants to expand but can't find employees or investment. She says people around Itambé would rather go hungry than work.

She also has a little shop where she sells clothes and shoes that are stylish, though no so much so that they cost much. She also stocks one each of a variety of odd products: a clock, an electric razor, a set of Barbie garden furniture, playing cards, a little roulette wheel. Customers are few. While she sits, she needlepoints flowers on towels.

My last night in Itambé is also the last night of Daniela's classes. They've planned a big party, a *forró* in the school gym. (Two or three sources have explained to me that *forró* is imitative of an English expression, "for all," possibly from an English mining company that held dances open "for all" the community to attend.) Daniela is making the event as big as it can possibly be. She and others have cut out decorations from newspapers and construction paper. ZeZé has made *feijão tropeiro*. The students have written some kind of drama that demonstrates the right way to care for the environment and tourists. They've brought handicrafts to sell. I show up with two boxes of candles to help with the atmosphere. When I arrive, the whole bunch of thirty or forty people is crowding around Daniela for a rather elaborate announcement of the best student or something. A gaily wrapped box contains several other gaily wrapped boxes. As each is opened, it names, in funny couplets, another person who has to open the next box, all to cheers and laughs. Daniela gets lots of hugs. She cries. Pretty soon I'm crying, too. The whole event is so friendly and human and warm, and there's no sign of Big Brother anywhere, no American soft drinks, no American music, no advertising. The little boom box may be from São Paulo or maybe even Japan or Taiwan, but the music coming from it is country peasant stuff. Every product I can see — the handicrafts, the decorations, the local *cachaça* that Adauto is surreptitiously offering to anyone who will drink it — is all local. No one is conscious of that fact. It's just happening, and everybody's just as happy as can be.

Chapter Nine

Morro do Pilar

Outside Itambé, about ten kilometers in the direction of Morro do Pillar, the *serra* turns rocky and sparse and eerie with huge, odd boulders that seem to have been thrust up as magma, frozen and cracked by ice, eroded for a millennium and left out to dry. The view to the west looks over a valley of hills washing up against the Serra Cabeça do Boi, with its stark, irregular humps, another range that starts at a cliff that must drop a quarter of a mile straight down to a narrow valley that separates it from Cabeça do Boi. From the looks of it, something ripped the ridge apart. The river that runs between them does not seem to have eroded its way through them. I'm at 3,100 feet, just below a layer of morning cloud that has risen from the earth and will burn off between nine o'clock and 9:20. The dawn light behind me slides a gilt patina across the bottom of the cloud. It's an unearthly sensation to be closer to the cloud than to the broad deep valley that spreads before me, rimmed at the far end by a ridge precisely as high as the one I'm on.

For most of two hours I hike uphill. The road changes from red clay to pink dust to sparkling quartz. Rock outcrops punched up through the sparse meadow loom over the road with Druidical mysteriousness. Under one of those outcrops, ten kilometers from Itambé, lives a well-known hermit named Domingos. To meet him, you have to know just where to stop — there's a little path heading uphill into brush and boulders — and there call out, as loud as you can, "Hooo, Seu Domingos!"

I find the spot and give a holler. Domingos answers with a hoot. I walk up the narrow path of granite sand to his home under a rock where he's got a living space of about thirty feet by ten. He's a stringy old guy wearing the remains of rags. His beard looks like it was trimmed with a dull knife in the dark. A ragged tuft of light whiskers sits above the center of his upper lip. On his head he wears the bottom of a plastic bag. He reaches out with his left hand to greet me. I reach out with my left. He touches it with one finger and pulls back. Then he squats on a rock behind his fence of jumbled bamboo and begins to talk in a voice jittery and slightly insane.

But he's lucid and curious about where I come from. He is under the impression that the United States is part of Brazil. He's sure of it and knows for a fact that the two areas are connected by a bridge, or maybe that Mexico is part of Brazil and is connected to the United States by a bridge. He asks me if I came to Brazil by land. As a matter of fact I did, about thirty years ago, hitch-hiking from Fairfield, Conn. to São Paulo, S.P. He asks me if I crossed a bridge on the way. As a matter of fact I did. Well, he says, there you go.

Domingos lives the most meager of lives. His brown shorts have a busted zipper and his shirt has only one button. The button is red. The shirt is a dirty rag. On his back he wears a shawl of plastic that used to be a shopping bag. He smells very bad. His knobby knees are scratched and scarred. As far as I can tell, he has no navel. He invites me into his broad narrow cave and in stuttering, maniacal chatter sets himself to looking for something clean for me to sit on. He finds some clean T-shirts that a woman gave him several months ago but which he's not yet gotten around to wearing. "I don't need much in the way of clothes," he says.

Most of Domingos' possessions are in two-liter soda bottles, tin cans and bamboo baskets that hang from his rock ceiling. They are tied with twisted strands of something sinuous that are pegged into cracks in the rock. The biggest thing he owns is a rusty milk can. He owns at least one small kettle, which also hangs from the rock overhead.

This is a man who can use some honey, and it so happens I've just lugged about 900 unneeded grams of the stuff up a long, hot hill. Would he like some? He's reluctant but not enough so to fully decline. His reluctance is in his having no food to offer me — a devastating deficiency in the Brazilian social context. Would I like some coffee? He could make some.

Noooooo...no thank you. I truly believe that you can judge a man's water by his house and garb. This man's water is hanging in age-old Coke and Fanta bottles, water probably from a clean source, a spring around there somewhere, but I'm sure the containers are veritable convention centers of germs and parasites. But that doesn't matter because he doesn't think he has any coffee anyway. He's mortified by his lack of anything to share. When might I be returning? In six months or year, I say. He says he'll have food for me then. So we pour, or try to pour, some honey into a plastic cup that had once held a retail serving of mineral water. But the honey's crystallized. It won't pour, so Domingos uses the broken blade of a pruning hook to shear the crud from a length of bamboo that then serves as a spoon. I say, "Don't let the ants get in there," but he knew that already.

Domingos talks and talks and talks, frenetically, sometimes stuttering with the urgency of getting a certain word out. He has a lot to say. He reviews his life for me, but his chatter is so quick and so scattered with peasant idioms that all I can really understand is that he's from São Paulo state and he's seventy-two years old. With pathological detail he recounts how he arrived in Minas Gerais, the time the train arrived, why it was late, where he went first, ad nauseam and beyond. I understand little of it, and I'm sure none of it matters. But a lot of what he isn't saying matters a lot – like why the hell does he live under a rock ten kilometers outside of a town which itself isn't much of a place to live?

A better question: Why didn't I ask him that?

I pretty much understand one thing: He may not be living under that rock much longer. The owner of that land died recently. Through convolutions of inheritance and deals, recounted now in excruciating and confusing detail, a woman has come to own the land. She has told him that he can stay for just two more years. Then he has to go find a rock somewhere else. Or so he thinks. I kind of doubt the reality of this danger. This land, too rocky for crops, to rough for cattle, too far from town for anything, is of no possible use except as a place to hide.

*   *   *

Morro do Pilar is over twenty miles from Itambé, farther than I can walk in a day. But Adauto and a man named

Hermínio, the town secretary of tourism, have assured me that if I turn left off the main road at a place indicated by a sign, I can reach the Fazenda Sobrado, owned by a fine fellow named João Brandão. The farm, about halfway to Morro do Pilar, happens to be on a shortcut that lops off a couple of kilometers, albeit at the cost of a steep climb. I'm neither enticed by the shortcut nor concerned about the climb. I am worried about having to sleep outdoors, subject to snakes seeking heat, scorpions wandering along, spiders biting, the touch of the venomous hair of the *lagarta* caterpillar, the thirst of a rabid, blood-sucking bat. Brazil is an inhospitable place for sleeping outdoors.

Around noontime, under a killer sun, I wind down into a river valley and soon arrive at a little farm that turns out to belong to Brandão's brother, Noinho. Brandão's farm is just up the road, but Noinho invites me in for lunch. He apologizes for his furniture, which is in a jumble while two guys paint his door and window trim a shiny colonial blue. He hands me a dish and gestures to his *fogão a lenha*. I load up with rice, black beans, boiled corn flour, collards, a stewed drumstick. I accept a dose of *cachaça* and ask for a drop of *malagueta* pepper. To quote Hemingway's immortal words, "It was good." Noinho, shirtless, shoeless, sleepy, fidgety with an urge to get back to something unfinished, watched as I ate, saying little, being polite, trying not to wake all the way up from a nap before I left.

João Brandão's farm is just a few hundred meters up the road. He receives me well, sits with me on the bench of his veranda while tell him how I come recommended by Adauto and Hermínio, who so generously invited me to rest at his farm for a while. We chat for a while as he probes me politely for my background and purposes. From him I learn that his house, once a two-story sobrado, was moved to its present location many years ago, losing its upper floor along the way. It's still a nice house of big windows with heavy shutters and no glass, wide floorboards, heavy timbers framing the doors, high ceilings and a kitchen outside under a slanting roof. He bought it relatively recently after achieving success with a trucking company and then as a director of a farm co-op bank. His wife prefers to stay in Itabira, a city of modern amenities that stops short of reaching the cultural and culinary variety of a true metropolis. Retired now, he spends his weeks on the farm, managing to wrest a little revenue from a few hundred head of cattle and cows. He produces milk and cheese and loves the down-and-dirty nature of a farm unencumbered with the tidiness and frill that a woman would insist on. This is a guys' house, not dirty but strictly utilitarian, a place where men eat off plates held in the laps while they're sitting somewhere comfortable, like on the porch or in front of the TV. There's no chicken in the freezer but there's a .22-caliber rifle leaning against a table. The pots and pans are shiny clean but have no handles. Everything is clean except for the ruddy veneer of dust that farm hands just don't have time to brush away. Most ceiling corners are graced with dark ropes of cobweb. The air smells of black tobacco, pasture grass, wood smoke, curing cheese and the earthy essences of the surrounding barnyard. I can see, hear and smell why Brandão's wife prefers life in Itabira and he prefers life here.

A farm hand brings a Thermos of coffee and a pair of cafezinho cups on saucers. We sip the coffee with audible satisfaction. Then Brandão shows me to a bedroom, introduces me to the bathroom, and gives me leave to wash up and rest. I shower up and in a delicious agony of muscular exhaustion sink to the bed and drift into the sounds of the surrounding barnyard, a cacophony of chickens and roosters, squabbling ducks, marauding geese, the intermittent bawl of a cow or calf, the clop-clop-clop of horse hooves, the shouts of farm hands explaining things to each long distance, the desperate yap and whine of a dog too long on a rope too short. How good it is – not just the beauty of a farm teeming with life but the generosity of a man who will open his house to a traveler who needs shelter from the reptiles and bugs. In fact, now that I think about it, this house, dating back to the days of the *tropeiros*, has probably been opened to hundreds, even thousands of travelers. They'd have nowhere else to stay, so, since they were humans, they were let in.

The distances between villages and houses gave birth to the virtue of generosity that is still a foundation of Brazilian culture. Even today, a friend or stranger at the door must be offered coffee, and once he or she is at the table, the host will quickly deploy every other available food, at the very least cookies, crackers, biscuits, cheese, and sweets. Anyone arriving at mealtime will be dragged to a place setting. People of inadequate generosity are called *gaveteiros*, a word derived from *gaveta*, meaning "drawer." *Gaveteiros* are people who quickly slip their dinner into drawers to avoid having to share it with unexpected visitors. I don't know a word meaning the opposite of *gaveteiro, gente boa* — good people — would cover the concept. João Brandão is *gente boa*.

*   *   *

The shortcut toward Morro do Pilar is indeed a steep climb. Having drunk most of my water on the first hill, I stop at a pretty little farm to ask if they can fill my bottle. It looks like a nice place to get water. Flowers grow all over the place, the main gate has a tile roof over it, and the corral is under a steep thatched roof. I clap at the gate and call out All-ooooh. A voice from the porch invites me to come in. It's an old guy with a permanent smile and no teeth, José Simões de Oliveira, 72, who's more than happy to give me some water. He insists that I join him on his porch bench and have a little coffee. He lives there with his wife, a Calvanistic-looking woman in a calf-length gray dress and white blouse. She sweeps dead leaves and bougainvillea petals from her yard with a palm branch as José tells me about the old days. He operated a pick for the railroad company when the tracks were laid from Belo Horizonte to Itabira. He brought the "best church bell in all of Brazil" from Rio to Itabira by ox cart. He had ten children, which he felt was not enough. All but one now live in Belo. They try to get him to leave his isolated little house and come to the city, but he won't go. "There I don't have *liberdade*," he says.

The whole time we talk, José smiles as if he's forgotten how to stop. He holds a leaf of corn husk in his hand, having forgotten that he was about to roll a cigarette. His wife keeps sweeping and sweeping. Avocados thump down around her. In their kitchen they have at least twenty feet of sausages draped around a rod over their wood stove. I take José's picture with the morning light coming in through the kitchen window. His wife refuses to have hers taken because she's unprepared, inherently plain, and she has a yard to sweep.

Until I meet up again with the Estrada Real, the trail is too steep for cars. No traffic passes. The morning fog burns off right on schedule, and by ten o'clock the sun is set on broil. The scattered puffy clouds, so pretty and evenly spaced, never come between me and the sun. I walk with my water bottle in my hand, tilting forward to keep the weight of my pack high on my shoulders, staggering from one shady patch to the next, stopping at each to suck down more water. It occurs to me that if I run out of water — my bottle holds only a liter and a half — and have to keep walking uphill under direct sun, I could well suffer heat stroke, fall down, go into a coma and die. The urubus would eat most of me before anyone found my parched remains. Indeed their shadows are gliding past my feet. They're circling me, their ragged wings stretched wide across the updrafts.

But they don't eat me. I make it into Morro do Pilar, urban population: 2,488. I book into the Hotel Monsenhor Matos. For some reason I don't expect to find much of interest in this town. The guidebook lists one church, four waterfalls outside of town, and the ruins of the Royal Iron Factory, where, in 1813 or 1814 or prior to October 5, 1815, or at one o'clock p.m. on October 15, 1815, iron was first smelted in Brazil. (This was 206, 207 or 208 years after it was smelted in Jamestown, Virginia.) The ruins consist of two sections of mud wall not much bigger than double doors. They are enshrined under concrete roofs. The plaque has little to say about this pitiful monument to this hugely important event. The blast furnace was allowed here after all hope of finding gold was gone. Today, Minas Gerais has several hematite mines, and Brazil is one of the world's greatest producers of steel. Brazilian steel is so good and produced so efficiently that President George W. Bush had to put a tariff on it, effectively trashing his dream of a free trade zone for the Americas.

With the gold gone and the mud blast furnace eroded away, Morro's biggest industry now is the weaving of *taquara*çu, a thick bamboo that can be sliced into slivers that can be boiled until soft, then dried and woven. This is the only place in the world where this is done, and the business is entirely in the hands of poor families with no other source of income. The men go out, find the bamboo, cut it down, bring it home. The women boil and dry it, then weave it into long strips an inch or two wide. Three generations of women will sit around doing this all day. They do it while walking down the street, gradually building up coils around their shoulders. These long ribbons can be made into purses, hats, belts, decorations. The weavers sell it by "the arm," a length as long as they can reach from one hand to the other, probably about five feet. They'll sell twelve arms for two *reais*, about seventy-five cents, a little more than the price of a beer. So far, *taquara*çu is safe from tariffs. George Bush doesn't know about it, and it isn't sold anywhere except here in Morro do Pilar.

Once I've looked at the ruins of the iron factory, I figure it's time to move on up the road to somewhere interesting. But I'll feel guilty if I don't at least stop by Town Hall to check in with the secretary of tourism, if for no other reason other than for the pleasure of describing the typical ne'r-do-well suckling at the municipal teat. Instead, I find no secretary of tourism there at all. But the town does have one, a woman named Fabiana, who lives just around the corner, down a steep hill of cobblestone. Someone calls her, and she agrees to see me if I would be so kind as to walk on down to her house.

As it turns out, Fabiana ranks among the conscienticized. She's the secretary of not only tourism but culture, recreation, history, and whatever else of a warm and fuzzy nature she chooses to take on. Her budget, of course, is minuscule, Morro being the eighth-poorest town, per capita, in Minas Gerais. But Fabiana doesn't care too much about budget. She wants to get stuff done, and she's got the cell phone to make it happen. What she needs right now is a car to take us around. Town Hall's cars are busy, and the town has no formal taxis, but a few guys with cars can be hired if they have nothing else to do, but they don't have phones, so Fabiana has to call people who live near them or know where they might be. Each call, however, seems to uncover a problem that she must at least temporarily resolve, usually with another phone call to someone else who isn't there but whom a child can be sent to fetch if Fabiana will just hold on for a moment.

Fabiana knows of the existence of three, possibly four, hand-written books — literally manu-scripts — that were written by slaves reporting on events in town. One such event involved a priest who became a little too adamant about the evils of adultery. His sermons got a little too specific about the different relationships that could develop. One of the Portuguese overlords took it personally. He had the priest buried up to his waist on the hill above town and left there to die. The priest screamed that no boy baptized in the Igreja Nossa Senhora do Pilar would ever become a priest. I am told that the curse has held true.

Another tale reports the collapse of a mine, crushing or trapping eighteen slaves. The hill above town, up where the town used to be, is still riddled with tunnels. The bones of the eighteen slaves are still up there somewhere.

Fabiana wants to go look for the slave books, which are in the hands of private citizens, though she doesn't know exactly whose. She also wants to go look for a couple of drums she has heard about. They were once played by slaves for the Brazilo-African dance called *catopé*. She knows who has these drums. All we need is someone with a car to take us there. Town Hall's cars are busy, and there aren't really any official taxis in town, but there are a couple of guys with cars who can be hired, but they don't have phones, so Fabiana has to look for them by calling other people who may know their whereabouts, but each call digresses into other problems that Fabiana has to deal with.

While she calls and calls and calls, I flick through a little book that tells the history of Morro do Pilar. I come across a certain character I'd heard about a long time ago, a fellow known simply as Juquinha. Some called him Juquinha da Serra, but that's really just a name and address. For reasons unknown, some called him Juquinha Chupa-ovo: Juquinha Egg-sucker, a name he did not like.

Juquinha lived under a rock way off in the mountains. Unlike Domingos, he was actually a very sociable guy who came into town and was widely loved. He sold orchids that he found in the mountains. He knew everything about nature, including the curative effects of roots and herbs. In town, he used to clown around with children and tell them stories. He was famous for being simply a nice guy, a man with a floppy hat and a walking stick, an armload of flowers and not much use for money, a hermit you could love, as poor as dirt and as happy as could be. In the 1970s he either disappeared or died in his cave or died in town — the stories vary. Someone who appreciated him sculpted a statue of concrete on a mountain overlooking a broad valley under big sky. It's a few hundreds yards off a dirt road I once went down. There's no sign indicating it, and it blends in with the surrounding geology. You really have to know where to look. It's about twice life-size, him sitting with one leg out straight, two hands cradling his other knee, his floppy hat on, his stick beside him, a homemade pipe in his mouth, a smile in his eyes.

I ask Fabiana what Juquinha was famous for, why there's a statue of him, why everybody assumes a look of fondness when they talk about him. She says he was famous for nothing except who he was. He was illiterate. He never held a position on anything, never offered aphoristic words of wisdom, never wrote a poem or a song, didn't do anything but be a nice guy.

Fabiana finds a car. Off we go to look for the old drums. They are in the possession of a very black man named Júlio Cesar, one of the last people in town who knows how to do the *catopé*. He lives with his very black and beautiful family in a little house on the outskirts of town. He and his family are all descendants of slaves from an old farm called Mata Cavalo. The second-to-last white owner of the farm was a little eccentric, if not downright deranged. He left his farm to his daughters under the condition that they not marry and not bear him grandchildren. He also freed all his slaves under the condition that they continue to live and work on his farm. Upon his daughters' deaths, the slaves were to inherit the farm. One of the daughters managed to preserve her chastity and her possession of Mata Cavalo. Quite predictably, however, the slaves were unable to maintain their possession of the farm. Other farmers nibbled at their land. The blacks, dirt poor and disrespected, undoubtedly illiterate, were unable to defend themselves against the encroachment. The issue has been in court for many years. Given the glacial bureaucracy of the Brazilian legal system, the case may never be resolved. Until it is, the descendants live in a little house on the side of a steep hill on the outskirts of Morro do Pilar.

Júlio Cesar brings the two drums from a little mud shed behind his mother's house. I've never seen drums like this, each standing on a peg-leg. One drum is named José, the other Maria. José's leg is stuck in a tin can. Maria's, unshod, has been gnawed by termites. Both have cracks edging up their drum cavities, but their skins are still tight. They used to cover buffaloes. Fabiana and Júlio Cesar agree that they need to find an excellent carpenter to fix these drums right. They may have come from Africa itself, and today they are needed for the resurrection of the *catopé*. Júlio Cesar says that when these drums were all fixed up, they used to shine at night while everyone danced. Fabiana herself will arrange some varnish and a carpenter.

Júlio Cesar is the only person in Morro do Pilar who remembers how to do the *catopé*. He wants to preserve the dance as much as he wants to preserve José and Maria. He agrees to give lessons. Fabiana asks him when. He says soon. She asks if next weekend would be good. It would. Fabiana will so inform the world. She'll even have the opportunity announced from the speakers on the church bell tower.

She has something else to announce from the church loudspeakers. While talking with Júlio Cesar's mother, we learn that someone is taking advantage of the dengue fever epidemic. The epidemic has been contained in Rio de Janeiro and São Paulo, but a few cases have popped up elsewhere. It's generally more of a problem in urban areas because it can spread only when a mosquito bites an infected person, then goes on to bite someone else. This requires a certain population density. A few cases have been recorded in Morro do Pilar, but they've been people who came into town from Itabira. To prevent an infestation, the municipal government is spraying insecticide around everyone's houses at no charge. But somebody has been coming around and telling people they have to pay to get it done. They say it costs twelve *reais*, then do it, then charge ten times that for the materials used. One woman got taken for more than a month's salary. Fabiana, aghast at such crookedness, will have the church loudspeakers announce that the city's spraying services are free for all.

I like Fabiana. She cares, gets things done, and she

likes to see them done right. From Júlio Cesar's house we take the car to see an old woman who may have one of the old books. We found the woman, but unfortunately the book has been lost. It got half ruined from being passed around town, and finally somebody took it to Belo Horizonte to show somebody. It never came back. She doesn't know who else has old books by slaves. She thinks no one. They've all been lost. Fabiana is visibly grieved by this, holding her forehead in one hand. "The waste," she says. "The loss."

The town still has a big memento of slavery, a labyrinth of narrow mines that riddle the mountain above town, up where the town used to be until it ran out of space and water. The town's first church, the Igreja do Canga, built in 1710, is still up there. Nearby, if you know where to stomp, you can hear the echo in a tunnel below. If you have a flashlight, you can go into the tunnels, some of which wander a kilometer into the same mountain that still holds the eighteen slaves who died in the cave-in. Fabiana wants the town to build a *pousada* and a museum up there near the mines so that tourists can come to appreciate the history, spend a little money, watch some *catopé* to the thump of José and Maria, and maybe think about the eighteen slaves who are still down there somewhere.

Later in the afternoon, I go to the pharmacy to by a few Band-aids for my sorer toes. I have one unused Band-aid I've saved to show to a pharmacist because I don't know the word for it in Portuguese. The town pharmacist, Rafael, knows the word: It's "band-aid," of course, albeit pronounced bon-DIE-jee. So I buy five, and then, on second thought, one more.

Rafael and I get to talking about what I'm doing in town and where I've come from, and pretty soon an old geezer comes along and the three of us are talking about the hermit Domingos. I'm very interested in Domingos's story because I've always had the suspicion — if that's the word for fear crossed with hope — that the odds of my ending up living under a rock on a mountain rather than in a retirement complex are about fifty-fifty. I can see myself fleeing to a cave, but I can also imagine being chased there. Domingos's case isn't clear-cut either, not even thirty-five years after the fact. Apparently he once had a girlfriend, might even have been engaged to her. She was the daughter of a rich farmer who didn't approve of her marriage to a man who had no money and was already discernibly nuts. The girl dumped him for someone more acceptable. There may have been a fight or some death threats. Domingos retreated to a rock cave on a mountain and has lived there ever since, no doubt still suffering an open wound on his tender heart. It wasn't the rock he lives under now. Every once in a while, when the visitor traffic gets too heavy, he moves to a new rock. The old geezer thinks Domingos's mother may have lived under a rock, too.

Right across the street from the pharmacy, the Igreja Nossa Senhora do Pilar resonates with the sweet sound of children singing. I can't resist a church of people singing, so I slip in a side door and hang out in a rear pew. The singers are little girls chortling a song about "*todas as raças...*" — all the races — doing something together. I can't quite make out what all the races are doing together, but I'm pretty sure it's not "calling each other names." Despite the angelic voices singing such a sweet message, the choir leader snaps at the little girls for crossing their arms as they sing and alerting each other to the presence of a stranger the color of stir-fried shrimp.

The only place that serves a meal in this town is under a roof behind a big sign that says "*Kaiser Bar e Restaurante.*" Kaiser is the name of a beer, not the place. Despite its Germanic sound, Kaiser is made in Brazil and owned by foreigners. In other words, the name is essentially a lie, a disguise, a trademark fantasy that does little to distinguish Kaiser from Brahma, Antarctica, Bohemia, Bavaria, Skol, Schincariol and Cerpa, all of which taste like Budweiser and such.

As if to complete the lie, the Kaiser Bar e Restaurante does not stock Kaiser beer. In all other ways, however, the establishment does not pretend to be anything it isn't. It has no false motif fashioned by fishing nets on the wall or faux Depression-era tavern signs or cowboy artifacts. It's just a floor of concrete under a roof of corrugated plastic held up by former tree trunks. The tables are plastic, all the easier to move out of the way of drips as a thunderstorm moves in. The lights blink a couple of times. I hope they go out for good so the bar can take on a colonial motif of candles and the human closeness that comes with candlelight. Four guys in four shades of skin ranging from dirty white to rain-slick black, come in and take a table to my left. They're weary from working outdoors all day. They order one dose of *cachaça* and pass it around. They order the *prato feito*, the economy plate stacked with whatever food the kitchen has available, most often rice, beans, a little beefsteak, a few leaves of lettuce, a slice of tomato, maybe a fried egg.

Speaking of commercial lies, there's a cigarette ad on the central post that holds up the roof. Except for the Kaiser sign and the Antarctica logos on the plastic tables, it's the only commercial message in the place. The ad is for a bargain basement smoke that goes by the name of Sudan. At first glance it seems a suspiciously honest name for a cheap cigarette, but by the miracle of post-modern advertising, it flagrantly puffs itself up to the glory of Mt. Rushmore (angled to imply endorsement by no less than George Washington himself), a quick stop at a flashy motel in Las Vegas air-brushed to blend into the excitement of a cowboy at a rodeo and a snazzy red sports car outrunning a backdraft of dust. Aficionados of Mother Nicotine can choose to peruse the collage further to note that Sudan comes in three yummy flavors: "Lite, Regular," and, under a noble escutcheon, "Luxo." At the bottom, the government's words to the wise and whomever else it might concern, in also Helvetica bold, black on white: "Cigarro causa impotência sexual."

As I walk home under my little umbrella, a bunch of little boys, soaking wet, catch up to me. They recognize me as a foreigner, and one proffers a memory dredged up from school: "Whatee eez your namee!" To their amazement, I answer with a complete sentence that they understand. They're silent for a second, then collapse in laughter, joyous and astonished at their own intelligence.

Chapter Ten

Conceição do Mato Dentro

Say what you want about stupidity, but one fact remains: It never sleeps. It's always waiting, ready to go. Picture it as a little dog lying on the floor, seemingly snoozing but really just waiting for a door to open, an opportunity to go for a walk. The little dog Stupidity is waiting for me when I awake at 3:50 a.m. for my hike to Conceição do Mato Dentro, eighteen miles away. It's a long way to walk, and it's important to me that I arrive there before lunchtime because I already know where I'm going to eat lunch. By four-thirty I set off into the darkness of a foggy morning under a new moon. After I pass the last of the street lamps, I have to use my cigarette lighter to read the guide book. I can't even see my feet. Once I follow my little dog right off the road, into a ditch and up the other side. I come to a bridge that the guide book refers to, though the mileage doesn't feel right. I come to a farm, but it's on the wrong side of the road. I come to a cattle guard that should have been before the farm, not after. Things just don't feel right, but I keep walking.

The sun rises, though I can't tell where. I hear a man in the fog at the lower end of a long pasture singing to his cows, but the cows are busy watching me walk by. A wolf, twice the size of any dog I've seen in this country, crosses the road in front of me, swaggering in the way of wolves, shoulders hunched, head low, not bothering to stop and look at me as all animals on this road do, especially dogs. It was a wolf, all right. I should get up early more often. But not before dawn.

When a little yellow pick-up truck comes out of a farm, I flag it down. The guy tells me I'd already be a quarter of the way to Conceição if I were on the right road. But I'm on the road to Guanhães, which would get me to Conceição, all right, but not for a couple of days. He gives me a ride back to Morro, tells me his story. He's a reforester. He plants eucalyptus for steel companies and has a little weekend farm right there where he picked me up. He says he thinks George W. Bush is pretty hypocritical to be putting a thirty percent tariff on

Brazilian steel. He's punishing Brazil for its efficiency. He's getting carried away with his unstoppable power.

The guy drops me off at the turn-off I missed in the dark, a road perfectly obvious in daylight, clearly marked by a sign with an arrow and everything, even the kilometers to Conceição: 25. It's a low and rusty sign, tucked in among weeds on the left side of the road, easily missed in the dark, yes, but still, I remember sensing a structure as I passed it but didn't bother to check it out. My reforester/savior offers to take me all the way back into town so I can get some breakfast, but no, I don't want breakfast in Morro. I want lunch in Conceição. And along the way I want to suffer. I want to get hungry. I want to ache. The road is perfect for this, a steep and steady incline gutted by rain, slippery with gravel, littered with rock. By the top of the first hill I've guzzled my liter and a half of water. I stop at a farm for a refill. I've barely begun this hike and I'm already sore and exhausted. I'll never make it to Conceição before lunchtime and the brutal noontime sun. A kilometer up the road, I come to a classic fork, a perfect bifurcation, neither road less traveled than the other. My guidebook has already informed me of various landmarks that did not require decisions. Now I need a decision, but the book makes no reference to a fork in the road. Burnt once today, there's no way I'm going to walk down one road until I reach someone who can tell me it's the wrong road. I'm going to wait, even if it takes all day. Somebody always comes along, right?

Within sixty seconds, a VW Gol comes rattling down the road from the direction I just came. When I motion for it to stop, it does. I ask which road. The driver asks if I'm walking to Conceição. As soon as I say "I am but...," he's out of the car and opening the trunk for my pack. I cannot resist.

He's a jolly young fellow named Renato. His big, loose African mouth peels back to his gums when he laughs, which is often. Renato is super-satisfied to have a job that pays US$ 180 per month and doesn't involve much more than driving a car. It's not much, he says, but it's enough and therefore better than most other people in Brazil. He distributes medical products for a pharmaceutical company. He doesn't even have to sell them; a sales rep does that. He comes along later and delivers the products. He covers hundreds of miles of dirt road, driving with the carefree urgency of someone young at the wheel of someone else's car. He drives slouched back, one hand low on the wheel, one elbow out the window, sliding through curves, spinning the wheels up gravel hills. Ruts and rocks — no problem. He's been stuck in mud before. He's spent time in ditches. He knows better than to slow down for the sake of somebody else's oil pan. He's got a seven-month-old daughter back home in Governador Valadares. He just wants to deliver his products and get back home to see her. His eyes soften as he pictures her.

I'm glad to have the ride but sorry not to be walking this particular stretch of the road. It's the roughest and woodsiest I've seen so far, passing under dense *mata atlântica*, part of the last of the forest that the Portuguese found five hundred years ago. We pass a turn-off where a sign indicates the Fazenda Mata Cavalo — the one once owned by former slaves. Either that road or the one we're on will take us to a state highway, which is just dirt but level and graded, a longer but faster route to Conceição. The guidebook says to stay on the main road, which could be either way. We turn right. It's soon obvious that not many vehicles have been on the road in a long time. The forest canopy has kept the road wet, but there are no tracks in the mud. We pass over a rickety bridge that would have collapsed had we not sucked in our breath as we crossed. We come around a bend to a dead cow in the road. Twenty or thirty *urubu* buzzards stand on and around it. Renato slows a bit to honk them out of the way, but they really don't want to retreat. Then the stench of maggot-ridden cow-flesh swamps the car. Renato slams the gears into second and floors the accelerator. The urubus in the road lift their wings and hop. The dozen on the carcass hold their ground. I'm very glad I'm not trying to walk through that scene, gagging on the smell and suffering the gaze of a carrion crew interrupted in the middle of a good cow.

With back-slaps and hand-shakes, Renato drops me off in Conceição do Mato Dentro, a town big enough to have stores, a gas station, and two banks, yet small enough for a dog to sleep in the middle of the street. When I was here a few years ago, I was introduced to a beautiful woman with a beautiful old inn, the house where she has lived since she got married some sixty years ago. During my brief visit, I shot half a roll of film in her kitchen. I can't remember the woman's name, but I definitely remember her helper telling me that the Dona never puts a meal on the table with fewer than nine hot dishes, all cooked on a fogão a lenha. So I've been thinking about lunch for almost three years now, and it was with that lunch in mind that I set out for Conceição before dawn. Though I've forgotten the name of the woman and her inn, I describe both well enough to various people. They know her. She's Dona Mirtila Generoso Lima, and her *pousada* is alongside the Mercado Municipal. And yes, upon arrival, I see that the shutters are still taxi-cab yellow. It's good I remember the shutters because she has no sign announcing her business.

I knock on the door, get no response, and finally open it and walk in. She's in there, still in black clothes, still mourning her husband, a truly good man, she's told me, who died seven years ago after a life of hard work and generosity.

Dona Mirtila says she remembers me, and she's delighted that I have brought the pictures I took when I visited before. She installs me in a room, shows me the bathroom and encourages me to take a shower right away. She also informs me that she hasn't made any lunch because she doesn't do that anymore. She sends her guests to the one good restaurant in town, just a few blocks away.

Her *pousada* is still beautiful, more than a mere inn, almost a museum of the good life of interior Minas. The house, built in 1784, once belonged to the church. She inherited it from her father, who had inherited it from his uncle, who had been a priest a long time ago. It's a classic one-story colonial townhouse, with *taquara* ceilings, long, wide floorboards, heavy-duty shutters, doors nine feet tall, a wide hallway passing between spacious bedrooms. The table in the dining room has been standing there since about the time Kentucky became a state. I try to lift one end off the floor. All I can do is make it groan a bit. Dona Mirtila made the seventeen-foot-long tablecloth. The other furnishings are stark and elegant, the furniture antique and heavy, the decorations reminiscent of yesteryear or the quiet beauty of nature in Minas Gerais – a bouquet of dried flowers in a crystal vase on a simple marble-topped table of *jacarandá*. Every inch of Dona Mirtila's *pousada* has been graced with aesthetic sensibility. Nothing would indicate the wear and tear I'd expect from the ten children she bore in this house nor from the other eight whom she adopted and nursed at her own breast. The eight came from women who could not afford to feed them. They brought babies to her the way my neighbors bring kittens to me.

On this day Dona Mirtila is teaching her new helper how to do things right. As the helper stands aside, hands behind her back, Dona Mirtila shows her how to roll a napkin correctly and slip it into a golden ring just right, how to lean the cutlery on the little silver horse that stands to the right of each plate, how to set the china tea cup on the saucer, handle to the right, and the saucer upon the china plate, how the napkin can be set at the upper rim of the plate or at a jaunty angle at ten o'clock or two o'clock, though she really prefers it up there at noon. The juice glass goes on the right, the fruit cup to the left. The doilies are for laying across the juice pitchers, beauty against flies.

Come Sunday morning, everything is laid out just right along with my breakfast of baked banana crisp, *goma* biscuits, toasted cream *rosquinha* cookies, *quebra-quebra* crackers, *bolinha* ball biscuits, cream biscuits, cheese bread, bread pudding, bread buns, gelatin, *queijo mineiro*, homemade orange cake, homemade guava jelly, homemade mango jelly, fruit salad, homemade butter, lime juice, mango juice, coffee, and milk from an actual cow and delivered in an actual milk can. Dona Mirtila apologizes for the lack of passion fruit juice and cheese fritters, the former being out of season, the latter unavailable on Sundays.

Conceição do Mato Dentro has a history of many names. Before it was anything at all, it was part of the region known as Ivituruí, an Indian word the Portuguese translated as Serro Frio, so called for the frigid, misty clouds that blow into the region. In 1702, a chapel of Nossa Senhora da Conceição was erected where the church of the same name now stands. The town held the name of its church until 1851, when the name was changed to Conceição do Serro. In 1925 it became just plain Conceição. In 1943, it became Conceição do Mato Dentro.

It was a grubby, down-and-dirty mining town until the Portuguese Crown realized that it would be losing a lot of gold unless it established a little order. By the middle of the eighteenth century, it had things under control. The Crown was collecting one fifth of all the gold produced. In 1764, it collected 99 *arrobas*, an *arroba* weighing about fifteen kilos — about 33 pounds. Ten years later, however, only 75 *arrobas* came into the government coffers. In 1777, it was down to 70. By 1811, it was down to 24. Seven years later, it was half of that.

In 1820, it was down to two. The Crown sent German mineralogist Baron von Eschewege to find out what was wrong. Was the gold petering out or was somebody ripping it off? Eschewege said it was a problem of geology and technology. The easy gold had been found. There was more, but it would demand more investment in technology processing systems.

By that time, however, Portugal itself barely existed. When Napoleon invaded Spain and Portugal in 1808, the Portuguese government fled to Brazil. Investments in mining technology were not a priority. Conceição has been in decadence ever since. Economic statistics are questionable and somewhat out-of-date, but town hall says that in 1996, the town's gross municipal product amounted to no more than R$ 18 million, pretty close to US$ 18 million at that time. (Five years later, the exchange rate has fallen from one-to-one to about 2.5-to-one.) The region produces about one metric ton of calf's foot jelly, three tons of butter, six tons of cheese and ten tons of molasses candy per month. There are many small *cachaça* stills, but only one, Bente Velho, is commercial enough to have a label and the AMPAQ seal of quality. That producer distills a hundred thousand liters per year.

Conceição is eighty percent mountainous, seventeen percent hilly, three percent flat. The highest point is on the Serra do Espinhaço, rising to 4,937 feet, the lowest at the Fazenda Rio do Peixe (Fish River Farm), at 2,066 feet. Belo Horizonte is ninety-six miles to the south. The average temperature is 69 F., the average high, 80.6 F. The highest temperature hits in February, about 84 F., the lowest in August, when it gets down to 50 F. Most of the rain falls between November and March.

The highest waterfall in the area, *Cachoeira* do Tabuleiro, plunges 895 feet straight down into a pool sixty feet deep. The *Cachoeira* de Congonhas falls 229 feet. The *Cachoeira* Rabo do Cavalo — Horsetail Falls — falls 390 feet, separates into two plumes and falls another 260 feet. The *Cachoeira* Três Barras falls 40 feet over a wall 130 feet wide.

Conceição has the highest rate of illiteracy in the state. Among children seven-to-ten years old, the rate is fifty-one percent. Among those fifteen to nineteen, the rate is twenty-five percent. The average for Minas Gerais is seven percent. Serious diseases have been generally eliminated though one rural area has a lot of dysentery. Rabid blood-sucking bats are a bit of a problem.

Speaking of rabid blood-sucking bats, I went to the bank to try to change a 100-real note, the equivalent of forty dollars. I needed smaller change because other than in a major city, any note larger than a ten is impossible to change. If you're stuck with fifties or hundreds, you're broke. I go to the Banco do Brasil first, successfully passing through the big revolving door that is actually a metal detector that automatically traps anyone who tries to come in with a gun. I didn't, but I get trapped in the line waiting for a teller. Brazilians pay a lot of their bills at the bank, and payments from various social programs come through the bank, so the bureaucracy at the teller window can get pretty dense. During the ten minutes I stand in line, not one person clears either of the two windows. One client has to go wait in another line to speak to the manager. I can't tolerate any line for more than three minutes, so I leave. I go to the other bank, Itau, which has just one teller but a shorter line. Unfortunately, they don't have enough cash on hand to change a 100-real note.

But I meet Dona Mirtila in the street and explain the problem to her. (Actually, this big note is her problem more than mine because I'm to leave the next morning and will have to pay her a quantity I still don't know but am sure will not come close to forty dollars.) She tells me to give her the note. She'll take care of it. She knows how to handle banks. She says that once when she was in northeast Brazil and wanted to withdraw money from her account, the bank manager said that the money had been deposited in her bank but had not reached his branch yet. She suggested that he take money from his personal account and put it into her account so she could withdraw it. He said, "*Sim, senhora,*" and did it.

Eager to have the story of her city told correctly, Dona Mirtila lends me a history written by someone she knows.

I'm delighted to find in the book a chapter dedicated to some of the town's more memorable nuts. One, named Bicudo, was most prominent in the 1940s. Bicudo was a big black man, strong, silent, watchful, respectful and respected. He was known as a hard worker, and though his nickname would refer to a wino, he never drank. But during a certain part of the year, he would go crazy, becoming "a furious Hercules." This tended to happen in May. His purchase of a brick of molasses candy was an indication of trouble coming. According to witnesses, he would break the brick into pieces, throw each up into the air and kick it when it came down. Shortly thereafter, eight or ten soldiers would wrestle him down to the jail and into a cell. He'd stay crazy for a week, and then they'd let him go.

A fellow called Levi Boi was a dapper *mulato* with straight hair that he kept well combed and slicked down with Vasoline. He went about in an old but clean and well-pressed white linen suit far too big for him. He always carried an old newspaper, the *Correio da Manhã* (The Morning Mail) over his arm or open in front of his face. He was illiterate and spoke with a stutter. When he wasn't "reading" his newspaper, he mumbled to himself with a concerned look, as if discussing with himself the morning news. He often held these discussions on the steps of the jailhouse.

Zebu was an inveterate drunk who loved music. It was whispered that he was the illegitimate son of a prominent citizen. Almost every day Zebu would tank up on *cachaça* and then go around giving one-man concerts in which he'd grab his nose with one hand while the other reached high up and pretended to play the keys of some bizarre instrument. He sang while doing this. After sufficient performance, he'd go fall asleep under a cattle guard. One historic day some society ladies were crossing the cattle guard when one, much in the way of a cow so foolish as to attempt to cross, slipped and got her foot stuck between the planks. Down below, Zebu woke up, grasped the situation, and took hold of the lady's foot in an attempt to free it. She released a scream of historical duration.

A fellow named Fina laughed all the time, without effort and without control. He had to be prohibited from wakes, burials, and the presence of the sick.

Magaridinha was a black woman a little over three feet tall. She wore several layers of colorful clothing and a bunch of medals on a ribbon around her neck. She carried a big piece of bamboo to defend herself against street urchins who picked on her. She used to hang around the jailhouse with Levi Boi until the jail was closed down and turned into offices. She never talked with anyone but held conversations with invisible people.

Lambreta, too, hung out on the jailhouse steps,

even after the offices were installed. He walked around barefoot with a big metal cup that he'd bang on doors to ask for coffee. But the coffee wasn't enough. Residents had to give him some cheese or cookies until he was satisfied. Otherwise, he'd never leave.

Conceição is not a town of nuts only, however. It has a living war hero, a rarity in a country which has generally managed to remain peaceful. Brazil fought with Argentina in 1851, then with Paraguay in 1865. Brazilians helped the allies in World War I and again in World War II, when José Pimenta, now 81, joined the Força Expeditionária Brasileira, 33,000 men sent to battle fascism in Italy. Second lieutenant José Pimenta, Soldier # IG292340, worked with long-range artillery under the U.S. 15th Army of General Eisenhower at the battles of Mazzarozza, Amaiore, Monte Prana, Bargo, and others. He remembers that the Brazilians were the only allied soldiers who shared their food with the starving Italians. It was prohibited, but they were Brazilians, so their compassion was maximal, their respect for prohibitions, minimal.

In September of 1945, Pimenta returned to Rio by ship, to Belo Horizonte by train, and to Conceição by bus. When he arrived, all the school children – the boys from the Brothers' school, the girls from the Sisters' school — were lined up at the entrance to town. His girlfriend was there, but she was no longer the girl for him. Within a month he was going out with Maria Pires, whom he soon married and is married to still. They have had eleven children who have had twenty-six children. One daughter married an American named Miller and had a boy named Harrison. She lives in Hyannis, Mass., but she's got a problem with depression, so José and Maria are raising Harrison, a good-looking brown-haired kid of 13 with Down's syndrome who likes to ride his bike around the neighborhood. One of these days he's going to get hit by a gravel truck if he's not careful, which he tends not to be. Neither are the drivers of the gravel trucks, which thunder down the street as if it were a highway.

José is a soldier still. He believes in the importance of the army. The most disciplined and honest men he has known were military men. They are of much better quality than the bums in the state and federal legislatures. It was the army that eradicated the communists in Brazil in the 1960s, just as armies had eradicated the Nazis in the 1940s, just as George Bush's army is eradicating terrorism.

Pimenta has been receiving an officer's pension all these years and has been messing with a small farm just outside of town. He makes a little charcoal, plants a little cane, raises a few cows, makes a little cheese. Now he's trying his hand at coffee, which these days few people plant in this region. Maria wants him to stop working so much, to behave more like an 81-year-old man, but he's not ready for that. He looks like he's 60 except when he has to get his aching back out of a chair.

Dona Mirtila has me talk with another octogenarian with a bad back, Inez Emanuela Ferreira Diniz, known about town as Inezinha. A woman of humble income, Inezinha has spent her whole life serving the community. Today she is so sore of ankle and back that she can barely get around. Nonetheless, she probably has more political power than the mayor himself. Inezinha has been caring for the priests of the Igreja Santo Antônio for the past sixty years. She's done all the embroidering for the church, stitching up and caring for every frock, mantle, towel, and tablecloth that plays a role in Catholic ceremony. She knows Catholic ceremony down to its infinitesimal minutia. Her walls and furniture are heavily invested with images of saints, saviors, crucifixions, candles, symbols, quotes, Bibles. It was Inezinha who embroidered the towel that must cover the cloth that must cover the altar during the sacrament, the corporal, she tells me. "You know that, don't you?" she asks. After hearing that slightly insinuating question several times, I just say, "Yes, of course." I don't want to interrupt her. She has a way of digressing through eighty years of memories, leading me down long trails that go from, say, the mayor to a certain priest to the priest's brother who went to study in Rio and married a woman who had a house on a certain *praça*...and there Inezinha bogs down, trying to remember the name of the *praça*, which, of course, has nothing to do with the mayor I had asked about.

Inezinha was married for twenty-one years to an ill-tempered diabetic named Diniz. Apparently his moods rose and fell with his blood sugar levels. Inezinha says diabetes is common in the Diniz family, possibly the result of inbreeding in the royal Diniz family of Portugal many centuries ago. He was the son of a white man from Cape Verde and a *mulata* woman from Morro do Pilar. He drove a gasoline truck for the BR fuel company. Jealous, angry and domineering, he kept his Inezinha on a short leash. He pulled her off a volley ball team because it required her to wear shorts. She shows me a picture of her and the team back when she was tall and thin and able to slam balls down over a net, quite the opposite of her current squat, shrunken shape and sciatic lumbar. She was childless when Mr. Diniz died, though she had informally adopted a boy who now drives a truck. She no longer eats meals, living instead off nibbles of cheese and crackers. She never drinks water. Her coffee is Nescafé instant.

Inezinha has been elected this year's *Rainha do Rosário* — Queen of the Rosary — an honor that comes with burden. The Festival do Rosário is a quasi-religious tradition dating back to a religious procession in Ouro Preto in 1733. Most towns have a Rosário church that was built for black Christians during the days of slavery. Though not usually as big and fancy as the *matriz* — a town's main church — the average Rosário dos Pretos — Rosary of the Blacks — compares well with other churches in town. Each has an image of a black virgin. The Rosários were built and financed by a brotherhood of devout blacks, the Irmandade do Rosário. Before Conceição had an Igreja Rosário, the blacks were allowed to stand at the back of the *matriz*. Slaves attending their masters, however, could accompany them inside so as to be ready to serve them. There were no pews in those days. The whites brought little rugs to sit on, and their slaves remained nearby. One fine day in 1727, a scuffle broke out between several slaves and a white guy. The white guy ended up dead. Today no one knows for sure what happened next, but the slaves were probably dispatched unto their maker at the Cruzeiro do Forcado, the Gallows Cross, next to the water fountain downtown, where misbehaving slaves were hung from the symbol of Christianity with the blatant hypocrisy that comes with unfettered power.

Once that aspect of the problem was resolved, it was decided that blacks should not be allowed inside the church. A black woman, Jacinta de Barros, the concubine of the Portuguese capitão Manuel Correia de Paiva, put up money for an Igreja Rosário dos Pretos to be built just two blocks from the house in which Dona Mirtila now lives. The church was blessed in 1730. The year 2002 finds it closed to the public, its interior stacked with scaffolding as a crew tries to save the altars and ceilings from dry rot and termites. One six-foot stretch of paintings of cherubs and saints is only paint, the ceiling that use to be behind it having completely rotted away. The workers have transferred it to a veneer of cork. The pillars of an altar, hollowed out by termites, have been repacked with a sawdust compote that should last a while.

Nossa Senhora do Rosário has been with the Portuguese since 1571, when she appeared at the battle of Lepanto, when the Muslims were ousted from Portugal. She became the protector of blacks — Nossa Senhora do Rosário dos Pretos – after hovering off the coast of Brazil. Indians and *caboclo*s — white-black-Indian mestiços — saw her. Being under the influence of Jesuits, they began to pray, sing, dance and play musical instruments to call her back. Apparently that was the wrong approach. It didn't work. Some sailors showed them how to do it right, but they had no better luck. Then some blacks thought of dancing the *catopé*. That did the trick. Nossa Senhora do Rosário appeared again, and to this very day, blacks have never suffered a problem that she could not resolve, and the *catopé* is still danced on special occasions.

Towns with a Rosário church usually have an annual Festival do Rosário, scheduled on a date that does not conflict with the same festivals in nearby towns. Today, neither the festival nor the church nor the brotherhood is exclusively black. Each year four judges from the brotherhood — two men, two women — elect a king and a queen — *um rei e uma rainha*. This honored pair is in charge of financing and organizing the event, which involves a ceremony, a parade with costumes and a band, and sweets for everybody — yes, everybody, the whole town, not to mention the country folk who come in from the hills, and the tourists who come in from the city, and former residents who return to town for the event. It's a big job, a job for a mover and shaker and consummate Catholic such as Inezinha, who has been elected in 1968, 1980, 1987, 1996 and 2002.

Sweets are a specialty of Minas Gerais. *Mineiro*s take their sweets seriously. Candied oranges, candied limes, candied lemons, candied melon rinds, candied coconut, candied cheese, candied egg yolk, candied guava, guava paste, pastes of fruits for which there is no word in English, *doce de leite* caramel paste, caramel candy, molasses candy, peanut butter candy. Inezinha may live off crackers and Nescafé, but in her first term as Rainha do Rosário, she and her friends made twenty twenty-kilo cans of sweets. The second time she made sixty cans, the next time eighty. This year she's figuring on a hundred. People know her sweets. This year, after the Rei do Rosário promenades to her house in suit and tie under a canopy on poles within a perimeter of glorified rope and takes her hand just so and holds it as they promenade to the church with costumed escorts, *catopé* dancers, a parade and marching band, a few thousand people will line up at the Casa da Cultura. There they will pass through a room where one by one they can load up on sweets that have been made under the scrutinizing eyes of not just Inezinha but God and ten generations of Rosário queens who know the importance of doing certain things right.

Just so. She shows me the precision and delicacy of the grasp, the grasp of the dreams of childless widows who may remember slamming volley balls over nets but now hobble with a hand to the lumbar. She has a picture of her husband, Rei do Rosário, holding her hand that way.

To do her festival as God wants it done, Inezinha will have to squeeze money out of all her friends, town hall, every business in town, every farmer who has fruit, milk or cheese to contribute. Somebody will have to donate the sugar and the cans the sweets are packed into. Everybody donates a little something. One big expense: the costumes, which have to be rented in Belo Horizonte. It's a lot of work for a woman in her eighties with a bad back, flat broke, but it will be worth it when the King of the Rosário takes her hand just so.

Chapter Eleven

Córregos

Maybe it's the distance, or maybe the heat, or maybe something in the cookies and biscuits that Dona Mirtila has provided me in lieu of a sit-down breakfast, or maybe the good air or the perfectly scattered clouds, I don't know, but something makes me awfully sensuous on my hike from Conceição to Córregos. After a strenuous hump up a hill of a few kilometers, I rise to a view so beautiful I have to sit down for a while and just look at it. The hills are sculpted as if for a painting that illustrates depth of field. The thin, brown ribbon of road meanders down into the valley, then up and across a hill and around the other side, reappearing on a even farther hill, winding around it, disappearing, reappearing impossibly far, seemingly near infinity as it thins to a scratch across a ridge purple with distance. I know I can't walk that far in one day, but I also know I don't have to. I just have to keep swinging one foot past the other, again and again, all day, watching the scenery go by. I could do this forever. My feet couldn't, but I could.

I'm sensuous all the way. I stop at cows standing on the side of the road, amazed at how beautiful they are, their tilted ears, their broad nostrils, their big brown eyes. I tell them how beautiful they are, but they don't seem inclined to believe me. I compliment a mule as she stands in the road looking at me. She's a perfect mule with a nice dark stripe around her middle. I tell three horses — one red, one white, one mottled — that they're beautiful, each more so than the others. Above me, urubus circle in perfect formation as they ride perfect updrafts in a perfect sky. They're probably hungry because no one could possibly die on so perfect a day. A nice truck goes by, and I think how nice it must be to earn a living driving a nice truck on such a nice road. I sit on a perfect little timber bridge over a gurgling brook to eat a bunch of Mirtila's perfect cookies. Along comes a perfectly out-back bus, dented, dusty, rumbling, squeaking. It holds its breath as it shivers across the bridge, which is of perfectly minimal width and strength for such a bus. The timbers chuckle but don't give way.

I reach the distant purple ridge and look back south at the distant purple ridge I've just come from. Only my feet can believe I've actually walked that far. To the north, the road keeps on winding up and around hills. Córregos is nowhere in sight until a little after noon, when I'm suddenly upon the place, a one-street town with cattle guards across the road at each end and a church in the middle. It has two vehicles, a VW bug, in Brazil called a Fusca, and a VW squareback, here called a Brasilia, both out of production in Brazil for several years now. The Brasilia has four flat tires. Cows, horses and mules graze on the grass between the street and the houses on either side. They outnumber the motor vehicles by at least five to one. The *Pousada* Estrada Real is easy to find. It's the biggest building in town, two stories, and the only wooden structure. I'm a little late for lunch, but the nice lady in the kitchen is glad to reheat the rice and beans and chicken. She fans the fire, slips the pots into the holes in the grill, sautés some collards. A slug of *cachaça* and a big glass of water from a clay tank satisfy me until the food is warm. I turn my dirty clothes over to a big woman named Fátima who says that due to a water shortage, she will have to wash them at the spigot. I don't know what that means, but I nod my approval and thank her for taking care of it.

To my disappointment, Cleonice, the woman who owns the *pousada*, has just left for Belo Horizonte. I was hoping to talk with her about the controversy over her new building. Built of wood, it's completely foreign to the town's ancient *pau-a-pique* architecture. It's not a bad-looking building, somewhat in the style of a chalet, but it just doesn't fit, and there's a law against architecture that doesn't fit. In fact, the IPHAN agency has already ruled against her and prohibited her from building it. She's still building it, though; IPHAN be damned. The woman in the kitchen tells me that Cleonice is a marvelous woman of dynamism and ideas, a divorced woman who comes and goes as she pleases — *uma mulher-homen*, a man-woman. She owns a lumber company in Belo Horizonte, which would explain why she isn't building her inn out of local mud. Except for the intrusion in the municipal ambience, she's been good for the town. Her *pousada* is the only business that employs anyone. At the moment, half a dozen men are banging and sawing, turning an attic space into guest rooms. Apparently the building has been under construction for over two years. The banging and sawing never stop, not even when I try to take a nap in my room directly under the work. The hammering loosens a shower of sawdust onto me and everything I own. Though exhausted, I abandon my room and look for something constructive to do.

I have the names of two reputedly intelligent people: Marilac and Odete, both teachers. When I ask a boy where I can find Marilac, it so happens she's walking by at that moment. She denies that she's one of the more intelligent people in town. She says I should talk to her husband. He's the smart one. He knows the history of the place. He's not home, however; he's out on their farm. If I watch for a man on a horse coming along at dusk, that'll be him. As for Odete, she has just left for Tapera on the school bus. That's where she teaches. She won't be back until ten o'clock tonight, unless it rains.

As far as I'm concerned, when enough things go wrong in a row, it's best to put the project aside and try something less productive. If a nap is not feasible, and if there isn't so much as a park bench to sit on, and if there's a grubby bar nearby with a saddled horse standing in front, it's probably best to go do some research there.

It's a grocery-bar that offers staples essential to a simple life, plus cold beer and local *cachaça*. I set up an office at one of the tables on the front porch, right in front of the horse, who just stands there staring at me. It isn't tied, but since it's standing with one rear hoof up off the ground and showing all the signs of a headache, I guess it doesn't need to be tied. It's a peasant horse, stocky, grayish, dusty, scarred, tick-laden, tough, an equestrian mutt that gets the job done without fuss or the complications of pride. I could get along with a horse like this. I wish I could invite this horse for a glass of beer. I wish I could hear what it has to say, though I'm sure that if it could talk, it would speak in the slurred peasant dialect I find so hard to grasp beyond the basic gist. If it could talk, it would tell me of pastures and flies, the weather, the dark side of saddle sores, perhaps the pointlessness of horse-work — things I could appreciate only with a certain cultural detachment, things I'd never really understand. And if a horse could understand talk, I'd tell it that I know how it feels to wait interminably, one sore foot raised. In my crisp, first-world dialect I'd try to tell it about flying United.

A boy on a horse drives two cows past the bar, his skinny dog in attendance. A man riding bareback bounces by at a gentle trot. A man on a one-speed bike with rusty handlebars goes by just as slowly as a bike can go. My horse keeps staring at me. It flicks an ear to dispatch a fly, but nothing else moves.

Back at the *pousada*, I find that Marilac has left me a history of Córregos, several typed pages stapled at a corner. It's pretty interesting for a place of barely six hundred souls. Córregos was settled shortly after the veins of gold were discovered at Serro Frio in 1701. The *bandeirante* pioneers there, led by Antônio Soares Ferreira, divided into two groups to search for more gold. One group went north while the other, led by Gaspar Soares, Manuel Corrêa de Paiva and Gabriel Ponce de Leon, went south. In Itaponhoacanga, they found quite a bit of gold, but they pressed on, beating the dark bushes of the *mato* dentro until they came to a river they named the Santo Antônio. The river had nuggets of gold scattered along its gravely banks. They also found diamonds. It was a good place to stay for a while. The men cleared the area, planted some crops, put up a chapel under the rubric of Nossa Senhora Aparecida de Córregos — Our Lady of the Appearance of Creeks.

They found a lot of gold at Córregos. They dug canyons that still exist. One marks the northern edge of town. They dug reservoirs to hold water they would release onto heated rock, to crack it and expose the gold. In 1714, when a mass was celebrated in Vila do Principe, today called Serro, most of the attendees were from Córregos. For the event, they donated 450 kilos of gold.

They found a lump of gold the shape and perhaps — this history isn't clear – the size of a saddle. Capitão Vincente Machado sat on it and declared "Let it never be said that I have never sat on a saddle of gold."

They found copper, too, and threw it all away, so much of it that horses could walk across the mine tailings for a league — 6,000 meters, a little over three miles – without touching any other kind of dirt or stone.

In the way of water in containment, gold and diamonds have a way of leaking out of government control. In the way of human nature, people white, black, and red were always looking for ways to divert the mineral wealth of Minas Gerais before it reached Lisbon. Fifty slaves in Córregos stole a great quantity of gold and disappeared forever. A soldier named Silvestre Gomes Correia Falcão got caught shaking down a smuggler and keeping the diamonds for himself. This history does not record his fate. Odds are he was decapitated on the spot, but if he had connections, he might have gotten off on several years of hard labor in Angola.

To prevent such leaks in the flow of mineral wealth, the Portuguese Crown had to control its movement. To control the movement, they had to control the roads, and to control the roads, they had to know where they were. From 1775 until 1778, the cartographer José Joaquim da Rocha mapped the roads leading to the *Arraial* Tijuco, today called Diamantina. One road goes through Piranga, Mariana, Catas Altas, Santa Barbara, Itambé, Morro do Pilar, Conceição do Mato Dentro, Córregos, Vila do Principe, and, finally, Tijuco. That's the road that goes past the *pousada* where I'm staying and the grocery-saloon where the horse was standing and staring. It was called the Estrada do São Francisco. Because it was the main route of the *tropeiros*, it was also called the Itinerary of Corrals.

An English businessman, John Mawe, traveled through the region in the first decade of the nineteenth century. He stopped for a while in Córregos. He described his trip in a book, Travels into the Interior of Brazil, in which he wrote (as back-translated from the Portuguese):

"I crossed harsh and dangerous terrain of quartzite

and schist and arrived in Córregos, a village with gold washes. Some years ago one of them produced a net profit of 800 c. even though only four blacks were employed for the month (...) The house in which I was a guest showed signs of ancient opulence. Captain Bom Jardim, the owner, a respectable old man, took me in cordially. He told me he'd been born in Porto (Portugal), left his native land at the age of seventeen, and had lived in Brazil for the past sixty-two years. He'd been drawn to establish himself here in the hope of participating in the riches for which the region is so famous, but he arrived two or three years too late. Seeing the decline in mining, he was obliged to go into farming. To this he applied himself with such perseverance and success that he acquired a fortune and educated several families."

Mawe reported that at the height of the mining activity, the local population was three thousand, but it then fell to a third of that. In 1823, the Cônego Raimundo Trindade found "806 souls" here. By 1925, the population had risen back up to 2,945. By the end of the century, it dropped to approximately 600, with young people tending to move away in search of work, and nobody but Cleonice moving into town.

In the 1950s, a hydroelectric plant was built on the Rio Tapera. For ten years it provided power to the town. Then it was shut down, and the town was without electricity for ten years, until CEMIG, the state electric company, brought in power lines.

As of early 2002, the town has just one phone, an *orelhão* (big ear) public phone. The number is 868-1340. When it rings, one of the several teenagers hanging around the phone will eagerly answer it and, if necessary, run to the house of the person called. A few people have cell phones, but the reception's a little too dependent on the weather. To use them, they have to go up to the cemetery, the highest ground around.

Córregos has had a music school since the late nineteenth century. It's right across the street from the *Pousada* Estrada Real, and just after dark, I can hear them practicing. It has always been directed by the Rocha family, the most recent of whom is Célio Edson dos Santos, adopted son of the deceased Maestro Luis Belarmine Rocha. The band practices every night, playing Brazilian marches such as O Vinte-Cinco de Maio, thumping them out on four drums, two coronets, three baritones, a tuba, a flugelhorn, a few trombones, and a pair of cymbals under the insistent hands of Maestro Célio himself. All the brass instruments are made of tin that bears the dents and dings of over a century's service. The current band, which several townspeople and I observe through the windows, has a total of twenty-five members, a rather impressive percentage of the town's middle-triple-digit population. During their two hours of practice, they did not play a single song I recognized.

They were all Brazilian songs composed, I'm sure, in the days before radio.

The sound of this band is sweet in its humility, a luscious blend of by-the-numbers left-right-left and a sloppy African two-step, a march crossed with a samba that plods along until interrupted by a momentary shift in upbeat and downbeat that is dropped into the song as if to help a soldier do a half-skip to get back in step. Oddly enough, this little upbeat-upbeat-downbeat, which seems to come only after several dozen measures, never catches anyone by surprise. The whole band gets it right. It's a beautiful moment.

It's even more beautiful to hear this music just up the street from the Igreja Nossa Senhora Aparecida dos Córregos, where ten women and two men are holding a pre-Easter novena without benefit of priest. Their slow, drawn-out hymns, echoing in the cavernous three-centuries-old church, rise behind the rhythmic, tin-brass paramilitary music that sounds as innocent and unsettling as a child's wooden rifle.

The town may have no priest, but it does have a bishop, Dom José Maria Pires, who, as it turns out, is a beekeeper and who, depending on whom I ask, is somewhere between the ages of 84 and 94. To my chagrin, he is out of town until next week.

Dom José Maria is the kind of dynamo that would not be expected in the outback of Brazil though not totally surprising in the town of Córregos. Towns in Minas Gerais are often known for having inhabitants of certain tendencies, such as laziness, tight-fistedness, industriousness, and honesty. They can be *gente boa* or vagabundas — good people or bums. Despite its history of quick-money gold-digging, Córregos is known for its hard workers, a tradition that dates back at least a hundred years to the time of a local priest named Cônego Antônio Madureino de Carvalho, who died an old man in 1931. The Cônego did not allow his flock the sin of sloth. He rousted them from bed. He made them think big and finish what they started. He got them used to it. José Maria Pires, a young boy when the Cônego was an old man, learned, and he became one of twenty-three priests who have come out of Córregos. He went on to become Bishop of Paraíba, a state in northeast Brazil. He has returned to Córregos, though he's elsewhere more than he's here. But he keeps a nice two-story house, the one where the band meets. It has a beautiful garden, orchard, and an apiary running up the hill out back. He arranged a grant from Netherlands that has financed a plantation of passion fruit, pineapple, guava, acerola, lime, and a pulp processing plant to go with it. The church donated the land. A community organization called VINOCOR — Vida Nova para Córregos — runs the operation and sells the pulp to juice producers via a middleman from Conceição. The project's going rather well, except that the freezer they bought and paid for never arrived because the supplier went bankrupt.

Dom José Maria also created the Alameda da Saúde, saúde meaning health. It's a row of palm trees planted on the way that leads up to the cemetery and the Senhor dos Passos chapel, up where people make their cell phone calls. One palm is planted for each fallen Córregense. Loved ones are asked to write a few pages about the deceased, and one day they will assemble all of the pages into a book of memories. Some 80 palms have been planted.

It is the teacher Odete who finally tells me about the water problem that is hindering the washing of my dirty clothes. The town has three springs, one named Kiana, one named Suzann, and one without a name. The one without a name also has no pump. Kiana and Suzann have pumps that send water to a tank on the hill of the cemetery. Both pumps, however, are burned out, and not for the first time. A few days ago they burned out and were sent to Conceição to be fixed. They were reinstalled but soon burned out again. Now they're back in Conceição.

I walked down to Kiana. She's right off the main street, around behind some back yards, a shallow pool of clear water within an off-kilter trapezoid of concrete ten or twelve feet wide. Her water bubbles up as gentle eddies. Her overflow trickles out the very spigot where Fátima so recently washed my clothes. I find the nearest pile of horse dung and pace off the distance from half the town's water supply. It's about fifteen feet. Far enough, I guess, as along as the pump stays broken.

*   *   *

Maria Odete de Alameda Avelar, a retired teacher, teaches the fifth through eighth grades in Tapera. She keeps teaching, she says, for the money. She goes to Tapera on the school bus every evening with about twenty of the local kids. The get back home after ten o'clock. If it rains, the bus can't make it, so they don't go. If they're in class when it rains, the bus won't be able to make it back, so the kids and Odete walk back, some twelve kilometers, over seven miles. They hike in flip-flop sandals over a mountain in the rain in the dark over a mud road, no raincoats, no umbrellas, no dinner, arriving home sometime after midnight. During a recent rain, they had to wade across the bridge over the canyon their forefathers' slaves dug at the edge of town. Odete and the children had to hold on to the railing so they wouldn't get washed away. While we talk, Odete is wearing a blue T-shirt with a picture of a grinning Sylvester the Cat in cap and gown, a diploma in his paw. Now that I think about it, I've seen a lot of these T-shirts around. The back of the shirt lists the graduates of the Tapera middle school class of 2001.

The elementary school in Córregos is a dilapidated house near the public phone. Odete describes it as "miséria." Before the last election, Odete went to Conceição and pressured a mayoral candidate to promise, a cross-his-heart-and-hope-to-die promise, that if elected he would build a school in Córregos. Odete promised him the village's votes, and she delivered them. He won by eight. So far, however, he has made no movement toward a new school. Now she's telling him that in the next election he will get not one vote out of Córregos, not one. Her mouth is bitter and twisted with anger when she tells me this, her forefinger stiff and pointing upward. The mayor is in more trouble than he knows. He's up against a teacher who walks her students home seven miles over a mountain in the rain in the dark over a mud road in sandals, no raincoat, no umbrella, no dinner. If he doesn't come up with a school for Córregos, he's going to be one very lame duck.

I stop by Marilac's house to return her history. There I end up in a long conversation with her and her husband, Renato. He's 63. For many years he supplied the *tropeiros* with mules. Until the 1950s, all goods were brought to or taken from Córregos by mule. Then, Renato says, with electricity and the improved road to Conceição, the world changed. He still buys and sells mules, horses, and donkeys. He has about forty animals right now. He also has good collection of authentic *tropeiro* gear. He shows it to me, then goes to fetch a mule so we can dress her up. He puts the fancy leather-and-tin muzzle over her snout. This was the apparatus the *tropeiros* put on the mule that would lead up to twelve others. He dressed her in the necklace of little brass bells that all the mules wore. They sound better than cow bells, clearer and sweeter. A train of these animals would be a line of music winding through the mountains. He slings the saddle onto the mule and over it hangs the big leather satchels that once carried coffee to Curvelo, a main point of exchange, four or five days west of here. He maneuvers this mule into the sunshine so I can take her picture. He praises her for her beauty, her docility, her willingness to just stand there. I don't know whether mules can think, but if so, this one is thinking "bullshit" as she stands there in the sun, all dressed up as if for church. She stands there while we sit in the house. We know she never moves because we hear no bells. We look at Marilac's collection of herbal *cachaça*s, at least twenty bottles, each different, corked, no labels, each with a different herb, root or fruit inside. Some of their smells are entirely new to my nose. Renato tells me that the lady across the street, a widow now, was given a wedding ring made of gold that her husband had collected from the gutters right there in town. This source of a little wealth is no longer available, however, because the old kind of gutter has been replaced with a new kind that doesn't trap the gold.

As we talk, Marilac keeps dashing into her kitchen, which smells strongly of garlic, to check the several pots bubbling on the *fogão a lenha*. I suggest that Renato start himself a little business of taking mule trains of tourists up the Estrada Real to Tapera, Itaponhoacanga, even to Serro or Diamantina. I suggest, quite without basis, that he could charge forty *reais* per person per day. Forty times twelve per day...he and Marilac get excited at the idea. I can see their eyes dreaming up a scheme. I suggest working with a tourist agency in Belo Horizonte, arranging *pousada*s to receive the people, farms to prepare good farm meals. Yes, they say, yes, that would work. I don't know whether the mule outside is listening and thinking, but we don't hear any bells. She isn't running away. Maybe she likes the idea.

Chapter Twelve

Tapera

The hike from Córregos to Tapera is an easy twelve kilometers. After a climb of two kilometers, the views are stupendous, with the *serra*s of Escadinha and Jacuba to the west and a hilly valley of dense forest to my right. Once I'm over the ridge, I take off my $75 shoes and put on 75-cent flip-flop sandals, the kind you grip between two toes. It's an improvement. My feet appreciate the air.

The road meanders past pastures without fences, the grass knee-high and laden with fronds of reddish seed. The cows, nearly up to their bellies in food, must think themselves in heaven, and maybe they are. I come around a bend and interrupt the opening moves of a wide-open tryst of three cows and a bull in the middle of the road. The cows bolt up the embankment and into the grass of a pasture, but the bull stands his ground. He's a big one, with big horns, his blank dark eyes looking down his snout at the stranger in backpack and six-bit flip-flops. I wonder what it is about the facial expression of a cow that seems to say, "What?" while that of a bull always seems to say, "No." Bulls like this can kill people, and the midway point between Córregos and Tapera, Minas Gerais, Brazil, is a lousy place to get gored, even a little. It's also a lousy place to get bit by a snake, so I'm reluctant to walk sandal-footed through the tall grass on the side of the road. Negotiation seems my best bet, so I explain in calm words and gentle gestures that I am a really nice guy, he a fine-looking hunk of beef, his cows most admirable, though not to a guy like me, I hasten to add, a guy who just wants to hoof on down the road and let him and his get back to their bovine business. I show him the palms of my hands. I tilt my head, raise my eyebrows, and coo, but it's obvious that this animal has nothing else to do today besides stand between me and Tapera, lunch, and a normal life expectancy. Speaking calmly — "You're cool with this, right? I'm just going to squeeze on by and be on my way, right? You cool with this? — and moving slowly, planning to let him gore my pack if gore he must, I edge on by him. He turns around and watches me go on down the road and around a bend.

Tapera

*   *   *

Tapera's another one-street town, albeit a longer street than the one in Córregos, enough of a street to sustain a population of 1,200. The street runs down the middle of a valley with a stream over on the western side. I note a sign that refers to a Rua São José, but there's really no street there, just a stretch of grass grazed short and peppered with enough dung to indicate a little traffic. I note a bus called the San Antonio Express, but it looks terminally parked. I note three public phones. The school looks respectable though it doesn't sound like there's a whole lot of traditional learning going on inside. I step into a grocery-bar to ask where I might find the *pousada* of Maria Eni. The man behind the bar and the guy sitting on the floor are more surprised at my presence than by the mule who's in there with them, her head over the bar, her tail end almost reaching the door. She looks for all the world like any stone-drunk *cachaçeiro* who has achieved a pleasant stupor. I'm tempted to ask "Why the long face?", but it doesn't translate well, so I try "I'll have what she had." The men look at her as if they've just noticed that they're not alone.

It's the bar owner's mule, of course. She gets lonely and walks on in for some company. The owner sprinkles some corn on the bar. She plucks it up with her beefy lips

215

and crunches it with her molars while her tail slaps the flies off her backside.

Maria Eni's *pousada* is just down the street. She calls it a *pensão*. I ask her what's the difference between a hotel, a *pousada* and a *pensão*, besides the price. She smiles and laughs and says she doesn't really know, but she thinks that her place isn't good enough to be a *pousada*. I tell her it certainly is good enough. If she puts up a nice sign — rather than no sign — she can readily upgrade to *pousada* status and charge an extra *real* or two. The rooms are small but well appointed with two beds and a little steel Brahma beer table between them. The bathroom is tiled and spotless and sports a nice toilet seat. Maria will be glad to make me a nice lunch, and of course a little breakfast is included in the price, which is the equivalent of four dollars, the same as your basic *pousada*. Call it what you may, it's home to me.

Maria Eni has the kind of sincere and humble smile and easy laugh that causes defenseless people like me to fall in love. She's been a widow since 1993. Shortly after that tragic date, her son, known as Baixinho – Shorty – moved back home from an industrial town on the outskirts of Belo Horizonte to help her run the *pensão* and the little grocery-bar that becomes a dance hall on weekends. She does all her cooking on a *fogão a lenha* wood stove and grinds her coffee by hand. Almost all the food she serves comes from local cows, chickens, pigs, trees, bushes and fields. Her corn meal gets ground at a water-powered stone grist wheel just up the street. The stove heat comes from local trees. She doesn't buy much more than salt and olive oil. She can turn a nice profit on an organic gourmet meal that she sells, with apologies, for about a dollar and a half.

At Maria's recommendation, I go across the street to talk with Dona Saudalita, former director of the middle school here, the same one where Odete of Córregos teaches. Saudalita wasn't born here, she tells me; she was born across the street. She's been a widow for the past six months. Her husband died of leukemia. There's no treatment for such a thing here. When you get it, you've had it. She's still in emotional recovery. Sadness still weights her cheeks and deepens her big, dark eyes. She wears a black dress.

Saudalita was primarily responsible for getting the town government – Conceição do Mato Dentro's town government — to build a middle school in Tapera. Until then, kids who wanted to study beyond the fourth grade had to go live in Conceição, at least two hours away by bus, weather permitting. Normally a town of only 1,200 people wouldn't offer such higher education. Literacy is the limit. Saudalita buries her face with both hands as she tries to tell me what a struggle it was to get a school built. "Power," she says, "always has other priorities."

Saudalita calls Tapera a place of *esperança*, which

could mean hope, waiting or expectation, a curious mash of concepts which, in my ignorant opinion, has something to do with the belief that prayer produces reality. But Saudalita means simply that the town is always looking forward to the next festival. They have a lot. The Rosário's a big one, and Carnaval, of course, and Semana Santa, which is next week. But the biggest is the Evento de Taparenses Ausentes, the Event of Absent Taperenses. On a weekend comfortably removed from other festival weekends, everyone who has moved out of Tapera comes home for two days of dancing, drinking, talking, laughing, catching up, and tending to their roots. The population swells to three or four thousand, everyone theoretically sleeping in their families' homes. In reality, no one really does any sleeping at all, not even if they try, which they don't. They stay awake, in the street, having a great time, all day, all night, all weekend. Everyone's home is open to everyone. The meals are constant, the *cachaça* free, the confusion a joy, the mirth, I imagine, overwhelming. You'd have to be from here, I'm sure, steeped in Tapera, to have any inkling of what everybody's laughing at, talking about, crying over. I haven't actually witnessed this, but I conclude it after hearing Saudalita and other people try to tell me about it but giving up as they squeeze their eyes together with one hand while holding their bellies with the other. They tell me I really have to be here to see it, but I think they mean I have to be from here to get it.

Tapera

Tapera isn't really the name of this place. The real name is Santo Antônio do Norte. Like every other place along the Estrada Real, it once thrived on gold. As the gold disappeared, so did the town until a guy built a clandestine hat factory here. It employed a lot of people and made a lot of good hats, but Dom Pedro found out about it and had it burned down. Nobody in town today knows why, but they suspect it had something to do with taxes. Whatever the excuse, it was practically the end of the town. Almost everyone moved away. A visiting Portuguese dignitary of some sort described the place as a "tapera," a run-down place of abandoned houses, a ghost town. The word described the place pretty well. The name stuck. But in 1932, some visiting church authorities came to see about fixing up the church. It didn't have a bell tower, the walls were crumbling due to lack of foundation, the graveyard surrounding it was a little morbid, the wall around the graveyard a little forbidding. They decided to have a bell tower built and a new cemetery established on the hill on the other side of the valley. The Taparenses dismantled the graveyard wall, replaced the church foundation by jacking up the *pau-a-pique* walls and packing the graveyard rocks underneath. They reassembled the rest of the graveyard wall around the new cemetery. The graves around the church, well, they're still down there somewhere.

The authorities also decided to change the name of

the town to something a little more optimistic. Someone suggested Santo Antônio das Aguas Numerosas, but another town was already using that name. Someone suggested Santo Antônio do Norte. Perfect. That's been the official name since then. But everybody still calls it Tapera.

One of the oldest guys in town, an artist named Jair Pires de Oliveira, takes me to the Igreja Santo Antônio to tell me of its history and show me some of his work. He's slight and short, with yellowish-white hair and gray eyes. He used to live with his sister in the oldest house in town. Neither of them ever married. Today, 82 years old, he lives under the care of a woman he raised when she was a child. As he takes me across town, he points out all the things that aren't there anymore — *praça* grass replaced by street, tall palms that have left behind only their circular footprints, a canal that ran right across the street, and vegetation that grew along the canal. Pigs used to come to eat the vegetation and wallow in the canal. They left a stink, and that's gone, too. The wall around the church, gone. The churchyard graves, gone. The parochial house behind the church, gone, replaced by an ugly building made of concrete and steel-framed windows. The only thing uglier in this town is the telephone tower erected beside the Igreja do Rosário, which stands just up the street at the far end of town. The tower is so close to the church that it looks like a prosthetic steeple with mechanically phallic intentions. Jair doesn't mention it.

We stop by the house of Antônia, a *ministra* who keeps the big iron key to the church. She comes with us. Jair knows the Santo Antônio to its most minute detail. He built and painted some of its altars, carved some of its images of saints. He shows me the patched-over hole in the wall where a hook used to hang to tie the pulley rope that raised and lowered a silver candelabra that somebody stole. Or maybe a priest sold it. In all, forty-five artifacts have been stolen from the church, including a marvelous carving of an angel with a trumpet that was once attached to an exterior wall. That was in the old days, during the several centuries when a church could be left open. Now you need to get Antônia and her big iron key.

Jair is also a homeopath. For many years, years that haven't come to an end yet, he's been the town's only on-site medicine man, though sometimes there's a doctor at the clinic. Other times, if you want a doctor with a medical degree, you have to go all the way to Conceição, which can take a long time since there may not be a car in town that day, and even if there is, the road may not be passable, and even then, the doctor will probably prescribe medicines that cost money, so the patient probably ends up trusting Jair's roots, herbs, and years of experience.

Jair used to be quite the *cachaçeiro*, too, a major consumer of the local hootch, as glum as a mule eating corn off a bar. At some point he bottomed out and joined a Protestant church. Protestants here tend to be very conservative and serious. And sober. And expensive. When he found out about the mandatory ten percent tithe, he returned to the mother church, the big mother with the graves around it.

He takes me to his old house, where a woodworker now lives. The man makes furniture and parts for wooden machinery. His bed and dresser are made of rare *jacarandá*. His floorboards alone are worth a fortune. His kitchen table is worth thousands of dollars, and the furniture he makes would be, too, if it were in New York. Here he sells hardwood armoires for as little as a hundred dollars. When we arrive, he's working on an axle as stout as a telephone pole. It's for a little grist mill being renovated, not because it's cute but because it's the town's only source of corn meal.

The grist mill is a small, cubic, *pau-a-pique* building with mud walls still waiting for a plaster finish. Below it, water shoots from a pipe to hit the blades of a horizontal disk that turns a vertical shaft that turns a disk of stone that's a good two feet wide. As it turns at a rate of about two revolutions per second, it rubs against a similar stone below it. A hopper above the stone holds the corn, which shivers down a little chute. A stick connected to the chute drags on the rock as it spins. A bump on the stone nudges the stick, which jiggles the chute which causes a kernel of corn to drop down. Centrifugal force throws the corn over the edge of the stone and down to be rubbed between the two stones. The rubbing slows the spinning, which slows the nudging of the stick and the jiggling of the chute and the feeding of the corn. Every piece of this machine was produced locally. It's a very slow process, grinding corn at a rate of about one or two kernels per second. But it can run all day and all night without attention, and the energy is free, raining down on the mountain, *graças a Deus*, and flowing down the creek to the pipe to the grist mill.

Back at home, at lunch, I'm thoroughly enjoy Maria Eni's *angu* (polenta made with corn ground at the grist mill I've just seen) with the thick broth of a chicken stew. While I'm eating, she brings me two swords that date back to the days of the Portuguese, genuine swashbuckler equipment that made men deadly in the days when firearms were so awkward that they really could only start trouble, not finish it off. The swords are rusty with a century and a half of disuse but in their busier days had been sharpened to about half their original width. These were swords used to apply Christianity to Africans and Indians, swords that kept the gold flowing down the Estrada Real toward Lisbon. I mention this misuse of religion to Maria Eni. She asks what religion I belong to. I admit Congregational tendencies. We talked a bit about the differences between Catholicism and Protestantism, neither of us knowing much about it but agreeing that they aim at the same God and practice the same morality. She says she can't understand how some people simply don't believe there's a God. I tell her that I know quite a few, and they are good, moral people. She agrees that they can be, but still, how can they not believe in something so obvious? I can't argue with her. The sweetest of rains, a silent, gentle mist, is falling all around us, all things growing are green, and they're all pointing in the same direction.

A little later in the day, a young man stops by to show Maria his wound. He was gored by a bull in the same abdominal spot where Jesus got jabbed by a Roman soldier. The scar is big and ugly. Somebody has stitched the wound shut with needle and thread. Now he's treating it with prayer and a bandage soaked with olive oil. He thinks it's getting better, but it still hurts.

During the evening, the silent, gentle mist thickens into a serious, swishing rain. The clothes I had washed in the morning are going to stay wet for a while, and tomorrow I'll be walking to Itaponhoacanga in wet clothes if not under wet skies. By nine o'clock, thunder is drumming up even more rain. A chattery flock of wet middle-school kids stampede into the *pensão* to throw their books and bags into an empty room, then chatter back out into the rain. They actually seem rather excited that the bus can't take them back to Córregos. No umbrellas, no hats on their heads, shod in flip-flops, no dinner in their stomachs, Júnia, Reginaldo, Romério, Jánia, Lucressa, Gleciane, Júnior César, Antônio, Junho, Idiné, Cíntia, Edison, Renaldo, Siro, Raquel, Sídia, Qui, Nilton, Adiwilson, Karine, Elvira, Robson, Luiz Henrique and Jaques gallop into the drizzly dark. It's twelve kilometers—seven miles—back to Córregos, and there isn't a single electric light between here and there. Across the street, Professora Odete, under a small umbrella with a bent rib, waves good-bye to Saudalita, who stands in her doorway behind the curtain of rain trickling off her roof, her arms crossed, her shoulders hunched under her black sweater. Odete says *"Tciao,"* and Saudalita says, *"Vai com Deus."*

Chapter Thirteen

Itaponhoacanga

It's neither raining nor not raining the next morning when I head for Itaponhoacanga. A drizzle seems suspended in the air, the morning mist part of the low clouds – perfect weather for hiking up a steep road under a dense forest. The road goes up the side of the mountain that rises from the edge of the backyards on the east side of town. Swatches of fog hang in the trees like the stuffing of milkweed pods. I can't tell whether the water falling on me is ongoing rain or rain stuck in the leaves since last night. The only reason it matters is that at some point I should decide whether to dig out my umbrella. Out of weird laziness, I'd rather keep walking than stop and open my pack. And anyway, the atmospheric dampness is so thick that it really doesn't matter whether its raining or not. In such humidity, rain is redundant.

After an hour or so I rise above the tree line to an area of gnarled brush and stark quartzite outcrops. My guidebook tells me that I should be able to see magnificent views to my left, but all I can see is gray cloud. The guide also promises prehistoric rock paintings on one of the outcrops, but it doesn't say which one. I wander around a few but can't find anything. But if I'd been a prehistoric artist, I would definitely have painted something in a place like this, where clouds blow around rocks the size of churches and the brush reaches up in shaggy black arms. The cloud parts below me. For half a minute I can see Tapera way down in the valley, almost directly below me. Then the cloud closes again.

At this highest point on the ridge, the road turns to the north toward Itaponhoacanga. Along the way, I meet two men and a boy, Enis, João, and Jackson, on horseback, driving half a dozen cows toward Tapera. Ill-kempt, unshaven, teeth black and twisted, wearing oilcloth hats dripping with condensed fog, bewildered to meet a stranger on the trail, they could be cowboys right out of the old West. They shake my hand from the backs of their horses, ask me where I'm going, where coming from, why I'm walking alone in the rain. They're quite amazed to hear that they are driving their cattle down the oldest road in the Americas. They say, "Vai com Deus."

A few minutes later, along comes a young guy from Tapera, whose name, Fabiano, is on the back of his Sylvester the Cat T-shirt. He's on a horse and driving a mule ahead of him, whacking it on the tail end every time it stops. Accompanying him are four hounds and a miniature Doberman with a limp. The mule has a saddle because Fabiano, who I belatedly remember I met just yesterday, is on his way to Itaponhoacanga to pick up a cousin. He offers me a ride, I'm glad to accept his hospitality.

It turns out that getting onto a mule while wearing a backpack when your legs are tired from a long walk uphill isn't so easy. I can't quite get my leg up over the back of the mule, nor the weight of my pack up over the center of gravity. With all my weight on one stirrup, the saddle slowly slides around the side of the mule until it's ninety degrees down from where it should be. Fabiano has to get off his horse, unstrap the saddle and cinch it on straight. I put desperate energy into my second attempt, and all of a sudden, there I am, up on top of a mule.

It feels pretty good up here. It would feel better if I had something between me and the saddle besides swim trunks, but fortunately this is a slow mule. As she walks along, I just rock back and forth. My pack rests nicely on the back of the saddle. The only trick to riding a mule, it turns out, is that every half a minute or so, you have to whack her on the ass with something. Fabiano, perhaps frustrated that his pace is now half what it had been, lends me his leather whacker. It's very easy to operate. The tricky part is the first ten or fifteen seconds after the whack, when the mule remembers her role in the scheme of things and shifts into a higher gear. The first time this happened, I came to understand the physio-etymological root of the word "whoa." It comes from deep within the scrotum, rising quickly through the throat and out to the lips, where it forms with a natural bounciness that exudes the joy and excitement of horsemanship.

Before long I get the knack of it. It's really a great way to travel. All I have to do is sit there and the scenery keeps going by at the same slow rate that I absorb it. The dogs scout ahead for us, moving as two units — the hounds one, the brave little Doberman another. They move into the bushes like a well trained SWAT team, freezing at any sign of the enemy, then baying like beagles and closing in fast for the kill, except there's never anything to kill, just the scent of something now long-gone. They burst back onto the road, weave around the hooves, sniff out more trouble.

Fabiano tells me a good mule costs around $160, about the same as a medium-good horse. The rough equivalence is due to the economic advantages of a mule. A horse isn't good for much more than human transportation. It can't go far without a decent meal, and if you're not careful, it can develop digestive problems. Mules can transport not only a person but cargo. Firewood is the common cargo these days, but of course it was the mules of the *tropeiros* that supplied Minas Gerais with provisions for almost half a millennium. And mules don't get digestive problems. They live on grass. They can stand around in the rain. And at $160 each, they're practically disposable.

By the time we ride into Itaponhoacanga, I'm swaggering in the saddle like a cowboy who's just ridden in from Comanche territory. Our gang of five probes ahead, clearing the way, starting dog fights off to the side, finishing them off and moving on. People in the street look at us. Others appear in windows to see who's riding into town. It would be nice to have a six-shooter for the occasion, but it would surely lead to trouble. Fabiano's asking where the *pousada* is, but I'm on the lookout for a saloon. I want to clomp in bow-legged and order a whiskey at the bar. Alas, we find the *pousada* first, a disappointingly suburban-looking house so new it still smells of wet concrete. It even has a little lawn out front. I dismount cautiously with the fear that the saddle will again slide around or the weight of my pack will tip me over. By the time I've steadied myself on the good turf of Itaponhoacanga, a curvaceous young lady by the name of Nídia arrives with the key to the *Pousada* Estrada

Real. The first words from her pumpkin-round face are a statement with half a question mark at the end: "You're hiking on the Estrada Real."

It's a clean, well lighted place — sterile, even – with nice tile floors and a modern bathroom attached to each room. Nídia runs the place for an Itaponhoacangense refugee who has made his fortune in Belo Horizonte. He built the *pousada* not for the profit as much as to help Nídia, who has the energy needed to oversee it, and the town, which has no other businesses besides a few meager grocery-bars, a little luncheonette trailer equipped with gas grill and refrigerator, a post office, and a public phone. The luncheonette trailer opens only at night, the post office opens for only a few hours each weekday, and the phone, to judge by the people squatting around it while no one actually uses it, is on the fritz.

Nídia is clever enough to have already alerted Dona Modestina ("Titina") Rosa da Cruz that a stranger's come to town and will in all likelihood be in need of lunch. Dona Titina needs an hour or so to get lunch going. Her meal is the antithesis of fast food. She adds a little wood to her stove, a little water to her beans, a dash of corn meal and water to her angu, some okra to her simmering chicken. She has enough for herself, her daughter, her grand-daughter and me. She's 63, with clear gray eyes and a face lined with the kind wrinkles of a blessed Virgin Mary smile. She is the incarnation of humility and goodness. Her pretty daughter runs the post office. Her pretty grand-daughter, Kalline, studies in the school where Nídia teaches. Neither of the offspring can join me for lunch, however, so I have Titina's kitchen table all to myself, which is good because it barely holds all my food, which, dish by dish, comes to include chicken, beans, rice, *chuchu, jiló*, fried potatoes, a salad, roasted manioc flour, and a pitcher juice of bitter-sweet orange limes, followed by a cafezinho, a thick slice of cheese, a dollop of caramel paste, and enough candied fruit in sugar syrup to please an army of dentists.

The next day is Palm Sunday. Here's how they do it in Itaponhoacanga. Early in the morning, everybody gets dressed up and walks to the chapel at the cemetery on the hill at one end of town. Along the way, each person picks a fistful of weeds. At the cemetery, they go into the chapel, perform a quick genuflection in front of the lifelike crucifixion, go into the cemetery to visit the dead and wonder about the miracle of resurrection, then go back out front to wait for the priest to arrive. He does so in a yellow VW bug, arriving from another town. He reviews the miracle of eternal life and thanks Jesus for dying for all of us and our sins. Everyone raises their weeds to the sky. He blesses the weeds, which are now destined to be stuck in jars back home. I don't know why roadside weeds, not flowers or palm branches, are the chosen symbols, but I suppose it might be because these poor people see themselves as weeds who, like Jesus, though neither beautiful nor worth much, are loved and blessed by God.

Then everyone walks their weeds across town to the Igreja do Rosário, singing along the way. They pass the Igreja São José, a medium-sized church without a bell tower. Built in the mid-eighteenth century, it was recently closed for renovation, or really for salvation. After deteriorating to a state of rot, IPHAN stripped it of its altars and images so they could be restored elsewhere. Now an owl and some bats live in there. The ceiling paintings are beautiful, possibly the work of Aleijadinho.

No one knows much else about the history of Itaponhoacanga, not even the dates when the Rosário was built. The name of the town is a Tupi-Guarani word meaning "Rock-that-looks-like-a-negro-head." You can still see the rock up on the hill above town. A naturalist named José Vieira Couto came through town in 1800 and described the place as having "fifty fires, insignificant houses except for one, which looks like that of a nobleman, its people living by farming and mining." Saint-Hilaire came through in 1817 and found the place "deplorable."

And that's about it for the history of Itaponhoacanga. It goes back no further than people can remember. If I might add my two bits of observation, I'd describe the place as having three parallel streets connected by two cross streets, houses with big backyards planted densely with fruit trees, mules and ragtag horses wandering around, chickens and roosters in constant communication, a general smell of woodsmoke, and a lot of stationary people discussing things. Except for subsistence agriculture, there is virtually no employment, and the phone doesn't work.

Somewhere along the way to here I've picked up a *bicho-de-pé* (tunga penetrans, in Latin), a parasite that enters the foot, where it becomes a sack of eggs. It looks like a faint white spot under the skin. It itches and hurts at the same time. Kids kind of like to torture themselves by picking at it. Me, I want it out. The normal procedure is to have your mother do it with a needle. Mothers-in-law can also do it — mine once did — but this is not recommended. I have neither on hand. Nídia, bless her, offers to take a stab at it, but I'd rather do it myself. Trouble is, my sewing needles were made in China and therefore are not sharp enough to puncture skin. I use the awl on my pocket knife, squeeze the bug out like pus, leaving behind a nasty little hole I'll have to walk on for either seven or seventeen miles, depending on a rather complicated Nídia scheme that begins with the phone that doesn't work. The alternative mileages depend on whether I have to walk all the way to Serro in one day or can arrange a place to sleep in a village along the way, a place officially named Deputado Augusto Clementino but known among people as Mato Grosso. Nídia knows a nice guy in Serro who has a farm in Mato Grosso. If the phone gets fixed, she can call him and persuade him to let me spend a night on his farm.

So she gives me his phone number and name — William Gomes — and come morning, off I go. For the first few miles, the road winds between foggy pastures and under tall, wet trees. Then it meets up with state highway 10, which is still dirt but wide and level. It's an easy hike to Mato Grosso. The hole in my foot doesn't hurt too much, though the Band-aid keeps coming off. Mato Grosso is up on a hill off to the left of the highway. At the turn-off there's a grubby little bar, closed, and a public phone. Unfortunately, my phone card doesn't work. Fortunately, along comes a car from Itaponhocanga. The driver has already received instructions from Nídia. He's to find William and have him call me on the public phone. Off he goes. Twenty minutes later, glory be, the public phone rings. It's William! He already knows who I am and what I need. He won't be coming to the farm this day, but I'm welcome to spend the night there. He'll send a key with the next person he finds who's headed in that direction by car.

So I sit to wait in front of the little bar. I wish it would open so I could get a little something to eat, but the owner, Valdir, who lives right across the street, has gone fishing. It's a trashy little spot to have to wait for an unknown duration. It smells of old excrement. Paper, candy wrappers, bottle caps and such litter the ground, as does a dog asleep in the dirt of the road. The flies here seem dirtier than flies elsewhere. They like me a lot but are especially fond of the sleeping dog. Another dog comes along, scratches up a little nest of cool dirt, curls up in there for a while, then gets up and scratches up a new spot over near Valdir's house. Valdir's trashy looking daughter comes out of the house. Her golden locks hint at a person who spends a lot of time in front of a mirror. Her bare belly is something that really shouldn't be exposed to the public. She uses the phone, goes back to the house without noticing me. A little later, her mother crosses to the bar, unlocks it, gets something, locks up, goes back to her house, all without acknowledging my presence. This is the first time anywhere along the Estrada Real that someone nearby has failed to bid me "Bom dia." Except for the dog, the dirt, and the flies, I could be sitting in a mall back home in Connecticut.

There I sit for a miserable hour. Logic works itself around in my brain until I figure out that: a) it's very possible the key might never arrive, or maybe not for several hours, b) I'm hungry and bound to get hungrier, c) it's only ten miles to Serro, d) whoever's coming with the key will probably recognize me on the road, and e) the sun isn't too hot and my foot isn't hurting too much. So I can make it. Three hours from now, I can be drinking cold beer.

So I explain the situation to Valdir's daughter, telling her that when a car comes along with a key for me, she should explain that I have already departed for Serro.

And off I go, hoofing hard on a flat road of auburn dust and pebbles. Ten miles, it turns out, is a long way to walk if you have even a small hole in your foot. Along the way I come to a little bar, but the only food the guy has is cookies, crackers, candy, and *cachaça*. I'm tempted to make do on the hootch — the lunch of many an exhausted peasant — but in my hunger I take a craving for a certain kind of wafer cookie in tutti-frutti colors that once entranced me in my childhood. As I recall, I was denied those cookies by a mother who believed snacks to be the food of the devil or something. I'm sure she isn't going to catch me here in a dusty little two-man bar halfway between Itaponhoacanga and Serro, so tutti-frutti wafers are my lunch. The nice man behind the bar fills my liter bottle with ice-cold water from his refrigerator. Within half a mile, as I walk along, chewing the artificial fruit flavors into a tacky wad and reading the list of chemical ingredients on the back of the package, I realize that my mother knew her food. I should have had the *cachaça*. When I come to some kids entertaining themselves with the dirt of the road that passes their house, I ask all their names and whether they've been to school today. They have been, so everybody gets a handful of tutti-frutti wafer cookies, though what they really need is dentures and a bath.

A car comes along from the direction of Serro, passes me, stops, backs up. The driver asks if I'm the guy who's waiting for William's key. I am. Well, he doesn't have the key, but he knows about it and is sure another car will bring it soon.

An hour later, I come upon a taxi with a flat tire, aimed at Serro but going nowhere until someone gets back with a spare. The driver asks me if I'm the guy waiting for the key to William's farm. He doesn't have it, but he's heard about me. If someone arrives with a spare tire soon, he'll give me a ride into Serro.

When I come to a sign that indicates Serro at a distance of only five kilometers, I decide to liberate my poor, hot feet and put them into sandals. They like it for the first kilometer or two. We're walking past Maciço da Pedra Redonda – Round Rock Massif — a bald dome with hairy vegetation around its lower slopes. It takes me two hours to walk by. Beyond it, a rain shower keeps promising to come in and cool me off, but it never delivers.

A boy comes walking along from the direction of Serro. He's about twelve years old, wearing a tattered shirt, ragged shorts, nothing on his feet. When we meet in the middle of the road, he regards me with all the incomprehensibility and suspicion due a man who comes out of nowhere with a backpack and a bright red face.

The boy says he's going to Itaponhoacanga. He's got a six-hour hike ahead of him, barefoot all the way. It's two o'clock in the afternoon. He's carrying no food or water, and I'm sure he has no money. I wish a bus would come along so I could buy him a ticket. As we part, I keep turning to look back at him. Each time, he's turning to look back at me.

Chapter Fourteen

Serro

The indicated five kilometers to Serro take me only to the outer fringe of municipal limits. My feet are tired of the sandaled life, but they won't go back into shoes. They've become peasant feet, broad, beefy, callused, darkened to the color of clay. They don't want to go into shoes. At the same time, they don't want to walk any more. They want to soak in cold water. They want cold beer in their veins.

With an urban population of about 11,000, Serro is the biggest town I've come to in several weeks. It takes me almost an hour to walk from its first houses to its historic district. By the time I'm staggering down the main street, I can barely lift my feet over some of its larger cobblestones. I book into the *Pousada* Vila do Principe, an old sobrado that was recently restored from a state of near collapse. In this building was born Pedro Lessa, a famous jurist who became a justice in the supreme court. Also born here was Valentim das Fonsecas. The *das* of his name means "of the," possibly a preposition of possession, for he had *belonged to* the Fonseca family. He was born in the *senzala*, the slave quarters that today serve as the dining room where guests take their morning coffee. It's an impressive building with posts and beams eighteen inches wide, doors nine feet high, ceilings fifteen feet high. A table in the hall between the rooms is fifteen feet long, three feet wide, four inches thick, all one slab of black wood. Two hundred years ago it was used to make cheese. It has a gully running down the middle to drain the whey.

They give me a room on the street so I can listen to a guy break up thirty feet of sidewalk with a hammer and chisel. If there's an indigenous sound indicative of Brazil, it isn't samba or the squawk of a toucan. It's somebody breaking concrete with a hammer and chisel, hour after hour, day after day.

After a real soaker of a shower, I go straight to bed, too tired to go out for food. I suffer chills, shakes, and nausea from sheer exhaustion. But I can't sleep. The guy across the narrow street keeps chinking at the sidewalk, and the cars that creep up the street sound like they're driving through my room. After a couple of hours I get up, go across the street for some caldo de *feijão* bean soup and a dose of *cachaça*. They go well together. The caldo comes with bits of fried pork fat and scallion sprinkled on top. It goes straight to my aching crux. I feel much better. I hobble up the street to a pharmacy to get some stuff to put on the hole in my foot. The kid behind the counter has to go in back to ask his father what's good for holes in the feet. He gives me some ointment. I go back home, watch thirty seconds of all five channels on my little black-and-white TV. There's nothing good on any more than there is on the hundred-odd channels I have back in Connecticut. I think how useful this little TV would be if I could throw it out the window and hit the guy with the chisel.

Semi-sleepless, I come up with a brilliant idea. Serro should prohibit all vehicular traffic from the streets of its historic district. Cars and trucks should park down near the bus station, where people with mules and carts can take riders and cargo where they have to go. It would be a great way to employ peasants whose skills are pretty much limited to those related to farming. Their investment would amount to no more than a mule and a cart. Tourists would surely love it, and the town would sound the way it looks.

And the idea might spread. Other towns might start

doing it. Streets would become full of people instead of cars. The noise would be of conversation and footsteps, the clip-clop of hooves, the rumble of carts, the cluck of chickens in the public space. When mules got lonely, they'd be allowed into bars. Wouldn't that strike terror in the heart of General Motors! Their stock would go into a tailspin. The Dow would go down the drain. The world economy would implode to isolated local economies like so many little towns along the Estrada Real. People would spend evenings talking with each other. When their televisions got rusty and stopped working, they'd convert them to chicken nests. They'd live on three dollars a week and sit around praying for rain.

Later that night I'm sitting at a table outside a restaurant on the Praça João Pinheiro, below the Igreja Nossa Senhora do Carmo and the Capela Santa Rita, considering the ramifications of that fantastical and carefree scenario — Would it lead to war? Plague? Starvation? — when a guy comes along and asks me if I'm the American who's supposed to be spending the night at William's farm in Mato Grosso. He's in his late forties, I'd say, dressed in clothes I'm sure he's been wearing for several days, if not weeks. He has a little mustache no wider than his nose. He's glad to find me here in Serro because he was given the job of driving out to Mato Grosso in the morning to pick me up. Now, to his relief, he doesn't have to go.

The least I can do for his troubles thus far, of course, is offer him a seat and a glass of beer from a bottle I really don't need to finish myself. He accepts. And he begins to talk. His name is Joubert but he's known as Juju. He lives alone on a mountain that's off in the direction of Milho Verde, the next town up the Estrada Real. He lives there in a small house. He lives at one with nature. Nature comes right in the door, sometimes right up onto his kitchen table. That's fine with him, though he feels compelled to kill the larger snakes that wander in. He's sorry that he has to, but that's what he has to do. He's practically a Buddhist.

I fear he may also be practically a pest, too. One thing I loath about travels in poor places is the occasional presumption that I'm there to buy beer for anyone pushy enough to grab my attention and take advantage of my courtesy. And in bars everywhere there are drunks who need to unload their minds on anyone too polite to shoo them away. Juju clearly has a need to talk, but he isn't drunk, and he barely touches the beer I pour for him. He isn't a pest. He's saying things of great interest to me — Marxist economics, Brazilian literature, cultural imperialism, the importance of nature — so I listen, wishing I could write it all down. His ideas aren't as new as he seems to think they are, but he puts just enough spin on them to keep me interested.

For a guy who lives on a mountain outside of Milho

Verde, the son of illiterate peasants, Juju's astonishingly intellectual. He praises the work of Flaubert, Mann and Hemingway, whose books he says he has read in their original languages. I would doubt this except that the few times I interrupt him to ask what a word means, he promptly gives me the word in English. When I ask what the verb *rogar* means — I'd seen it on an oratory card in a church — he put the word into the phrase I'd seen on the card and translates the phrase as "pray for us." When I ask what *besta* means, he puts it into the phrase *Êta vida besta* and translates it as an expression that boils down to *bullshit*. It's the kind of phrase a character in a book by Guimarães Rosa would use in the grunty, sing-song dialect of the outback *sertão*. Juju wants me to understand the importance of the work of Guimarães Rosa, a *mineiro* writer of literary complexity akin to that of James Joyce. I'm interested because I've tried to read Rosa and never managed to understand a complete sentence.

Rosa's sertão narrative is the earthiest of dialects rendered with an artistic twist. It's a language difficult for urban Brazilians to understand, impossible for foreigners. Rosa's sertão vocabulary produces brilliant metaphors and images. He weaves in elements of Aeschylus and the Bhagavad-Gita. He has scruffy illiterates speaking in raggedy pentameter and onomatopoetic quasi-verse. This is probably why I have enjoyed reading Rosa's *Grande Sertão: Veredas* out loud even though I understand almost none of it. Juju recommends that I try *Sagarana* and *Primeiras Histórias,* Rosa's earlier works, which should be a little easier to grasp.

Juju talks of the world's utter failure to create and live a philosophy that accommodates nature. He doesn't see any movement in that direction whatsoever. He speaks in an unending sentence, so there's no way I can ask whether he knows about the widely popular desire to reach an environmental balance, or about the Green movements in Europe and North America. Maybe he doesn't know about them; maybe he sees them as ineffective, maybe he knows all he wants to know about everything. He talks and talks and talks. I know better than to force people like this into dialogue. I just listen.

Juju, it soon turns out, is a graphic artist. He draws cartoons and illustrates children's books. He also carves. He hints at some degree of success and renown and great opportunities that he has had to decline because he will not live in a city. A friend in Boston has said that he could easily sell his carvings there. But there's just no way he's going to Boston. He has his place on the mountain, and there he stays.

He presents me with one new and rather disturbing thought. As he's talking the fragility of cultures before the bulldozer of the corporate/commercial culture of the United States (Motown, Hollywood, advertising, Disney), he says that Brazil's best defense is its general illiteracy.

Urban Brazil has already embraced the American culture. Rare is the shop or T-shirt that doesn't bear English titles. Rare is the bestseller that isn't a translation of an American book. The average song on the radio is either American or Americanoid. English words pervade the conversations of people who listen to that music, see those movies, tour the internet or mess with technology. Rural Brazilians — peasants — on the other hand, retain their national culture and the purity of their language. Their vocabulary is that of their parents and grandparents and Guimarães Rosa, their accents those of their local areas, their myths, stories, and heroes the products of local culture, not corporate cross-promotions. The strength of the Brazilian culture, its last rampart, is its ignorance.

*   *   *

I'm stuck in Serro for a week during Semana Santa, which ends on Easter Sunday, because this is when city folk flood into small towns for a little vacation and a chance to see how the holy week is supposed to be celebrated. If I leave Serro in the middle of the week, I'm likely to end up in a town with no place to sleep. So here I stay, gladly stuck in one of the prettiest places in the world. The week's events include a community confession for women, another for young people, a palm leaf procession, a mass of unction for the ill, a Last Supper mass, an enactment of the washing of the feet, a midnight mass, a baptism mass, the Good Friday Via Sacra enactment of the stations of the cross, and, on Easter Sunday, the procession and Mass of the Resurrection.

The Via Sacra is the world's oldest tear-jerker, and it didn't fail to jerk a tear or two from a philosophical cynic like me. Whether Jesus was a God or a regular guy, the story of the Crucifixion — story in the sense of either fiction or the slant of good reportage — has yet to be equaled for sheer drama. The ending may stretch credulity a bit, but credulity is strongly present in the faithful as Roman soldiers drag the figure of Jesus from the Igreja Nossa Senhora da Conceição and condemn him to death. They whip him, beat him, and kick him until he rolls down the granite stairs into the street. The protagonist here could pass for a consummate pothead, his hair to his shoulders, his beard a mess, his eyes glazed over with godly vision. Someone told me that the Jesus character wants the full Jesus experience, so he asks his friends the Romans to really make it hurt. Though their whips are just frayed rope, they whip them hard, making them snap. Dye on the rope leaves blood-red scars on Jesus' back. They don't kick him hard, but they do push him down with their feet. Children cry at the violence of it. His cross is real, heavy, big enough to fit, and he's really shouldering it up and down a steep half mile, his knees on the cobblestone. He wears a crown of thorns, and one soldier crams it on tight.

As we proceed from station to station, a priest narrates the action through a microphone connected to a megaphone on a pole carried by a choirboy. We see Jesus fall, and it seems to me he really does hit his head hard against a curbstone. We see Jesus meet his mother, a moment in history unmatched by the drama of any opera, book, poem, or made-for-TV drama. What did she say to him?, I wonder. I knew you'd turn out this way? What did he say to her? I'm innocent? We see an apostle help Jesus to his feet. We see Veronica wipe his brow. We see him fall a second time. He consoles the children of Jerusalem, then falls again. He is stripped of his garments.

This really happened. A man was condemned to death for being a nice guy. He was flogged and beaten in the street, then tortured to death. All because he had a really great idea and just wouldn't shut up.

And then it happened a few million times more, not necessarily as Jews nailed to crosses but as blacks lynched, slaves flogged, leftists imprisoned, unionists beaten, students disappeared, children chained to sewing machines, all with less publicity than Jesus got, but somehow the idea stays alive. We know. And just in case anybody needs reminding, each Easter week, it gets acted out in the streets of Serro. The crowd sure knows what's really going on here, and they empathize. The priest reminds us that we all have our crosses to bear, but everyone already recognizes the personification of all the pains that fall on the innocent – the field workers, the unwed mothers, the spouses of alcoholics, the misunderstood, the falsely accused, the permanently poor. Brazil is rich in these people, and they spend a lot of time in church. They know what's going on. Beside me, a skinny young *mulata* bearing a boy on her shoulders — her shoulders! — weeps loudly, one hand on the boy's bare knee, one covering her face, her soggy eyes peeking between her fingers to watch what she does not need to see. A wrinkled old woman in a dark blue T-shirt, smiling and crying, holds a wrinkled hand out toward the cross as if feeling something. The back of her shirt says, in Portuguese, "Next time you tell me I was bad, I'll kill." It has a cartoon picture of a student holding an ax.

At the *Praça* João Pinheiro, the crowd gathers below the Igreja Nossa Senhora do Carmo, where two thieves have already been crucified. Soon Jesus is hoisted up into the sweltering late-morning sun like so much jerked beef. He is gouged by a Roman. He suffers visibly. He dies. He's taken down. The priest with the megaphone on the pole says he rises to Heaven. In this case, he does so to the accompaniment of poorly recorded harp music.

I kind of knew it would turn out that way, but I didn't know about the Penitential Liturgy that the priest would read, with the crowd responding in unison. I never expected to hear such words from the infallible Church.

I could not have phrased the confession better, I cannot think of anything to add, and I cannot think of a better occasion for its reading.

The Church invites us to put fraternity at the service of the life and dignity of the indigenous peoples. The sins committed against these people, our brothers, from the arrival of the colonizers, still continue in our day. We must seek the conversion of our heart to live the gospel today.

For all the sins of the old and new colonization which has been encroaching, over centuries, on the indigenous people of our America, we ask forgiveness...

FORGIVE US, LORD, FORGIVE US.

For the sins of the Church itself, so often the tool of old and new colonization...

FORGIVE US, LORD, FORGIVE US.

For the pride and ignorance with which we struck down the culture of the indigenous people, in the name of civilization, hypocritically called Christian...

FORGIVE US, LORD, FORGIVE US.

For the spoiling of Indian lands and the destruction of nature where they live, caused by farming, the interests of large national and multinational corporations, and by disrespectful tourism...

FORGIVE US, LORD, FORGIVE US.

For the inhuman violence with which we tried to transform Indian communities into new victims of our society of profit and consumption under the pretext of illusionary integration...

FORGIVE US, LORD, FORGIVE US.

For our inability to see the roots of the gospel in the simple and communitarian life of the indigenous peoples...

FORGIVE US, LORD, FORGIVE US.

For the lack of national solidarity of consciousness, the lack of honesty or efficiency in the responsible authorities, for the missions of the Church, for all the sins of the Brazilian people against the rights of our brother Indians...

FORGIVE US, LORD, FORGIVE US.

For so often trying to isolate the indigenous peoples' problems from the global problem of all the marginalized of the country, from the rural areas to the cities...

FORGIVE US, LORD, FORGIVE US.

For the lack of calling to engage ourselves, like Jesus, in the culture, martyrdom and hopes of the indigenous peoples...

FORGIVE US, LORD, FORGIVE US.

For those who killed our brothers, Simão and Rodolfo (Galdino), for those who covered up these crimes, for those who kill, day to day, the Indian, our brother...

FORGIVE US, LORD, FORGIVE US.

For our lack of hope in this new world that we must build, where all people, being our people, will be free and brothers...

FORGIVE US, LORD, FORGIVE US."

Lord, if you look on our existence with feelings as poor as ours, who among us can stand? Counting on your forgiveness and your mercy, we want to forsake always what displeases you, and happily fulfill your law. For Christ our Lord.

FORGIVE US, LORD, FORGIVE US.

*   *   *

Here's Serro's place in history. It all started a long, long time ago, when darkness lay upon the earth. Pretty soon along comes Adam. He gives a rib to Eve. One thing leads to another, and soon Pedro Álvares Cabral sails out of Lisbon, bound for India. Off the coast of Africa, he gets blown off course, possibly on purpose. He lands at a place he calls Porto Seguro. Thus Brazil begins its history by either subterfuge or error. The coast of Brazil turns out to be a great place to grow sugar cane, and Africa is a conveniently close source of cheap labor. Unfortunately, the Caribbean is also a good place to grow cane, and soon the competition drives down the price of sugar. In search of other sources of easy money, Portuguese *bandeirantes* hack their way into the interior. They find gold in Minas Gerais. In 1697, they start building a road inland, the Estrada Real. In 1701, the first *bandeirantes* pressed into the area the Tupi-Guarani Indians called Ivituruí, which the Portuguese also spelled as Ivituruy and translated as Serro Frio, Cold Ridge. Among the Portuguese are Sebastião Fernandez Dourinho, Fernão Dias, and Antônio Dias Adorno. With them is an Italian political refugee out of Genoa, last name Ottoni. But it is a Paulista, Antônio Soares Ferreira, who comes to Minas Gerais to discover gold at Ivituruí. Prospectors soon set up camp – two camps, really, an upper and a lower, one named Ivituruí, the other Gambá, Portuguese for Skunk. Skunk and Cold Ridge are connected by a path called the Rua dos Flores – the Street of Flowers. The two camps grow into each other to become the *Arraial* das Lavras Velhas de Iviturui. The *arraial* is home to the usual mining camp clashes and conflicts. In 1711, the Crown name sergeant major Carlos Mascarenhas Superintendent of Mines and gives him the authority to establish order. He has a palm-roof chapel put up and dedicated to Santo Antônio. He probably cuts off a few heads or in some other way establishes sufficient order for the *arraial* to be bumped up to the rank of Vila, the Vila do Principe. In 1720, Vila do Principe is included with other *arraiais* in the area, such as São Gonçalo do Rio das Pedras and Milho Verde, in the Comarca of Serro Frio, comarca being a jurisdiction akin to a county. Comarca status means that the region is for the first time under direct Portuguese government administration. In 1724, Vila do Principe becomes a parish. By 1728, the Igreja da Nossa Senhora do Rosário is up and running, serving as the *matriz* until the Nossa Senhora da Conceição gets built sometime after 1776.

In 1751, the Crown establishes the Casa de Fundição, the foundry house where all gold had to be taken to be processed, weighed and taxed. Manuel Vieira Ottoni, the son of the refugee from Genoa, is its director. The tax is twenty percent. Within twenty-five years, people who consider themselves Brazilian consider people who consider themselves to be Portuguese to be a bit greedy. In 1789, several liberals in Ouro Preto conspire to oust the Portuguese. They are betrayed, arrested and tried in Rio de Janeiro. Most are sentenced to prison, but the itinerant dentist Tiradentes is hanged and beheaded.

Meanwhile, things are not going well in Europe, at least not for the Portuguese. In 1808, Napoleon, at odds with the British over control of Iberia, takes over Spain and Portugal. The British ship Warspite takes Dom João and his mother, Queen Maria I, to Brazil. Twelve thousand other members of the court soon followed. They set up camp in Bahia but within two months move to Rio de

Janeiro. Dom João then sees the expediency of allowing manufacturing and free trade in Brazil. The British get special tariff rates and trade rights. He establishes a royal library, a royal press, a military academy. When his mother dies in 1818, he becomes emperor of Brazil and Portugal.

When two German scientific explorers, Dr. Johann Baptist von Spix and Dr. Friedrich Phillipp von Martius, come through Serro at about that time, they find an uninviting has-been mining town with poorly paved streets and a church still under construction. In *Viagem Pelo Brasil, 1817-1820*, they write, "The number of inhabitants has declined in recent decades, in consequence of the decline in gold production, so that today, the region has no more than 2,000 souls, and on this scene of ancient opulence, one finds only the vestiges of misery."

But all is not dark and dying in Serro. Manuel Vieira Ottoni's son, José Eloy Ottoni, is becoming a nationally prominent intellectual, writing poetry, perfecting his Latin, translating the Book of Job, the Proverbs of Solomon, and the Georgias of Virgil. He has a son, names him Ernesto Benedito Ottoni, a boy who will rise up from a mining camp to become a doctor and medical researcher. He had another son and names him Teófilo. Teófilo learned to read and write.

In 1821, with Napoleon ousted from Iberia, the

Portuguese parliament calls King João back. He goes, leaving his son, Pedro I, as emperor of Brazil. Pedro agrees to rule under a constitution, a concept that will slowly ferment over the next century. In 1822, João, under parliamentary pressure in Lisbon, calls Pedro back to the homeland. Pedro is unsure what to do until September 7, 1822, when, returning to Rio from São Paulo with the probable intent of sailing for Lisbon, he reputedly says, "*Independência ou Morte*" and declares Brazil a nation. Some versions of history hold that under a debilitating bout of diarrhea, Pedro essentially just says to hell with a trip across the Atlantic. Independence was a lot easier. It's not known for sure whether "Independence or Death" are his words or those of a public relations guy.

In 1823, Pedro changes his mind on the constitution. It's still there, but he disregards it, a legal precedent that survives to some extent into the twenty-first century. In 1826, Dom João dies. Under the absurd rules of succession, Dom Pedro's son becomes emperor of Portugal, a big job for a five-year-old who lives on the other side of the ocean. Until he's of legal age, however, his father's supposed to do the job. But his father's having enough trouble just trying to rule Brazil. Uruguay declares its independence in 1825 and claims Cisplatina, an area Brazil had annexed in 1821. Pedro sends troops to secure it, but they are fought off. Meanwhile, in northeast Brazil, several provinces declare an independent country and must be taken back by force. Pedro tries to support the commercial and military bureaucracy of the old Portuguese, but liberals resist him. After he has a liberal journalist assassinated, he loses political support. He goes to Minas Gerais in hopes of bolstering support, but he is received coldly. Lacking the support of Minas, he resigns in 1831.

Brazil now tries to form some kind of semi-autocratic nonmonarchical government. Over the next nine years, several combinations of conservative juntas try to maintain power. They all fail. Brazil's politically concerned divide into three main groups: the moderate liberals, who think some kind of limited monarchy will work, the real liberals, who espouse the constitutionalism of the United States, and the conservatives, who think things were find under an emperor.

Back in Serro, Teófilo Ottoni reads Hobbes, Locke, Hume, Rousseau. He goes to the newborn United States, visits Philadelphia, sees the glories of democracy. He returns, eventually to found a city called Filadelfia. He starts an underground organization called Clube Secreto de Amigos Unidos. They discuss liberalism. He starts a liberal newspaper called the *Sentinal do Serro*. On September 4, 1830, he writes, "The purpose of all political association is the preservation of the nature and inalienable rights of man. These rights are liberty, security, property and resistance to oppression."

He's serious about this. Over the next two decades he slams the conservatives and the monarchy again and again and again. He slams Dom Pedro II when at the haughty age of 20 he declares himself emperor and begins to regain the ground the monarchy has lost since 1831. In 1842, Teófilo slams Dom Pedro for retracting certain inalienable rights. Plots ensue. Liberals in São Paulo start talking revolution. Liberals in Minas Gerais back them but with traditional *mineiro* reluctance can't quite decided to back up their beliefs with arms. In 1848, São Paulo rises up. Teófilo gallops down there to rally the liberals and promise the support of Minas Gerais, which has pretty much decided to rise up, too. Federal troops push the Paulista liberals into the woods. Teófilo slips away, gallops north, hoping to tell Minas that all goes well in São Paulo and that the uprising should go ahead as planned. In his view, this is the only hope for liberalism in Brazil. As he races toward Minas, he's a wanted man with a white cape on his back and false passport in his satchel. He stops at a farm to spend the night, is recognized but not betrayed. Nearing the São Paulo-Minas Gerais border, he stops at another farm. He is warned that the bridge over the Rio Paranaiba will be dangerous. Federal troops guard the São Paulo side. Liberal rebels guard the other and are prepared to shoot anyone who attempts to cross without the password. No one at the farm knows the password, but Teófilo isn't worried. This is Brazil, nothing if not flexible. He arrives at the check point, hands down his passport but does not wait to see if it's accepted. He gives his horse a mighty kick in the slats and takes off across the bridge. The troops have time to fire only a few shots into the darkness. He thunders across the 400-meter bridge, hollering *"Viva a revolução!"* It works better than a password. The sentinel in Minas shouts back, *"Viva o capitão da capa branca!"*

Despite this brave and dramatic moment, this uprising, as all uprisings in Brazil before then or since, fizzles. Its leaders are arrested. Teófilo Ottoni goes to jail. A year later, however, in a trial of amnesty, Ottoni defends himself in court and is unanimously exonerated. His son goes on to become a doctor. After Dom Pedro II abdicates in 1889, Brazil becomes a republic, Filadelfia is renamed Teófilo Ottoni, and today it's known as a moderately miserable place to live, dusty, poor and unenlightened.

Today a bust of Teófilo stands on a pedestal in Serro's *Praça* João Pinheiro, the town's main plaza, just below the Igreja Nossa Senhora do Carmo and the Capela Santa Rita, just across the street from Town Hall. During most of this week, the Semana Santa, the town's big tourist week, the Casa dos Ottoni is the only tourist attraction that's open to the public during set hours. The old Casa de Fundição, now the Casa de Caridade Santa Teresa, is a hospital not prepared to receive tourists unless they are ill or injured. The Casa do Pedro Lessa, former home of a famous jurist, is now the Pousada Vila do Principe. The Casa do Barão de Diamantina is now a high school. The Chácara do Barão do Serro, the old house of a baron who first ran the town, is open only when Guido Pascoal is there, which is apparently when he feels like it and when there isn't some special event happening that needs the service of the popcorn cart he operates. The Casa de João Pinheiro, former governor, is a residence now, so all you can do is look at it from the outside. All the churches are closed except for scheduled masses. In other words, even though tourism is the biggest industry in town, there is really nothing for tourists to do but walk around and, tiring of that, choose a bar and drink beer.

Lariane Telles Mendonça would like to change that. She's a pretty, bright-eyed woman with freckles on her cheeks, a full complement of intelligence, and an inn she calls the Hospedaria Ares de Serro. She's fixing it up nice, historically correct except for the addition of a few bathrooms, one of which has a stone bathtub that used to be a horse trough. The beds and furniture are ancient and beautifully bedecked.

Lariane's been working hard to get the town organized to attract and support tourism, to preserve its better traditions, such as good cheese and beautiful festivals, and to avoid certain others, such as burning trash in the streets and closing tourist attractions on holidays. When I mention the advisability of banning cars, she is delighted to hear the idea because she's already proposed a similar idea, one which exceeds mine in brilliance. She's promoting a voluntary banning of cars from the historical district on just one day of each month. On that day, the town would sponsor a photo contest for anyone who would like to photograph a town that would look quite as it did in the late eighteenth century. There would be a monthly photo exhibit, with prizes not only to the best photographers but to the owners of the buildings that are in the photographs, thus promoting preservation of historical integrity.

This idea hasn't gone down very well with the powers that be. Lariane says there are about five conscienticized people in town. Among the unconscienticized is the secretary of tourism, a sluggish and cackly woman whom Lariane has seen toss lit cigarette butts out the window of her office, which is just above the sidewalk of the town's main street. Lariane's group dreamed up the concept of the Bolerata, a concert played by Serro's excellent marching band. The band plays from the second stories of colonial houses around a junction of streets where tables have been set up on the cobblestones. I'm blessed to witness this beautiful event. Cars have been prohibited since early that morning. People spend the evening at the little tables in the street, drinking beer, eating Serro cheese and other snacks by the light of little candles, getting into a good mood by midnight, when the band plays. The conductor, Danilo Briskievicz, stands in the middle of the ad hoc *praça*, waving his baton upward in three directions as the brass, drums and woodwinds play from little wrought iron balconies. Many of the musicians are children, so all we can see from our tables is the tips of their trombones and baritones as they sway back and forth. On the night I'm there, the moon is full, so it's straight above us at midnight. The effect is most glorious and entrancing. Lariane, draped in white apron and dreamy smile, dances as she weaves among the tables to serve beer, wine, cognac, and cheese. If there's any smile bigger, it's of the Briskievicz as he gestures applause upward to the houses around him. Every song they play is Brazilian, and "Brazil" is the only one contemporary enough for me to have heard. When the band plays "Brazil," people sing along. When the band plays the town song, people rise and sway, their hands on their hearts, as they sing along.

I get all goose-fleshy and teary-eyed. I cannot imagine such a beautiful thing happening in my own town. I cannot imagine my town mustering up a marching band. (It can't even muster up enough kids for a Little League team.) If by some miracle they did, they would not let children stay up till midnight to play in a concert. The adults themselves wouldn't stay up that late. They wouldn't allow beer to be served in the street. They wouldn't ban cars from a downtown intersection. I'm sure my town has never had nor ever will have a town song. If by some miracle it ever does, people will certainly not hold two hands over their hearts as they sing and sway — not unless maybe they find themselves in a situation where they can drink beer at tables in the street while twenty or thirty local folks play uncommercial music under a full moon at midnight. That just might do it.

The next morning I go visit Lariane at her inn and tell her that I now fully understand that I come from an impoverished nation and that Brazil — Serro, anyway — is wealthy beyond the dreams of most Americans. She's glad to hear it. Events such as the Bolerata are hard to produce because the political and commercial powers of Serro are in two factions. One wants to bring in industry, asphalt, and fast food. The other believes that growth is not necessarily improvement and that beauty, tradition and cultural purity will bring in more money and fewer problems than a mine or factory. Last night's Bolerata, as a matter of fact, happened with virtually no support from the town government, which failed to deliver tablecloths, more tables, cheese, a freezer, and other accoutrement and supplies that would have made the event even better.

Lariane and her team have planned other events, one of which is the monthly Festival of Cheese, which will happen tomorrow, again with virtually no help from the town beyond tolerance. Serro's cheese is the most famous cheese in a state famous for its cheeses. Apparently the local grass carries a certain bacterium that makes its way through a cow and into her milk. The cheese is good and so special that the United Nations has declared it a cultural heritage of humanity. Lariane puts both hands over her heart and all but swoons when I come up with what I must admit is an utterly brilliant concept. What is the moon made of? Cheese, of course, and on a clear night, the full moon looks exactly like a white wheel of *queijo mineiro*. Serro has a logo orbiting the earth. With her eyes rolling to the heavens, Lariane declares that henceforth all Boleratas will be held on the weekend closest to the full moon, and every table shall have at its center a wheel of Serro cheese to reflect the light of the moon.

Lariane is working on one project that is becoming truly huge. She and others are organizing a *cavalgada*, a cavalcade along the entire length of the Estrada Real. Ten people ride *mangalarga* and *campolina* horses from Rio de Janeiro to Diamantina over the course of about three weeks. It's a pretty big operation involving forty-eight horses, a number of support cars, a string of farms prepared to receive the horses and their riders. Sometimes the riders will sleep outdoors, sometimes in *pousada*s and spas. Bands will entertain them at night. Towns will roll out their red carpets. Television will cover their progress. Lariane would like to see horse trips become a regular means of transporting tourists into the interior of Minas.

The Festival do *Queijo* turns out to be less than I had hoped. It isn't very festive, and there's little in the way of cheese. The original idea, I'm told, was to have dozens of booths offering local cheeses and cheese dishes as well as other special foods, crafts, local *cachaça*s (sugar cane moonshines), and so on. This is only the first or second festival, however, so the concept hasn't caught on yet. It consists of half a dozen booths in the *Praça* João Pinheiro selling beer, *cachaça*, *churrasquinho* shish kebobs, home-made fruit liqueurs, T-shirts, flaky fried *pasteis* with actual cheese inside, and way down at the end, a couple of peasant women, as short and black as Pygmies, tough as gristle, offering fresh collards, scallions, bananas, and blue-green chicken eggs from their farm, which, to judge by their broad, cracked feet, must be rather far away. The only brand-name product here is the beer, Skol.

But who cares if there's no cheese? Any festival is a good festival, even a festival so sparsely attended. By noon no more than fifty people are sampling the *churrasquinho* kebobs, washing down the little chunks of blackened beef and pork with beer, bolstering the experience with doses of *cachaça* from a jug. A few of the more persnickety attendees sit at two little tables crowded into the patch of shade cast by a low tree of dense foliage. A family of tourists, Brazilians though certainly not from Serro, saunters along. I wonder how I can tell that they're tourists. Maybe it's the man of the family, a pasty fatso who obviously belongs in a business suit, not Bermudas. Maybe it's his wife, who looks annoyed to be so far from her sofa. Maybe it's the kids, who look so bored. Maybe it's because they're the only people who aren't in the general conversation, which seems to include everyone else in the *praça*. They're as foreign here as I am. They're just waiting for lunchtime to come around, I can tell. They really just want to go home.

I acquire a can of Skol and spit of *churrasquinho* and retreat with my notebook and pen to the shade a tall palm. I lean back against the tree, pull my elbows into the narrow strip of shade, set the beer between my feet, and try to describe the peacefulness of the scene, the simple pleasure the people are having at their little no-cheese cheese festival. I wonder how long it will be until Kraft finds a way to put synthetic Serro cheese in a squirt-can with a label that says "New! Improved!" This simple culture seems so fragile, so besieged by the bulldozers of commercialism. It's just a matter of time. These people are babes in a porn shop. They're doomed.

A boy of about 14, André Orandi Figueiredo, arrives, turns on an electronic keyboard, fiddles with some wires, tries a few chords, adjusts a background rhythm, then plays bossa nova, Brazilian pop, a *chorinho*, an Elton John song, pumping the sound out speakers meant for an audience of thousands. He switches to clarinet when a pretty girl with dark eyes and straight black hair comes along and tries her hand at the keyboard. Her sneakers, stylishly tattered around the ankle, have orange laces. He wears a white shirt with a collar. They make beautiful music together. Both have eyes of intelligence and maturity. I hope they get married and have a lot of intelligent children who play music together, write brilliant editorials, and translate classics like the Ottoni family that put Serro on the map. That isn't a matter for me, a stranger over here in the shade of a palm, to hope, but I hope it anyway. When they play "Imagine," my stomach gets all wobbly with the peace of the place and moment, imagining how the whole world could be like this, wondering if it ever was like this, with people sitting around a plaza below a church on a hill, everybody just yakking and eating and listening to a couple of local kids play music. It isn't like this where I come from. Where I'm from, half the stuff going on here — the open-air liquor from untaxed, unlabeled bottles, the bare feet, the grubby barbecue grill, the cheese never inspected by anybody but flies — would be illegal. Everybody would be home watching TV.

It isn't even like this where I'm sitting, over to the side, under the palm. I'm over here; everyone else is over there. I'm drinking beer from a can; they're drinking from big bottles that get passed around to the glasses of their friends. They're living; I'm watching. It's been this way for as long as I can remember, from high school on. For the last thirty years or so, I've been sitting off to the side, pen in my hand, essentially talking to myself by putting my thoughts on paper. Yesterday's Via Sacra procession, in which a man in a loin cloth lugged a cross around town, falling, meeting his mother, getting whipped and kicked by Romans, has me wondering what cross I have to bear, and now I decide it's this: I will always be on the outside of the fun, looking in, observing, writing about it, a sad detachment that began in youth and evolved into a profession.

So be it. I can bear that cross. I don't mind sitting here watching. It's not such a bad job at all. I just have to pay attention. When the duet cranks out the Beatles' "Yesterday," I realize that yesterday is exactly what I'm writing about as I wander down the Estrada Real, 750 miles through the nineteenth century, a yesterday when troubles seemed so far away, a place where I can hide away, there's a shadow hanging over me, oh I believe...I believe I shouldn't drink beer so early in the day. It just makes me all mushy, gleaning wisdom from pop songs and imagining myself a turncoat refugee from an evil empire where the dollar rules almighty.

*   *   *

Serro

Oration to Maria, Untier of Knots

Virgin Mary, Mother of beautiful love, Mother
who never fails to come to the aid of an afflicted
son, Mother whose hands never stop serving her
beloved children because they are driven by
divine love and the immense mercy that exists
in her heart, return to me your compassionate
look over me and see the knots tied up in my life.
You know my despair well, and my pain, and
how I am tied up by these knots. Mary, Mother
of God, charged with untying the knots of the life
of her children [sic], I trust today the thread of
my life to your hands. No one, not even the Evil
One can take me from your precious protection.
In your hands there is no knot that cannot be
undone. Powerful mother, by your grace and your
intervening power together with your Son and my
Liberator, Jesus, receive in your hands today this
knot. I ask you to untie it for the glory of God
and forever. You are my hope. O my missus, you
are the only consolation given by God, the fortress
of my weakness, the wealth of my miseries, the
freedom, with Christ, from my chains. Hear my
supplications. Guard me, guide me, protect me, o
safe refuge! Maria, Untier of Knots, pray for me.

Pray 1 Our Father, 1 Ave Maria, and make the sign of the cross.

In thanks today send away to have 1000 Orations printed and distributed to spread the benefits of our Grandiose Our Lady Untier of Knots. Send for the printing right after your petition. HELP TO SPREAD THE FAITH.

United By Faith Press. SEND YOUR ORDER. R$ 37,00 for the thousand with 2 blessed medallions Free. CALL FREE: 0800.55.4116 or (0xx11) 6731-2852. Free delivery to your home anywhere in Brazil. 04/2000 Edition. Subject to change.

Chapter Fifteen

Três Barras

The Estrada Real heads northwest out of Serro toward São Gonçalo do Rio das Pedras. It's a fifteen mile hike that starts off badly with a wrong turn attributable to my stupidity and the vagueness of my guidebook. I end up taking a paved highway out the wrong side of town and circling around, down a long hill, then up another before turning left onto dirt. By the time I'm on the right road, I'm pooped, and I've still got fourteen miles to go. The road meanders through a low valley of lush, wet pastures, following and then crossing the Rio Peixe. Then it starts to climb. The vegetation evolves from pasture to thick forest to thin forest to *cerrado* brush growing among weathered outcrops of rock. At the highest point, I cross the divide of the watersheds of the rivers Doce and Jequitinhonha, both of which empty into the Atlantic, some 270 miles east of here as the crow flies; twice that as the fish swims.

I'm ready to call it quits when I come into the village of Três Barras, some eight miles out of Serro. Três Barras isn't much of a village. It has no stores, no bars, no restaurants, no place to sleep. It's just a little church and a few houses scattered along the Estrada Real where it crosses the Rio Jequitinhonha, just a stream at this altitude. I've been told there's a woman here who will prepare a meal for any traveler who really needs it. I come into town asking everyone where I can find Dona Rosa. No one knows. But finally one imaginative genius asks whether I mean Dona Flor. I do. But which one? There are two. The one who prepares food for people, I say. Oh, yes, Dona Flor de Maio; she lives up there to the left of the church.

As I probe the path to the left of the church, Lady Mayflower is just arriving from the river with a load of stone-washed, sun-dried laundry on her head. She's of classic short-and-stout stature but upon seeing me shifts into high gear to catch up and lead me to her little house. Yes, yes, yes, of course, she can make me some lunch, of course, of course, of course. She's a fretting and protective hen of a woman who on sight has adopted me as a son and is apologetic for not having lunch ready when I arrived. Working with a dynamism I wouldn't expect from a person built along the lines of a tea pot, she huffs and puffs her wood stove to life, sets rice to boil, dashes out to the garden for greens and vegetables, cuts up half a chicken, chops up an onion, some scallions, slices and fries potatoes, minces garlic, dices a *chuchu*, shreds and sautés collards, assembles a salad, squeezes enough orange-limes for a pitcher of juice, produces a chicken sauce from thin air and within twenty minutes serves me a meal fit for half a dozen kings. Again, she's very, very sorry for the delay; she didn't know I was coming.

Dona Flor de Maio sits with me at the little table in her little dining room. In the center of the table stands a lovely bouquet of artificial flowers that her daughter made from folded corn husks. Behind her, a television babbles with a really stupid game show that involves the humiliation of its contestants. In another room, a baby cries. Dona Flor's daughter tries to shush it. She calls for a diaper, but her mother hollers that they're all wet. She tells me the house is crowded with the daughter and the baby and the son-in-law and herself. The whole house has only four rooms, all of them small, the doors consisting of strung beads.

As I attempt to eat a respectable portion of all the

food Dona Flor has prepared, she keeps her eye on my supplies. When I run low on collards, she moves to get up to make more. I insist that she has prepared far more food than I can eat. I ask her if there's any place in town where I can sleep, which I will need to do momentarily. She says that unfortunately Três Barras has no such place. She'd love to open a *pousada*, but she has no way to finance such a thing. A *pousada*, she says, is exactly what the village needs. Tourists often come here to enjoy the river and the waterfall, but there's nowhere to sleep, so they either camp or leave, in neither case leaving any money behind. If the village had an inn, people would stay longer, buy meals, bait, beer, *tira-gosto* appetizers to go with the beer, maybe pay someone to wash their clothes or their car. It would give the town a little economy. Right now they have no economy. There's a little bar over on the other side of the river but it's usually closed because no one has any money. Probably all the cash in town wouldn't be enough to build an inn. People here suffer, she says. Life is a struggle. Either you have a pension or a little job from the municipal government in Serro, like the guys who are cutting the grass around the church with clippers, or you're living off your garden and your chickens.

With perceptible guilt, Dona Flor suggests that the price of the meal would be about four *reais* — not quite two dollars. I give her a five-spot and ask her to keep the change for the inconvenience of me showing up after lunchtime. She blushes and says that if I need a place to stay for the night, she could find some room for me.

I'm not sure whether I can or want to press on to Milho Verde today. At the moment, I'm too full of food and the sun's too hot for me to do anything but take a nap in the shade. The best shade around seems to be in a little cemetery with a wall around it and a big tree leaning in. I unfurl my bed sheet across dusty ground six feet above and slightly to the side of a dead person and try to sleep. I get nowhere. Bugs keep touching me, not a lot of them, but there's always an ant finding me or a fly coming in for a taste of my sweat. I decide to pack up and go check out the river, which is what I should have done in the first place. It's a lovely stream of clear water sliding across sculpted sandstone. From a tub-sized pothole of swirling bubbles and cold water I watch a woman fifty feet upstream scrub laundry with a brush and whack it against the stone to beat the dirt out of it. It's such a lot of work! Is it worth it? I feel guilty in my whirlpool tub but not guilty enough to help her wash her family's clothes. But if I were a politician running for office, I'd buy Três Barras a community washing machine and earn the votes of every woman in town.

And once elected, I'd rally every unemployed man in town – which is to say all the men in town — and have them build a simple building where tourists could spend the night. I'd have them build it they way their forefathers built with trees, mud, grass, and water, with no nails, no power tools, no glass in the windows. I'd have them build beds with logs and rope. The whole thing could probably be built and furnished for somewhere between nothing and a thousand dollars.

I have a wicked urge to write and diminishing interest in my whirlpool bath. I'm starting to burn. I really should head for Milho Verde, but the sun's still dangerously hot. Better I should head for a bar, have a beer, sit at a table and write down everything Don Flor has told me.

Up at the road I meet an old man, a young woman and a little girl — uncle, niece and daughter — sauntering along behind a cow. I ask them where the little bar is, if there really is one. There is, and the woman says she's going that way and will be glad to take me. Her name is Cleonice and her daughter's name is Alana. That's almost the same as my middle name, Alan! Cleonice's big brown eyes get bigger. Alana...Alan...we're practically family! As we stroll up a grassy lane, she opens her life to me. It's been a hard one. She lived in Belo Horizonte for a year, working as a maid. Then she married a guy from Diamantina and moved there. He was a bum, she says, though she won't specify exactly what kind of a bum.

The little bar is closed. The owner, her brother-in-law, is in Serro shopping but should be back soon. He lives right next door to the bar. His wife, Cleonice's sister, says she doesn't have the key. Cleonice and I sit on a log to wait. A little pile of garbage smolders beside us. She continues the saga of her life. Her bum of a husband accidentally ran over their little son in the garage, killing him. That was the beginning of the end of the marriage, and soon she was back in Milho Verde with two daughters. She can't afford to feed both, so only Alana lives with her; the other lives with her mother. She has no income. She lives in a little house that some friends built for her on church land. "The Association" built her a bathroom. She doesn't know anything about this association except that it's good, it's in São Gonçalo do Rio das Pedras, and it came and built bathrooms for everybody in Três Barras. She wishes it would come back and build a *pousada* so a little money could come into town.

Cleonice is thirty years old. Her skin is dark and her hair Negroid, but her facial features are Caucasian. She's missing her four upper front teeth, though the others look white and healthy. Her blouse is orange, her skirt blue, faded, unhemmed, and crudely stitched in places where it has torn. She wears the common flip-flop sandals. While we sit on the log talking, she keeps tugging her skirt down over her fuzzy, knobby knees.

After about an hour, the door of the bar suddenly opens, unlocked from the inside. Cleonice's sister has remembered that her bar has a back door that wasn't locked. To my immense disappointment, however, there are no tables inside, just a counter of concrete blocks in front of a few shelves that hold perhaps twenty dollars worth of staples. I get a bottle of Brahma beer and sit on a box to write, holding my pad in my lap. I pour Cleonice a glass of beer. She says cold beer is good. She gives little Alana a sip.

By the end of the beer, it's five o'clock. The sun is low enough to tolerate. Now the problem is to arrive in Milho Verde before dark — about five miles in about two hours, neither easy nor impossible but certainly not something to put off. I put on my pack and shake the hands of everyone present, holding Cleonice's for an extra long time. I feel very close to her because she has told me so much about herself. I thank her for her friendship. Her skin's too dark to blush, but her eyelids dip with a bit of embarrassment. I wish I could give her a little money, and she's probably wishing I would, but I can't think of any polite way to do this. Society's myriad rules on propriety does not give us a way to just hand somebody a little cash. Nor does it allow me the silliness of kissing her hand, which for some strange reason I'd like to do. I just give it an extra squeeze that only she and I know about, then let go, turn around and walk back toward the road.

Chapter Sixteen

Milho Verde

The road out of Três Barras gives me a beautiful view of a long ridge of stone as the descending sun warms it to the hue of lukewarm lava. The ridge seems to point northeast to the Pico do Itambé, the highest mountain in this part of the state. It's high enough to create its own cloud, which at this time of day is the color of a dumpling in beef stew. The road climbs and climbs until it reaches a cattle guard at its highest point. From there I can see the sun settling behind mountains that must be fifty miles away. To the north, the few lights of Milho Verde drape across a plateau. To get there, I have to wind down into a valley, then wind up the other side.

Along the way, in the failing light, I stop to watch a god-awful tarantula creep across the road. It's as ugly as any bug can be. It moves slowly, it's front legs reaching forward to feel around before its other six tip-toe ahead. I consider killing it but can't think of a good reason to do so. We're far from a house. It won't bother anybody. Besides, I'm also a little afraid that it won't die well, that it'll squeak, and that I'll have to pound it with several rocks to make its legs stop twitching.

I spend far too much time watching this fuzzy little monster cross the road. I'm just barely starting the climb up to Milho Verde when full darkness comes down. I can't see a thing on Earth, not even my feet. At one point I walk right off the road, over a ditch and into a bush. The hill is very steep, my legs too tired to take more than a few steps without resting. I'm not about to sit down in the dark because I know I'll sit on the tarantula that is almost certainly following me. Above me, the full froth of the Milky Way blazes across the center of the sky.

Perhaps because of its elevation and 360-degree panorama, Milho Verde was once an important military outpost of the Portuguese who controlled traffic along the Estrada Real. In Viagem Pelo Brasil, Spix and Martius wrote:

> The soldiers posted [in Milho Verde], of
> the Dragoons of Minas Regiment, have the

right to impede the entrance of anyone, no matter who they are or where they're coming from, whatever their title, who is without special order of the general superintendent. The inhabitants of the Diamantina District, every time they cross the borders, must present a written permission of the general superintendent. Not even the governor of the province himself is exempt. Upon leaving Diamantina, every person is submitted to a rigorous inspection by the soldiers. The soldiers are authorized to inspect, with extreme detail, not only the travelers' possessions, every nook and cranny of their baggage, but every accessible part of their bodies and those of their pack animals, to see if they have hidden a diamond. In case of suspicion, the traveler can be detained for twenty-four hours to see if he has swallowed precious stones. No one is exempt from this inspection. This depends, however, on the soldiers on duty. To ensure that these checkpoints not be bypassed by pedestrians, patrols cover the interior and borders of the District and are equally authorized to detain anyone.

Today — this evening — Milho Verde is a dark little town, its street lights dim and far between. Its three or four streets are paved with grass. I find the *pousada* of a man named Dilson, who is a *vereador* on the town council in Serro. His inn has only three rooms, but his dining room is set up for a dozen or more people. Dilson and I sit at one table to drink beer and talk politics while his wife whips up a late dinner on her big gas stove.

Dilson informs me that the road I came in on is not the authentic Estrada Real. In Três Barras I could have taken an older trail. There are no signs indicating it, no maps to show the way, so I'd have had to hire someone to take me. I wish I had, though I'd have missed the tarantula and the astounding sunset view. Of course on the other hand, who knows what else I might have seen on the trail? Who knows what a guide might have told me? Who knows what I might have come to know? I'll bet Confucius has the answers to these questions.

Dilson was elected *vereador* (town councilman) in 1992 in the Partido Socialista Democrata do Brasil. During his four-year term he got the Serro town government to improve the road to Milho Verde and provide a little public transportation in VW vans. He got a middle school built. But in 1996, three other candidates from Milho Verde ran against him. He won forty percent of the vote but not enough to beat a candidate from elsewhere. Milho Verde was without representation for the next four years, so town funds went elsewhere. In 2000, he got the other local candidates to agree to a nonbinding primary election. The three losers would decline to run so that the more popular candidate would get more votes. Dilson won. The others went against their word, but he won the election anyway. He hopes to continue improving the village.

Life in Milho Verde has improved tremendously in the past three decades. A public water supply was built in the 1960s. Electricity arrived in the seventies. There's still no doctor in town, but at least there's regular transportation to Serro and Diamantina. A new health clinic opens on a regular basis. Until it was built, the town relied on homegrown homeopaths. The local dentist was an amateur named João Nunes. Dilson says he was pretty good. He wasn't just a guy with a pair of pliers. He had "all the equipment," though no formal education in dentistry. People didn't come to him unless they had a truly unbearable toothache, which probably meant they had a lot of other bad teeth. Dr. João's personal philosophy of dentistry was to extract not just the aching tooth but all the teeth that looked rotten. Good old Dr. João. He's dead now.

The town has a midwife, too, Dona Maria dos Santos Faria. She's a beautiful woman with holy confidence in her clear blue eyes, a trace of blond in her silvery hair, kindness written in thin creases on her face, love in her smile, 78 years under her belt, and as far as I can tell, all her teeth. She has been delivering the town's babies since about the time I was born, about fifty years ago. Over five hundred citizens have issued directly from the womb into her devout and loving hands. The first was her son. In the agony of unassisted childbirth, she promised God that if He got her through the pain, she would never deny help to other suffering women.

He got her through it. She was 23 years old at the time. She lived in a place called Ribeirão Profundo — Deep Gulch — a village a little bigger than Milho Verde but still not much of a town. It was a district of Serro but had no effective government, Serro being several hours away by horse. At night, drunken prospectors would come into town and shoot the place up. She had bullet holes in her house.

Dona Maria lived at a mining operation for over twenty years. Children were always hanging around her house. She taught them things, the alphabet, the significance of vowels. Town Hall in Serro heard about her and asked her to be a teacher. She said she couldn't, that she herself had only three years of schooling. But they insisted, so she said she'd do it until somebody told her she was doing it wrong. She did most of her teaching under a big tree. She taught the children how to read, write, add, subtract, multiply, divide. She had them memorize poetry. For twenty-seven years no one told her she was doing it wrong.

Dona Maria is a very devout woman. "Dos Santos" is the right middle name for her. Her house is populated with pictures and statues of saints, especially Santo Expedito, patron of rescues and emergencies, and São Gonçalo, protector of women. But she doesn't claim to have a favorite, except maybe the Virgin. Once she built a little sanctuary to the Virgin in a cave on the side of a mountain. She squeezed castor beans for oil and used it for a little lamp. She cleared a pathway to the sanctuary. People came to see why there was a little light on the side of the mountain. Alone in the night she prayed one thousand Our Ladies. Despite being up there alone in the dark, she was never bothered by snakes, scorpions, spiders, cougars, or men.

Soon after her child was born, another woman called her to pray for her during childbirth. All the woman's sisters had died in childbirth. Now, on the big day, all the midwives in town were drunk, so the woman figured she'd be better off trusting God. She called Dona Maria because she was very devout. Dona Maria went, God in tow. She told the woman that death had not passed her house yet. She noticed that the woman's feet were cold, so she warmed up a clay roof tile, wrapped it in cloth and put it under the woman's blanket. She prepared a basin of warm water and bathed the woman. She prepared the swaddling clothes. She prayed. The baby arrived without complication.

Because the other midwives were often drunk, mothers-to-be started calling Dona Maria. Thus began her education in obstetrics. She would ride her horse for hours over the mountains to help women in need. She asked for nothing but a blessing. She figured things out as she went along. One woman gave birth, but the placenta wouldn't present. Fortunately, Dona Maria had a chicken feather in her pocket, so she stuck it into the woman's throat The woman gagged, coughed, and the placenta presented.

Dona Maria's husband didn't want her helping other women. He said he hadn't married a midwife and didn't want to be married to one. She therefore had to do it secretly. She had to lie to him. She'd say she was going out to cut firewood. She'd go to a woman's house to borrow corn meal or something, but while she was there, she'd deliver a baby. Sometimes she followed up when other midwives had failed to deliver the goods. When she arrived and said a prayer, the baby would soon come along. The other midwives said she was wiser and more faithful than they. She also knew her herbs and roots. She learned a thing or two from João Nunes, the amateur dentist.

At one delivery, the woman was in great agony. Dona Maria arrived and began to pray the Salve Regina. The woman said, "Save me first, then pray," but Dona Maria said, "First we take care of God, then we take care of ourselves."

Dona Maria's midwifery was hard to keep secret from her husband. The whole community knew, of course, but they all kept it secret from her husband. If just one person blabbed, Milho Verde would be back in the hands of drunk midwives. But one day her husband's cousin threatened to tell him. Dona Maria told him to go ahead and do it. She didn't care anymore. Someone else told the cousin, however, that if he blabbed, he'd stick a revolver in his mouth and blow him away. The secret was kept. When she was 32 years old, her husband was apparently struck by lightning, which caused him to fall into a river and drown.

"I've suffered a lot," she says, "but I took advantage of life. God has been good to me."

She remarried and had one more child, who was younger than her grandson by her first son, a nephew older than his uncle.

Dona Maria's kitchen is a clutter of cheeses and crackers, well scrubbed utensils, coffee in a thermos bottle, people coming and going to drop things off, pick things up, touch base with the woman who brought them into the world. Flies, too, are at home here, mostly with interest in the cheese. While I talk with Dona Maria, another woman cooks lunch over the wood fire. The woman's son was Dona Maria's last delivery. Her second-to-last is here, too, a little girl in a T-shirt that says "Butterfly" on it. Her current husband, an old geezer with no teeth, his trousers rolled, does a lot of snuff from a tin he keeps in his pocket.

Chapter Seventeen

São Gonçalo do Rio das Pedras

The Estrada Real from Milho Verde to São Gonçalo do Rio das Pedras is a piece of cake, just over four miles from the Capela do Rosário to the Igreja do São Gonçalo. The road is generally level, the air cool and clear with altitude. The quartz pebbles in the sand of the road could be confused with diamonds, and several times I'm confused enough to pick one up and wonder how am I supposed to know this isn't a diamond? No doubt a lot of them are, millions and millions of carats passing under my feet, unnoticed, left behind. If they are diamonds, it's a good thing I don't know it. Even though I don't especially want diamonds, I wouldn't be able to pass them by. I'd feel obliged to gather them. I'd spend the whole day combing pebbles. I wouldn't get anywhere, and where I'm going is better than diamonds.

In 1967, a young Swiss woman named Anna and a German woman friend walked into São Gonçalo do Rio das Pedras and decided to stay. They bought an old house on the *praça* of the Igreja São Gonçalo and fixed it up. There they started a summer camp for kids from the city. They did a good job, earned a good name, charged a good price to give city kids the country experience. They took the kids on hikes of hundreds of kilometers, climbing mountains, camping near springs and streams. Anna remembers the meeting of urban and rural cultures in the *praça* and the consequent confusion of values as the city kids traded their Swiss knives and fancy mess kits for handmade sling-shots and drums. Good liberals both, the women made sure their camp always included a few less-than-rich kids.

Eight years later, along came a German named Martin Kuhn, who was teaching at a university in Rio de Janeiro. Anna married him. They ran the summer camp for a while, then opened the *Pousada* dos Cinco Amigos, a place better than diamonds if your preferences lean toward whole grain bread cooked in wood-fired mud-brick ovens and slathered in local butter and homemade mango jam. This is the only *pousada* in Minas Gerais that has bookshelves bearing the work of Cicero in French,

292

published in Paris in 1918; Führung and Geleit, printed in Austria in 1978; Characteres de De La Bruyete, published by Gillparzers Pamfliche Werke, Stuttgart; a 21-volume Meyers encyclopedia, printed in Leipzig in 1907; and many more, books in at least five languages, their authors ranging from Goethe to Nabakov to Defoe to Bellow to Jorge Amado. Not that someone like me could actually read most of these books, but I do enjoy being in their presence, especially in a room with a large fireplace, a big old farm table, hooked rugs, odd carvings, and grass baskets of river stones, dried flowers, colorful gourds, and whatever else Anna has recognized as beautiful.

So it's straight to the *Pousada* dos Cinco Amigos I go, aiming for the church tower as I come down into town, cross the bridge over the Córrego Prata, and trudge up a steep street of granite stones that have been lying there for hundreds of years, maybe because they're just too big to lift. I find the *pousada* just as I had left it a year and a half ago, when I felt so much at home that I forgot to pay Anna before I departed for Diamantina. The next day I sent her some cash and an explanatory letter, but I never knew whether it had reached her hands. So it is with trepidation that I walk into her living room, pack upon my back, and with all due humility remind her of who I am. To my relief she laughs, says she remembers the incident well and in fact recently re-read my letter of groveling apology.

Anna has one of the world's loveliest smiles, sincere and humble, reinforced by hairline creases in her cheeks and forehead that seem to trace a life of serious thought, complex emotions, and lots of sun. Her silver-brown hair parts in the middle and falls straight to her neck. Her sharp blue eyes are sharp enough to see things that other people can't. Her face is unmarred by cosmetics. She's been in São Gonçalo for a long time, long enough to see the village emerge from the dark ages before electricity to the age where a telephone company would have the capitalistic audacity to try to erect a telephone microwave tower in the yard of a church so old that no one knows when it was built, except that it had to be before 1787 because that's the last time the ceiling was painted. The phone company, Telemar, tried to pull a fast one, driving into town and beginning construction without asking anyone. The church yard was the only place the tower could go, they said. Most people were delighted. São Gonçalo had only one telephone, the one at Ademil's bar, where Ademil himself would pass a telephone through a little hole between his office behind the bar and a booth where the caller could sit in privacy. Ademil would time the call and charge accordingly. With the new tower, everyone who could afford a phone could have one.

Anna was outraged that they were going to build a naked steel tower alongside a mud-and-wattle church. The same thing had happened in Tapera, where a tower stands within spitting distance of the Igreja do Rosário. The local town council member was all in favor of the tower. But "someone," Anna says with fingers indicating quotes around the word and a wink shifting the letters into italics, notified the IPHAN cultural protection agency. Within two weeks, breathtaking speed in a land of glacial bureaucracy, IPHAN put a stop to the project. After a brief flurry of corporate lies about the absolute necessity of building on that particular site, the company discovered a nearby hill that would serve just as well, albeit at the extra cost of an access road and power line. It's still an eyesore well within town limits but at least it's a little better than the intended blasphemy.

Anna was therefore not especially sorry to hear that the new public phone across the street, in front of Ademil's bar, was allowing people to make calls for free. Half the town queued up to call people all over Brazil, relatives in the United States, friends in Japan and France. Anna kind of liked that, but she wasn't too happy when her own phone, too, started acting up. She couldn't dial out, and she was receiving a lot of wrong numbers. By bizarre coincidence, many of them were trying to call the public phone in front of Ademil's bar. In an avalanche of belated epiphany, she realized that her line was crossed with that of the public phone. People were calling the whole world, day and night, on Anna's tab. She's not too sure the lines got crossed by accident. The local Telemar guy knows her and the story of the tower. This had happened shortly before I arrived in town, so the issue has not been resolved. To keep her service from being shut off, she has to pay her phone bill and argue about it later.

Anna has spent her entire adult life trying to get São Gonçalo to appreciate itself, its own beauty, and the wisdom of its simple people. Bit by bit people are becoming more aware. What irritates her most is the practice of dumping food, paper, plastic, cans and other trash on the side of the street, setting it afire and letting it smolder for a day or two. The smell goes beyond bad. It taints the nostrils and rips at the throat. "They don't even smell it," Anna says. "How can you get them to improve their lives if they don't even know how bad their lives are?" Her soft and loving face sharpens with ripping anger when she sees people too crude to appreciate beauty. She cites the case of a woman who dumped disposable diapers in the street and every few days went out and got them burning. People like that, she says, aren't likely to notice anything wrong with a phone tower next to a church.

And another thing: the noise of music on holidays. For celebrations in the *praça*, just in front of Anna's *pousada*, huge speakers pound out music until almost dawn. A *danceteria* on the other side of the *praça* plays disco music all night. The owner denies that it can be heard outside of his building. Anna has had guests leave her inn after a night or two without sleep. She has complained to Serro town council member Jilson, the same guy who wanted the telephone tower next to the church, but he says that loud music is necessary to attract people to São Gonçalo on the holidays. He can't grasp the concept of people seeking peace and quiet and bringing money when they come, money that trickles down into many pockets.

Even though eighty percent of the town (by Anna's estimate) is against the noise, when it comes time for a massive complaint, they back down, don't really see it as a problem, figure they can put up with it until it goes away. This is probably because they've remembered that their complaints will create enemies, sometimes whole families of enemies.

Another thing that bothers her: Tourists who come to town, party all night, then sleep in their cars right in front of her inn. They toss their garbage into the street, then leave town without spending any money.

And another thing: People build ugly concrete additions to their old houses, ruining the ambiance of the town.

And another thing: School teachers lead their children in punky pop songs that glorify violence and demean women.

And another thing: the television in Ademil's bar, turned up loud 'til all hours of the night. Anna and her guests have to listen to the passion of the *novelas* and the repulsive excitement of the commercials.

Many years ago, Anna and Martin helped found the Associação Cultural e Comunitária Sempre Viva. (Sempre Viva is a wildflower indigenous to the region, its name meaning "always alive.") This is the Association that built the bathrooms in Três Barras. It also has a nursery school run by the Clube das Mães, the Mother's Club, and a little workshop where women make hooked rugs, a skill Anna taught them. The Association always lacks money, and now the situation is worse because an incompetent bookkeeper ran up a big tab at the gas station in Serro and never paid it off. The Association's only revenue comes from rug sales, the services of a truck the Association owns, and a token membership fee of one real per month, which doesn't add up to much. At the moment, the nursery school can't afford to pay all its teachers. Someone's going to have to get laid off.

Aparecida Souza Ribeiro, president of the Association and wife of Ademil, says the Association would like to do more things, but the lack of money always stops them. They want to get a machine to flatten cans. They have a whole recycling plan in place. Kids will bring cans to certain locations on their way to school on certain days of the week. A truck will pick the stuff up, crush the cans, and take them to the town of Curvelo, where they could be sold at a break-even price. The machine costs just US$ 2,000. Aparecida would also like to know more about the process that turns plastic bottles into something that can be woven into textiles. She has seen socks and sweaters made of plastic. If São Gonçalo could turn soda bottles into clothes, no one would burn plastic in the streets, the unemployed would have something to do, and people would have clothes that last a long, long time. For now, all the Association wants is the machine that crushes cans, low technology but not low enough that anyone but the government can afford it. To get government funding, they need elected officials who object to the smell of burning garbage. Unfortunately, there are no such elected officials in São Gonçalo, so the Association just makes plans and waits.

A woman unscathed by global capitalism, Helena Sigueira Torres, lives in an ancient house right next door to Anna Kuhne's inn. Helena is a storyteller of some renown. A German woman from São Paulo came to hear some stories and published them in Germany in a very fancy book of the world's fairy tales. Three women came from the state of Goiás to hear stories for a research project. Someone came from Divinópolis, MG, to gather stories she could tell to patients in a nursing home. I went to hear stories about her life.

Dona Helena, short, center-heavy, happy, sixty-something, her face a smile of bliss, has me come right into her little house and have a seat on the bench of the little table that all but fills her little dining room. Her great-grandfather built this house of straw, sticks, and mud. I presume it is invulnerable to wolves. The clay roof tiles have been there since Helena was a little girl. They're black from the smoke of the fires her father used to build on the earthen floor of the dining room so the kids could sit around and hear stories. That was in the days before electricity, before television. I can just barely imagine the magic of a campfire on a dining room floor, the vivid images in the coals and flames and shadows as father and grandmother and aunts told stories.

Helena remembers the good-old days of fires on the dining room floor and walking to the well to fetch water in 20-liter cans she carried on her head. Until 1949, all imported goods — goods imported from outside of town — came in on the backs of mules. After the road was put in from Serro to Diamantina, the people of São Gonçalo had access to a little medical help. If they needed to go to the hospital, they could send a telegram to Diamantina, twenty miles to the north, requesting that a taxi come pick the patient up.

She remembers the concept of "milk brothers." By tradition, a newborn baby's first milk will be taken from the breast of another mother. The babies are then milk brothers, another thread through the warp and woof of the community tapestry. Unlike blood relatives, in-laws and god-parents, a milk brother is made almost at random, the available choices defined by whoever is currently nursing.

Life was hard back then, Helena says, but people were healthier. They had no running water, no toilets, no bathtubs, no medicines besides roots, herbs, and *cachaça*. But everything they ate was natural. What little they bought came home in bamboo baskets or sacks woven of string or tree bark. They had no garbage. None. They therefore had none of the ill health associated with the smoke of burning plastic or the mosquitoes born in abandoned cans and bottles. They didn't have television, but children knew how to pay attention. All you had to do was build a fire on the dining room floor. Today, Helena won't share her stories with children. They squirm too much. She tells adults and lets them tell the children. Children can't sit through catechism, either. They're losing their faith and, with it, their morality. On the other hand, women don't die in childbirth because they're depending on midwives with chicken feathers. They can go to the hospital and get a cesarean. It all balances out, Helena says, her face a dreamy smile. "Back then, we did what we had to do. Today we do what we can do, and everything goes well."

Anna gets word that somebody is cutting trees, or maybe even clear-cutting, around a spring just outside of town, a spring she's never heard of before. Springs and wetlands are protected here, at least in theory, but it's a theory not often put into practice. Local politics, including the kind that have nothing to do with government, complicates issues. To turn someone in means making an enemy. Anna already has many such enemies, and they speak badly of her. When one of her guests stopped in at the danceteria, the owner of the place spoke all kinds of horrors about her. But Anna hates to see people making things worse in São Gonçalo, which already runs short of water during the dry season. We decide to go look for the spring and get some facts about what's happening. Then Anna will figure out what to do about it without getting shot. Maybe she'll have FUNIVALE make an impersonal, institutional complaint, which is the least they can do, given all the water they use for their hothouses.

So we put on shoes and broad-brimmed hats and hike out of town, down a street strewn with rocks. The rocks soon break down to a sandy lane. We pass a classic case of stupidity, a nice new house surrounded by beautiful flowers. The back of the house looks out over a stunning vista tens of miles deep. The residents have built their water tank, a stack of bricks with a big, blue basin atop it, in such a way that it completely blocks the view out their kitchen window. "Why?" she asks, shaking he head hard enough to make her hair whip around. "Tell me, why?"

As we turn right toward Grota Seca, the road goes up across a hill into dense old forest. On the uphill side, to our left, we can hear the chop of an ax or two. On the downhill side, beyond somem trees, an area has been cleared. We can't see where the spring might be.

We walk farther up, then turn left on a path that takes us to a barbed wire fence. We climb through it, holding the strands open for each other. I realize that while other men have fetishes for women in pumps or leather or cheerleader outfits, I love a woman who can thread herself through a barbed wire fence.

From the highest point on this hill we can see hundreds of square miles of Minas Gerais. To the north we can barely make out the radio tower just outside of Diamantina, all the way out at the horizon, beyond several hills and two rounded mountains reminiscent of Corcovado, where the giant statue of Christ stands, or Pão de Açucar, the Sugar Loaf Mountain that stands above Rio de Janeiro's Guanabara Bay. Tomorrow I'll have to walk past all those hills and mountains. I don't see how. It seems too far even to drive in a day. In the other direction we can see the Pico do Itambé, which I've been gradually walking past ever since Itambé do Mato Dentro, almost a month ago. In all the vast area around us, only one place is cleared and planted. Most of the rest is gray rock, tan-green scrub, or dark green forest that has probably never been cleared. Here and there the purple flowers of the *quaresma* and the yellow flowers of the *ipé-amarelo* beautify the green like amethysts and topaz.

We return to town on a path that runs across the side of a rocky ridge. Anna tells me how she likes to go hiking alone so she can stop and listen to the birds and the wind, the near silence. The beauty of this place overwhelms her. Though she speaks German, Portuguese, French and English, she has no words for the beauty, and though she's a painter, she has no capacity to paint a picture of it. She has no way to do anything with it except to experience it. She also likes to take people with her so they can see it and know what she has seen. I ask her when she knew São Gonçalo do Rio das Pedras, not Bern, Switzerland, was her place in the world. She tells me a long story.

In 1991, she returned to Switzerland for medical treatment that would take a few years. Martin stayed in São Gonçalo. She recovered from her problem, then studied nursing because São Gonçalo needed someone who really new medicine. She'd already been the practitioner of last resort, the one people went to when the homeopaths ran out of cures. She had a good relationship with a pharmacist in Diamantina. They devised a system by which she should could visit a sick person, gather the necessary symptoms and information, call it in to the pharmacy and have the appropriate medicine sent to São Gonçalo. She remembers one case where the pharmacy could not help. A dirt-poor woman had just given birth to her eighth child in her little mud house. Her husband was a drunk who did nothing in the way of housework or caring for children. Anna doesn't know exactly how it happened, but somehow a pig got hold of the baby and ate it. Ana had to take the remains to the police in Serro and persuade them that there was no point in punishing the woman.

So Anna took a one-year program in nursing, then got a job in a hospital in Switzerland. She had her life pretty well planned out. She was going to work until she was 64, save her money, retire, then return to live out her days in São Gonçalo. But something went wrong. Her body became very painful for no diagnosable reason. Her flanks got stiff and hard. She could barely walk, soon barely move. A friend, a nurse who dabbled in Buddhism, said that her problem was in her spirit and that if she didn't get it straightened out, she would soon be paralyzed.

That was when she realized that what she really wanted to do was live in São Gonçalo. She finished out her contract at the hospital and returned to Brazil. Here she discovered that Martin had fallen in love with someone else. They separated. She kept the *pousada*. Soon her illness cleared up. Now she can hike through the mountains all day.

Hike through the mountains all day is pretty much what she does the next day when I leave for Diamantina.

Journey on the Estrada Real

The road, over twenty or twenty-two miles long depending on which sign, guide, or map you believe, begins with a big loop around to the west before it straightens out and heads north. Anna knows of a trail that cuts across that loop, though she's never seen it. We decide to look for it. She'll accompany me to the point where it starts. It's going to be a painfully long walk, so one of Anna's employees will send my backpack ahead on the morning bus. The plan is to set out at dawn. I start off the day by misreading my watch and getting up at 3:15 instead of 5:15, but I get it right the second time and find Anna making sandwiches of whole grain bread and cheese. She wraps them neatly in cellophane and puts them in a plastic bag.

And off we go under a dark-blue dawn, down the Estrada Real for a mile or so, across a concrete bridge high over the Jequitinhonha where the rivera narrows and swirls over dimpled rock.

Anna says the water looks pretty clean, though it's a bit cloudy at the moment, probably from diamond miners panning upstream. Then we turn up into the woods on the real Estrada Real, the old Estrada Real. The first fifty meters is paved with boulders of granite laid down by slaves about twenty years before George Washington was born. Anna notices that some of the smaller cobbleboulders have been dug up and taken away, probably by local folk who have nothing lighter to do for a living. The pavement soon peters out to become a trail so narrow that we have to push aside branches to get through. The trail wouldn't even be identifiable if it hadn't been cleared last year for a group of horse riders who were following the trail that Spix and Martius had followed in 1817. Peasants use the trail, too, and Anna picks up the little trash they've left behind. We may be taking a shortcut, but as it rises into the mountains, it's surely more exhausting than the road that goes around the mountains. What word for the views of hills and clouds and distant ridges? Stunning. Astounding. Breathtaking. I know why Anna is starting her day off with a five-mile hike. There are no words for the things we see. She has to show me so I know.

We emerge from the woods and arrive at pasture surrounded by a barbed wire fence with a gate. The main trail seems to run suspiciously westward. We kind of want to go north. We're aiming for a farm, the Fazenda Córrego do Mel — Honey Creek Farm — where we hope to get directions to the rest of the trail. But if we go too far west, we'll end up on the road. Half sure we're wrong, we follow a cow path down through the rocky pasture. The pasture is overgrown with ferns, which Anna tells me are a veritable weed that takes over open land. This always happens. Peasants clear more land than they can handle, then abandon it. The ferns take over, and then it's almost impossible to get grass to grow again.

The cow path doesn't seem to be taking us toward anything besides, at best, a cow. We wander back up to the fence, try another cow path, back-track, climb up on a big rock to see what we can see. When two dogs come along, descending from the gate we just came through, we interpret their arrival as indication of either a trail up above the pasture or the farm down below it. We decide to walk downhill.

And there we find the Fazenda Córrego do Mel. It's a nice little farm that's doing a good job of taking care of itself. They have a herd of cows, a field of corn, some sugar cane, a patch of manioc, a decent garden, a good stand of banana plants, several outbuildings of bamboo and thatch, more than enough chickens, and fences in good repair. Anna knows the owner, a beefy and very animated man with dark skin, a booming voice, a gentle handshake, a cowboy hat of straw, his chest as big as the sail of a ship, his shirt unbuttoned to the gut. His big, loose mouth jabbers in excited peasant dialect. He and Anna review what's happening with his family, friends, cows and crops. He's a fine model of a human being, big and strong, friendly as can be, getting by in the outback. He knows where the trail is, and he directs a kid named Valdimir to take us there.

Valdimir is about 14 years old, a fourth-grade drop-out who's helpful, humble, and moderately smart in the ways of the place where he lives. He takes us up a narrow path pressed deep by hooves. It becomes as rocky as a stream bed. A dense forest closes in over us. It's cool and humid in there, a place to expect to see a snake. I take up a length of bamboo that's about right for a walking stick, good for perhaps warding off a snake, and certainly for clearing cobwebs from the grass and branches that reach into the path.

We cross a stream with a tricky little leap from a rock to a rock. On the other side we find an old *rancho*, a way station of the old *tropeiros*. It consists of an old house, its doors and shutters well shut, an old barn, and an area of short grass, a lawn for parking pack animals. When Anna asks who owns it, Valdimir only says that his family is watching it. Anna thinks it would be a perfect place for a little *pousada*, a place where hikers could rest and get a good meal. But hikers don't come along every day, or even every month. A family would have to live there, sustain themselves with a little farm while they waited for someone with sore feet and a little cash. But what a great place to live while waiting, beside a clear stream under some trees along the oldest, and, here, least-used road on the continent.

From there we cut up across an area with no path whatsoever until we intersect the slimmest of trails. We keep heading uphill, passing outcrops the size of castles. Their unlikely shapes look like huge scapulas, towering grave stones, beat-up shoe boxes, craggy ghosts of rock dressed in lichen and amulets of flowered brush. Valdimir's brother and some other kids were up on one of these stacks of rock recently, hunting *mocó*, a jumpy little rodent resembling a guinea pig. The *mocó* jumped from a rock to a rock. Valdimir's brother jumped after him, missed his footing, and fell to his death.

At some unremarkable point on the side of the mountain, Valdimir points the way to go and tells us there can be no error. He overestimates our intelligence. Error is well within our capacity.

We climb to a high, level meadow of thin grass and confusing junctions of cow paths. It's a beautiful place of sweeping views. The most distant hills are so far that we can hardly distinguish them from the late-morning haze. The sky is trite with evenly spaced clouds on a background of undiluted blue. The meadow teems with sempre viva and bolinha flowers. The sempre viva are tiny dry buds on long, slender stems, prized as decorations. The *bolinhas* are astonishing star-bursts of thread-thin spines with minute buds at their ends. Bolinhas must be appreciated in the field, and not fields easily found. If you pick them, their spines almost immediately wilt and fall off.

We get a little lost as we wander down all the wrong cow paths, but it's a great place to get lost. I wouldn't mind being lost here forever. It seems a place where cows get lost and people never go, but sure enough, as we probe to the east, we come across a man and a woman as purely peasant as people can be. The man is maneuvering a squeaky, rusty little wheelbarrow through the grass. The woman carries a pruning hook on a long handle. He wears ratty old shoes. She wears the standard sandals. Their handshakes are as soft and gentle as cotton. The man holds one hand to his heart and smiles as if the Mother of God Herself is smoothing his hair. He has only one tooth. The woman gawks with an uncomprehending squint. They are taking a bag of corn to the Fazenda Córrego do Mel to have it ground into *fubá*. I can't imagine how they will get their wheelbarrow down the rocky path through the woods. They will surely spend all day going to the farm and returning to wherever it is in the hills they live. The economics of it perplexes me. How can two people survive if it takes them all day to produce nothing more than ten pounds of corn flour? How little can these people live on? Why do they look happier than anyone – anyone — I know?

In a rural dialect both slurred and rackety they explain which way we have to go to find the road. The instructions don't involve a trail. We just go that way, up over a rise, across a field, through a barbed wire fence, onto a dirt farm road, and around a rocky ledge until we see the sandy-white straightaway of the Estrada Real, a kilomeeter distant, beyond cascades of boulders and sheets of sculpted bedrock.

311

Journey on the Estrada Real

Anna hadn't meant to come this far. We've walked six or eight miles or more. I have twelve or fifteen to go, and so does she if she goes back by the road. She opts for the road because she might be able to thumb a ride. She wants to get back by four o'clock because she's supposed to meet with her band of flutists, some twenty-odd children learning to play plastic recorders. Anna is the conductor, so not much fluting will happen unless she's there. We spread out a little picnic on an expanse of granite, eat our little sandwiches, drink the last of our water. Anna tells me I will come to clean water if I angle northward toward the road. She knows because she and Martin and a bunch of kids camped there once. She's going to follow the farm road southward until it meets the real road. We hug. I kiss her cheek, tell her I adore her *pousada* and her. Then I go northwest and she goes south.

I have to walk about a mile to reach the road. The terrain is fascinating, smooth rock that seems to have been poured there, some of it slick with water and algae. Boulders seem to have rolled in from nowhere. Outcrops stand as if they had erupted from the earth and frozen. The path sparkles with quartz. It rises into a meadow of stiff, pale grass. A woman is there, knee-deep in grass, an arm holding a bunch of sempre vivas as if they were a baby. A kid sits nearby, fooling around with a sling-shot. A nasty little dog, part Chihuahua, part pit bull, part rat and at least half alligator, comes after me, his little incisors mincing viciously. I defend myself with thrusts and parries of my water bottle, holding it down in front of the dog's nasty little face. The boy does nothing until the woman yells at him. He shoots a stone at the dog, gets a yipe out of it, buying me enough time to slip by.

The woman apologizes. She is so beautiful with her arm of wildflowers. She's picking them to sell in Diamantina, she says. There's no work there, no gold left in the streams this time of year, no diamonds left. She gets two *reais*, abut 80 cents, for a kilo of sempre vivas. Ten or twenty of the flowers might weigh a gram. Yet this woman doesn't seem hungry, and her kid doesn't seem inspired to do anything but wait for her to finish working and take him home. Her life is hard, no doubt, hand-to-mouth, toothaches constant, no end to troubles, no hope of anything better than rain. But what miracle of reincarnation might have blessed her with the job of picking wildflowers in a meadow on a high plateau? What did she do to deserve this? In a former self did she waste a life at an investment brokerage, working furiously all day for an armful of ephemeral cash? Or is she being rewarded for a life that spread peace and comfort? I don't know how reincarnation works, whether it's a matter of just deserts or a balancing out of prior pains and pleasures, nor do I know enough about this woman's life to declare her in a state of grace. She has a lazy kid and a nasty dog and a long walk home with a load of flowers which at best will weigh a lot. But her job at the moment, the only one she can find, is a picture of paradise.

My job's not so bad, either. At the moment, all I have to do is keep walking. I do this with my head turned to the right. The view for the next two hours is a tableau of geographic and atmospheric drama. At the far end of the valley that reaches all the way back to São Gonçalo, a rain shower graces the sky as it drapes purple gauze along the ground. I am on the other side of the mountains I saw yesterday with Anna when we looked off toward Diamantina. I've walked all the way around them. I have two hours to decide that the only way I can describe one of the mountains is as a fist that has punched up through earth. The other could be described as an angel food cake that didn't work out. The thin pale line of the Estrada Real winds wide around the western edge of the valley. I just can't believe how far I've walked. I tell my feet; they say they know.

For two hours I pass no houses, no barbed wire, no sign of cattle, and no cars go by. A lush meadow of grass and flowers rises to my left, another descends from my right. I pass a single tree that bears pink flowers that rival the rose. I pass a single white orchid nudging up from a shady place under a bush. The sun is hot and direct, but the breeze is constant and close to cool. I have hope that the little rain shower will come my way. I drain my water bottle but soon come to a stream that slinks down a winding channel, passes under the road and hushes down a ten-foot cliff of pink rock. I go down to the stream, sit on a bank of gravel, fill my bottle, soak my feet. It's good.

The guidebook refers to a bar called Cantinho do Céu — Nook of Heaven — beside the Ribeirão do Inferno — Hell Gulch — some six miles outside of Diamantina. It sounds like a really, really, really, really nice place to sit and drink a really, really, really, really cold beer, possibly even spend the night. I don't think of much else for a long, long time. I waste a lot of scenery just picturing that frosty bottle, imagining the effervescent wetness, the mild euphoria, the birth of sublimely useless thoughts on the significance of a bar called Heaven on the banks of Hell.

Alas, the Nook of Heaven is closed, and Hell Gulch isn't something I want to stick my feet in. I keep going, now vowing to stop at the first bar I come to, one of few vows I'm confident I can keep. Soon I'm passing naked little concrete block houses that would probably fit, depth, width and height, in my living room at home. One — just one — is lush with back-yard plantation of banana, coffee, oranges, limes, manioc, collards. A young woman in a blue dress scrubs clothes in a concrete tub behind the house. I admire her industriousness. Transplanted to Manhattan, she'd probably make a killing in real estate. Left here, which is surely what will happen, she'll probably end up picking wildflowers for a living.

The first place with cold beer that I come to isn't the Bar São Tomé I'm hoping for. The São Tomé is the end of the line of Diamantina's municipal bus. I want to reach the São Tomé, perhaps indulge in some celebratory suds, then grab that bus, get off at the bus station, go to the *guarda volume* to bail out my pack, which according to plan is already sitting there waiting for me, and then head for the Hotel Dália.

But the concrete shack with the roof of corrugated asbestos isn't the São Tomé. It isn't a bar of any name. It's just a bar, and barely that, no more than a dispensary of Kaiser that can be consumed at any of three tables that say Antarctica on them or taken home for transfer to a clean glass. Besides the three tables, the bar has a short counter of concrete blocks, a refrigerator with a poster of the Kaiser chick in a t-t-t-t-tight and in a certain sense effective little bathing suit, and four shelves that hold a scant inventory of *cachaça*, Chiclets, lollipops, a pack of Sudans open for single sales, and a whole bunch of dusty little bags of popcorn embalmed with God-knows-what miracle of modern science. Here I sit to take my requisite beer, a 600 ml bottle that's really meant for two people. The first glass is good and cold and wet, but the rest, it soon occurs to me, is a little too early in my sojourn. The owner of the bar tells me I still have another hour's walk to the São Tomé. That's a long way to lug a belly of beer.

But what are my other choices? Hold out for squatter's rights to a table in a bar with no name? Stagger back to the industrious little woman in the blue dress and see if she's already married?

I slog on. I reach the São Tomé. It's not only a bar but a regular restaurant with its own little fliers fancied up on a computer, black on white in eight different fonts with clip art of a chef's hats, fork, knife and spoon, salt and pepper shakers, a roast turkey, a municipal bus. It lists every possible reason to take the bus to the end of the line:

> Bar Tome
>
> Picturesque place
>
> for you and your family.
>
> A bar in the tradition of the best in typical home-made meals offering clientele delicious dishes such as:
>
> Country chicken a lá chicken blood
>
> Pork ribs with gooseberries
>
> Complete *feijoada*
>
> Pork with *tropeiro* beans and collards
>
> Ragout á la Chica
>
> Fern tips with pork.
>
> All of these delicious and diverse home-style appetizers accompanied by the best aperitifs.
>
> Tomé is your bar

Journey on the Estrada Real

temple of good eating
come who believes
(Paulo Matta)
New World Bus Stop at the Door
Straw Bridge – Diamantina – Minas
Gerais
Beside the Chica da Silva Camping
Area
On the road to Salitre Cave

It's a *bar-restaurante* trying just as hard as it can.
The owner insists and insists that I have a meal, but I
can't do it. Not yet. I drink my water and keep an eye on
the bus stop across the street. That's the end of the road,
right over there.

Chapter Eighteen

Diamantina

In Diamantina each evening at six o'clock the Catedral Metropolitana rings a bell six times and then plays Ave Maria out a set of loudspeakers. This is the hour when people are leaving work, going home, walking while thinking about food and what to do after dark. In surprising numbers they come into streets. One reason they walk is that cars can barely toddle over the old slabs of granite paving. They walk in relatively straight lines that cut across the cathedral *praça* and take sight-lines down narrow streets that curve around things that haven't been there for hundreds of years. Only their need to greet a lot of others walking on the street or leaning on window sills breaks their homeward stroll. The common salutation is to raise the eyebrows and ask, *"Tudo tranquilo?"* The common response is to smile and say, *"Beleza."* In Diamantina I always book into the Hotel Dália because from a certain second floor window I can watch all this happen.

By seven o'clock the sky begins its shift to indigo. Street lamps attached to the baroque buildings come on. The tone of the talk in the streets turns to *tchiaos* and *boa noites*, good-byes and good wishes for good evenings. After a brief readjustment of cars, traffic tapers to a snooze. You can hear the soft shuffle of people walking down the street in sandals. The place is so quiet, so beautifully lit, the streets so stony, steep and curved, it feels like a place of make-believe.

If there's one thing the United Nations has done right in the past few years, it was to encourage this diamond of a city to straighten itself out, clean itself up. While São Gonçalo was barely beating off a cell phone tower beside its church, and Tapera never even bothered trying, Diamantina put its utility wires underground and in every way possible returned itself to its nineteenth century condition, minus the mule dung in the streets. The town thus became a UNESCO World Heritage site. The honor has saved the town from the otherwise inevitable ravages of unfettered commercial development. In time, the Heritage title may nudge the town out of its natural state and into the thematic hype of a tourist spot owned and operated by investors raising conditions closer to first-world standards. Until then, however, it's a place not quite yet geared up for the relatively benevolent tourism industry that the town is betting on. No one is hawking Diamantina T-shirts. There are no racks of post cards on the sidewalks, no golden arches in the sky. Advertising is kept off the streets. The many historical sites offer little written information. The tourism office has no sign, and even if it did, it has virtually nothing to offer a tourist. The few foreigners who find this town are received with the friendly awkwardness of restaurateurs and hoteliers who don't speak English but are adept at interpreting broken Spanish and well-intentioned gestures.

*　　*　　*

On the evening I arrive, a young woman of bright eyes and irresistible smile stops me in the street. Her name is Cristina Figueiredo. She has heard, from a friend who saw me in the Bar do Pescoço back in São Gonçalo do Rio das Pedras, that I am hiking the Estrada Real. Cristina is a reporter with TV Diamantina, which broadcasts locally. She'd like to interview me. Though looking as worn out and unkempt as Domingos the hermit, I agree. I meet her the next day at the TV station, an old house on the *praça do mercado*, which once bustled with mules and merchants. She sits me down at a table. Her cameraman sets up a digital camera no bigger than a paperback book. She asks me what I'm doing, then tilts a microphone to my face. I tell her I'm writing about a beautiful culture all but unknown to the world, a way of life that may be doomed in the face of global economics. She asks me what Diamantina should do to divulge its beauty to the world. I tell her to do nothing.

It was poverty that kept this place beautiful long enough to be saved. With the gold and diamonds gone, the region has few natural resources, and it's inconveniently distant from big cities. Since the early nineteenth century, the people have had little to sell and less with which to buy. Business and industry have shown little interest in coming here. There's been no reason to replace antique houses with strip malls, chain restaurants and parking lots. The town of 1830 was still here when they decided to preserve what they had and say no to what they could have. They retained their beauty without getting cute. None of the beauty is imported, artificial, commercial, or thematic. Diamantina hasn't had to follow the course of New Orleans pretending to be Cajun, of San Francisco fabricating pretensions of a lingering gold rush, of Boston flaunting icons of patriots, tea parties and beans. It isn't like Minas Gerais' other main baroque town, Ouro Preto, which is beautiful, to be sure, and not artificially cute. Like Diamantina, Ouro Preto holds the title of Heritage of Humanity, but Ouro Preto is a university town now, and the local-born are a quiet minority.

Diamantina's roots go back a long way, and deep. Two billion years ago, a continent called Gondwanaland broke into several big pieces, one of which would become Africa, another South America. On a subterranean pool of magma they floated apart. Water filled the space between the new continents. After a few hundred million years, they floated back together and gently collided. The collision raised the mountains of Minas Gerais and created tremendous heat and pressure deep in the earth. As the continents crunched against each other, they heaved up the Serra do Espinhaço, the serpentine mountain range that runs up the middle of Minas Gerais at three to four thousand feet. Deep below, the heat and pressure of the collision pressed carbon into diamonds. Then, as the continents recoiled from the megamillennial shock, the subterranean magma gushed to the surface, carrying diamonds with it.

Millions of years later, in 1714, in a gulch called *Arraial* do Tijuco, Portuguese adventurers came upon the little chunks of crystallized carbon. Until then, diamonds had been found only in India and the Far East. Tijuco was rich, but, being a mining camp, it wasn't a decent place to bring women. Diamonds aren't of much use if you don't have women, so the men had their slaves build a city at a comfortable distance from the camp. They called it Diamantina.

João Fernandes de Oliveira ran one of the most successful operations at Tijuco. He arrived from Portugal in 1753 and, as foreign men have been doing ever since, soon fell in love with a Brazilian girl. The object of his obsession was the daughter of a farmer and his slave, the vain and seductive Chica da Silva. Civil and religious law prohibited the marriage of a white and a *mulata*, but nothing could stop him from building her a nice house a block from his. He succumbed to her every desire, bowed to her insane jealousy. He built her a church. She bore him thirteen children.

The church, the Igreja da Nossa Senhora do Carmo, is right across the street from de Oliveira's house, squeezed onto what was an empty lot in a residential neighborhood, rising from street level without the plaza and elbow room found around most churches in Minas. He built it there for his own convenience. The architecture, however, was designed for the convenience of his famously picky Chica. In unique aberration to the standards of the region, the single bell tower rises from the back of the church, behind the altar, putting the bell an extra block farther from Chica's house. Rumor still holds that she demanded a little distance between her Sunday bed and the annoying ding-dong-ding.

The rear bell tower was also a legal loophole. The churches of Diamantina were designated to social classes.

The Nossa Senhora do Rosário was for blacks. Nosso Senhor do Bonfim was for soldiers. Nossa Senhora da Mercês was for *mulato*s. The São Francisco de Assis was for poor whites, and the Nossa Senhora do Carmo was for rich whites -- the likes of João Fernando de Oliveira...but not his beloved concubine. By law, no one of color could enter any church beyond the bell tower that normally stands at the front, near the door. For Chica to enter the Carmo — and penetrate white society — she needed a rich white church with a tower at the back. As usual, she got what she wanted, a church built to her specs.

Maybe that social penetration explains why this is the only church in Latin America, perhaps in the world, with paintings of angels demonstrably female. All others are asexual. If you sit in a pew, tilt your head all the way back and look at the right two angels in José Soares de Araujo's celestial ceiling painting, you can see two cherubim with frocks casually lifted, revealing what all due scholastic attention has confirmed to be vaginal labia.

The rear bell tower also allowed a black organist, Lobo de Mesquita, to perform in the church. The organ was placed in the center of the loft behind the congregation. The organist sat behind a wall so that the congregation could not see that he was a black. The wall had a little hole in it so the organist could see the ceremony and know when to play. Mesquita was the adopted son of the church's priest, who taught him music. He not only played *música sacra* but composed it. One fine Sunday he played a piece that suddenly shifted into an African tempo. He was charged with heresy and run out of town. He fled to Ouro Preto, then to Rio de Janeiro, where he was respected as a composer and musician — but only because he powdered his face white and wore a wig and gloves so that no one would know his race, a veritable preincarnation of Michael Jackson. Out of costume, in the streets, no one recognized him. He died an anonymous pauper. Today, though his name is known and his music still extant, there are no commercial recordings of his compositions.

It's a little too late to do Oliveira, Chica and Mesquita any good, but for whatever it's worth, South America and Africa are again floating toward each other on the seas of subterranean magma, slowly but at least moving in the right direction.

The Igreja do Nosso Senhor do Bonfim dos Militares is a little less exciting than Oliveira's Carmo, but as every church in town, it has its history. Built for the military class, its interior is as tight as the hull of a Portuguese man-o-war and its walls tilt out slightly. The altar and the wall behind it, like South America and Africa, bear matching tectonic scars. They were separated when Rome asked priests to face their congregation during the sacrament. The altar was ripped from the wall so the priests could stand behind it. The icon of Christ of the crucifix behind the altar has no fingers, and its torso seems not just tortured but deformed. The sculptor is unknown, but in all likelihood it was the leprotic Aleijadinho who, with carving tools strapped to the stumps of his arms, created an image in his own likeness.

When I visit the Bonfim during an evening mass, the faithful more than fill it. As many fit inside as outside on the brief, raised patio. The faithful outside raise their arms toward the icons inside. They sing to the music of a drum, a tambourine, and an accordion. They kneel on the stone. They pray and cry at the gilded icons, and they feel better for it. Their faith in God and sacred icons brings them more happiness than others find in their faith in television and commercial icons. I wonder which will win in the end – God or television? It's hard to say which is winning now.

In Diamantina, I'd say God still holds a lead. Sure, everybody has a TV, but the churches still fill to overflowing, and a good portion of the population still finds bliss at the sight of Jesus, Mary, and the assorted saints. The churches are by far the most magnificent and beautiful things in Diamantina, though nothing more magnificent has been built since the end of slavery. The churches are works of art and craft that will likely never be matched. I spend most of my time here wandering from church to church to study the altars, rest in the pews, listen to the hymns, look at the people. They come in bearing their crosses of dead children, pains here and there, mouths without teeth, exhausting labor, lives entertained by nothing but nature and each other. But at the sight of their Jesus on His cross, or His Mother with her tilted head and gentle little smile, they are filled and satisfied. They receive the power to love people who would steal from the poor if the poor had something to steal, and they themselves would sooner go hungry than steal.

I'm alone in the cool cavern of the Igreja Metropolitana, the biggest and newest church in town, the *matriz*, when an wiry old black man comes in. He's as dressed up as he'll ever get, I'm sure, with sky-blue pants and a clean, white, long-sleeve shirt buttoned up to his neck. He picks out a pew, crosses himself, and with the slow soreness of someone who's been working hard every day of his life, he lowers himself to his knees. Before he begins to pray, he lays his crooked, callused hand on his heart, says "*Bom dia*" to me, and dips his head. His humble smile reveals more gum than teeth. In his pew, he eases down to his knees, joins his hands on the pew in front of him, and sets his forehead to his thumbs. He prays in an inaudible whisper. I don't think he's asking for something. I think he's just giving thanks. Or maybe I'm just imagining it. Maybe it's just me.

Glossary

abobrinha	a type of squash
aguardente	see *cachaça*
alambique	a *cachaça* distillery
AMPAQ	*Associação Mineira de Produtores de Aguardente de Qualidade* -- a trade association dedicated to improving the quality of cachaça (aguardente).
angu	polenta, corn flour boiled in water
arraial	an encampment or rudimentary settlement. Plural: *arraiais*
bandeirante	an early Portuguese pioneer and slave-hunter, so-called because they put flags (*bandeiras*) on the hills they claimed.
barzinho	a little bar serving not just alcohol but soft drinks and such, often very informal, often half outdoors, possibly a few cooked snacks, perhaps meals and

staples, too.

batida — a drink of blended fruit and *cachaça*

beleza — beauty

benzedeira — a (woman) faith healer

biscoito de polvilho an airy biscuit of fine manioc flour

bom dia — a greeting, literally "good day"

boa — feminine of "good"

boa noite — good night

caboclo — *mestizo*s of black, Indian and white blood

cachaça — an alcoholic beverage made of distilled sugar cane juice, also called *pinga* and *aguardente*, normally 80 -1 00 proof.

cachaçeiro — one who drinks too much *cachaça*

cachoeira — waterfall, cascade

cafezinho — a little cup of coffee

caipiri — a small farmer, hick, hayseed, etc.

caipirinha — a drink made of pressed lime, sugar, and *cachaça*

caldo — soup or stew

campo — the countryside, rural area

casa — house

cerrado — tropical savanna

chafariz — a public water spigot for horses or people, often flowing into a stone basin

chorinho — a lively traditional music played with

	accordion, flute or piccolo, drums, a guitar the size of a ukulele, sometimes brass and woodwind instruments
chuchu	chayote, a light green, pear-sized fruit that grows on a vine, tastes a bit like cucumber, eaten as boiled chunks
churrascaria	a restaurant that serves *churrasco*, or barbecue
churrasquinho	beef, pork, or chicken barbecued on a stick
companheira	a female companion
conscientizado	made conscious or aware of something
CVRD	Companhia Vale do Rio Doce, a mining company, now known as "Vale."
doce de leite	a soft caramel often served with cheese for dessert
Dona	a respectful courtesy title for a woman
dona de casa	housewife
dormitório	a very cheap place to sleep, with limited amenities and possibly several guests sharing a room
estrada	highway, road
esperança	hope or the act of waiting
farofa	a side dish of sautéed manioc flour with bits of bacon, egg, onion, etc.
feijão	bean(s)
favela	slum or area of poor housing
fazenda	a farm or ranch

feijão tropeiro	a hearty mixture of beans, manioc flour, egg, chunks of sausage and other ingredients, the food of the old *tropeiros*.
fogão a lenha	an open-top wood-fueled cook-stove
forno de barro	mud brick oven
forró	a lively dance event, possibly originating from the English expression, "for all."
fubá	corn meal
fumo de rolo	a strong black tobacco bought in chunks cut from a coil, often rolled in corn husk
gente	people
galeria	a gallery or mining tunnel
garapa	sugar cane juice, the raw material of *rapadura* and *cachaça*
guarda volume	place to store baggage, the trunk of a car
hino nacional	national anthem
igreja	church
igreja matriz	a town's main church
incrível	incredible
IPHAN	Brazil's federal agency responsible for preservation and restoration of antiquities and historic buildings
graças a Deus	by the grace of God
jiló	*Solanum ovigerum*, a small, green, bitter fruit similar to the Easter white eggplant
liberdade	liberty, freedom
malagueta	a small, very hot pepper

mata	the general vegetation growing in the wild
mato	forest, or any uncultivated areas outside of town
matriz	the *igreja matriz*, a town's main church
mercado	market
mestizo	a person of mixed race or an animal of mixed breed
mexido	literally, a mixture. As a food, a mixture of leftover rice, beans, shredded collards, perhaps some manioc flour and other things
mineiro	from Minas Gerais, or a person from there
mulatto/a	a man/woman of mixed African and European descent. Brazilians use the word with no intent to disparage.
não	no, not
orelhão	a public phone
ovo	egg
ovo caipira	the egg of a free-range hen
pau-a-pique	a mud and wattle style of construction
pedra pintada	literally, painted rock; an archaeological site outside of Cocais
pensão	a boarding house or simple hotel of small rooms and limited amenities
pinga	see *cachaça*
pousada	a small inn or "bed-and-breakfast"

praça	a plaza, a square, an open area often found in front of a church
pracinha	a small *praça* (-inha being a suffix for the diminutive)
prato feito	literally, "made plate," the low-price dish at a restaurant, served with the food already on the plate rather than served in serving dishes
prefeito	mayor
queijo mineiro	a soft, white, moist, salted cheese typical of Minas Gerais
quaresma	a flowering tree that blossoms (traditionally) during Lent
quintal	the area behind a house, usually filled with fruit trees, flowers and vegetable gardens, perhaps a few animals.
rainha	queen
rancho	a way station for the *tropeiro* mule teams
rapadura	molasses sugar
reais	plural of real, the currency of Brazil)
real	real or royal, also the currency of Brazil, worth 40 - 50 cents U.S. during the trip related above. (Plural in Portuguese and English: *reais*)
rei	an old Brazilian currency (Plural: reis). Also, king.
rodízio	a meal deal at a *churrascaria* whereby waiters keep coming around with meat

on spits. You can eat all you want.

rua	street
sabiá	a thrush famous for its lovely song
SENAC	a state agency that trains people for the tourism industry
senzala	slave quarters
serra	a high ridge or mountain range
sertão	deserted outback badlands
serpentina	a water pipe that winds through the masonry of a wood stove to feed hot water into a tank
sim	yes
sítio	a small farm, often used only on weekends by city residents
sobrado	a townhouse of at least two stories
Sr./Sra.	Abbreviations for *senhor* and *senhora*, Mr. and Mrs.
taquara	a type of bamboo that can be splintered and woven, often used to make ceilings
tchiao	good-bye (as in the Italian *ciao*)
tira-gosto	appetizer
tropas	the old mule and donkey trains that once brought supplies into Minas from the coast
tropeiro	a person who worked with the tropa mule trains; see also *feijão troperio*.
tudo tranquilo	all calm

tutu	a dish of pureed black beans thickened with manioc flour
vagabunda	a bum, someone who doesn't want to work
Vale	short for Companhia Vale do Rio Doce, or CVRD, a major international mining company.
vai com Deus	go with God
vereador	an elected municipal legislator

The Author

Glenn Alan Cheney is the author of over 25 books, hundreds of articles, and several op-ed essays, short stories, and poems. He has written on such disparate topics as Chernobyl, nuns, Gandhi, nuclear proliferation, the Pilgrims, the Quilombo dos Palmares, Swaziland, Central American politics, Abraham Lincoln, and Brazilian issues. He also translates Portuguese to English and edits translations.

Made in the USA
Charleston, SC
13 September 2015